W9-CQZ-211

"In *Nobody Cries When We Die* Patrick Reyes vibrantly presents our common yearning to embrace a vocation to life. What God wants for us is life in abundance, to walk the life of justice and compassion with joy. Reyes anchors his narrative at the margins and in this, we all find the 'good soil' and invitation to live fully."
— Gregory Boyle, Founder/Executive Director of Homeboy Industries, Author of *Tattoos On The Heart*

"Patrick Reyes offers a brilliant mix of theological reflection and biographical snippets to demonstrate how 'narrative can be used to discern vocation.' Reyes grounds us in his firsthand accounts of ministry of *la lucha* among *la comunidad* in a way that is not gratuitous but instead ensures the reader gets a sense of both the struggles and the ingenuity of oppressed people. This broader and necessary education will help us remember the way the call of God shapes our lives. What is more, it will implore us to commit our lives, according to Reyes, to helping call our communities to life."
— Pamela R. Lightsey, Boston University School of Theology, Author of *Our Lives Matter*

"*Nobody Cries When We Die* is a captivating narrative of redemption. Patrick captures the reader's attention with compelling stories of tragedy and grief while pointing us towards God's triumph and grace. *Nobody Cries When We Die* lifts up the voices and stories of people who often suffer in silence but whose voices deserve to be heard. Patrick has provided us with a gift. His transparency shares both pain and purpose on a journey to turn wounds into scars (the evidence of healing). God has clearly used Patrick's journey as an instrument of redemption."
— Romal Tune, Author of *God's Graffiti*

"*Nobody Cries When We Die* is an outstanding journey. Reyes's collection of stories offers an eye-opening window to Latinx life in the US. Written in a beautiful prose, the author recounts his experiences in a community forced into violence and finds a common thread in the permanent struggle for justice and healing. It is his Christian vocation that makes him keep strong in his convictions in front of heartbreaking stories. This is a must read for anyone who trusts we can build a better world."
— Santiago Slabodsky, Florence and Robert Kaufman Endowed Chair in Jewish Studies, Hofstra University, New York

"With a riveting writing style, Reyes's memoir invites readers to explore their own inner labyrinth of Christian vocational discernment. At each twist and turn on the journey, questions abound: How am I going to live? Who is calling me to life? Can anything good come from my neighborhood? His approach to examining the depths of wisdom in the lived experience of ordinary, often overlooked people is a breath of fresh air for theological writing and a gateway for readers to encounter the Divine in the seemingly mundane."
— Gregory C. Ellison II, Candler School of Theology, Emory University, and Founder of Fearless Dialogues

"Patrick Reyes has given us a beautiful witness to the power, creativity, and resilience at the heart of Christian community. This is a book that every young person needs to read to be encouraged and enlivened in their call, and every leader in churches, theological education, and non-profits must listen to if they are going to adequately create space for the future generation of leaders."
— Brian Bantum, Seattle Pacific University, Author of *The Death of Race*

"A compelling narrative, practical theology, and vocational formation book all in one. Reyes is a scholar who courageously intertwines the reality of his life with deep and serious theological and theoretical reflection with the purpose of guiding one in vocational discernment. It is about time that a scholar need not leave his life aside to do theology and theoretical work, which comes from the core of one's life. Now this makes sense and will make sense to every generation reading it as mentors and prodigies, ministers and parishioners, or just people sharing deeply about faith matters around their coffee. This brings a full community around the table to discern, to heal, and to know God more profoundly. I will use it for my Christian ministry students for sure."
— Elizabeth Conde-Frazier, Dean of Esperanza College, Eastern University, and Author of *Listen to the Children*

"Walter Benjamin once said, 'It is only for the sake of those without hope that hope is given to us.' This book is the best interpretation of this saying to our days. Patrick Reyes writes about 'the world and himself,' showing the inside and the outside world in which the Latin@ community lives. There, without hope, we learn what hope is all about. This is a book to cry, rejoice, and ponder with at every page. I will read it to my students, to my community, and to my family."
— Cláudio Carvalhaes, Union Theological Seminary, New York City

"At times both poetic and prophetic, *Nobody Cries When We Die* is a passionate hybrid of autobiography and theological reflection. Reyes writes such that biblical stories and theological ideas that are often flattened are fully rendered with depth, flesh, and feeling. To read this book is to enter into the world and experience it through the lens of a faithful Christian who sees struggle and injustice all around him, and there, in the midst of it all, finds God calling out for mercy and change. Reyes has heard this call. *Nobody Cries* embodies God's demand for justice and prophetic transformation, and does so in a voice that never veers from compassion. It belongs on every shelf that holds Willie Jennings' *The Christian Imagination* and Ta-Nehisi Coates' *Between the World and Me*."
— Callid Keefe-Perry, Author of *Way to Water*, cohost of *Homebrewed Christianity*, cofounder of the journal *Theopoetics*

"Patrick Reyes provides us with a way through some of the most difficult questions of our time as a theologian, a scholar, and a community-accountable activist. His book will be a classic text in the canon of literature produced by liberation theologians and speaks to students who often are invisible in the seminary classroom. Teach it, read it, and maybe most important of all, live it!"
— Najeeba Syeed, Founder and Director of Center for Global Peacebuilding, Claremont School of Theology

"Reyes does not pull any punches as he takes his reader on a journey that can be a both heartbreaking and profoundly affirming story. Through a powerful retelling of his own spiritual autobiography, Dr. Reyes demonstrates how through God's redemptive power, his sense of calling and vocation have emerged, even in the midst of trauma, pain, loss, and oppression. The text challenges the reader to consider how one's own vocation can be heard and expressed in the messiness of everyday life."
— Michael W. DeLashmutt, Vice President and Dean for Academic Affairs, The General Theological Seminary of the Episcopal Church

NOBODY CRIES WHEN WE DIE

GOD, COMMUNITY, AND SURVIVING TO ADULTHOOD

PATRICK B. REYES

chalice
press

Saint Louis, Missouri

An imprint of Christian Board of Publication

Copyright ©2016 by Patrick Reyes

All rights reserved. For permission to reuse content, please contact Copyright Clearance Center, 222 Rosewood Drive, Danvers, MA 01923, (978) 750-8400, www.copyright.com.

Scripture quotations marked (NIV) are taken from the HOLY BIBLE, NEW INTERNATIONAL VERSION®. NIV®. Copyright © 1973, 1978, 1984 by International Bible Society. Used by permission of Zondervan Publishing House. All rights reserved.

Scripture marked NASB is taken from the *NEW AMERICAN STANDARD BIBLE®*, © Copyright The Lockman Foundation 1960, 1962, 1963, 1968, 1971, 1972, 1973, 1975, 1977. Used by permission.

Scripture quotations marked (NLT) are taken from the *Holy Bible,* New Living Translation, copyright © 1996. Used by permission of Tyndale House Publishers, Inc., Wheaton, Illinois 60189, U.S.A. All rights reserved.

Scripture quotations marked KJV are from the *King James Version.*

The cover art for *Nobody Cries When We Die* is an excerpt from *Quetzalcoatl,* a mural at Chicano Park in San Diego, California, created by Mario Torero. Established by Chicano activists in 1970, Chicano Park has received international recognition as a major public art site for its commanding mural paintings of the past and present struggle of Mexican and Chicano history. Fernando Vossa photographed the mural for this cover. Art used with permission from Mr. Torero and Chicano Park.

Cover design: Jesse Turri

ChalicePress.com

Print: 9780827225312   EPUB: 9780827225329
EPDF: 9780827225336

Printed in the USA.

Contents

For Grandma and all those who bury los inocentes.

Series Foreword

Cultivating Faithful, Wise, and Courageous Leaders for the Church and Academy

Welcome to a conversation at the intersection of young adults, faith, and leadership. The Forum for Theological Exploration (FTE) is a leadership incubator that inspires diverse young people to make a difference in the world through Christian communities. This series, published in partnership with Chalice Press, reimagines Christian leadership and creates innovative approaches to ministry and scholarship from diverse contexts.

These books are written by and for a growing network of:

- Partners seeking to cultivate the Christian leaders, pastors, and theological educators needed to renew and respond to a changing church.

- Young leaders exploring alternative paths to ministry and following traditional ways of serving the common good —both inside and beyond "the walls" of the church and theological academy.

- Christian leaders developing new ways to awaken the search for meaning and purpose in young adults who are inspired to shape the future.

- Members of faith communities creating innovative solutions to address the needs of their congregations, institutions, and the broader community.

This series offers an opportunity to discover what FTE is learning, widen the circle of conversation, and share ideas FTE believes are necessary for faith communities to shape a more hopeful future. Authors' expressed ideas and opinions in this series are their own and do not necessarily reflect the views of FTE.

Thank you for joining us!

Dori Baker, Series Editor

Stephen Lewis, FTE President

Foreword, a Letter from a Friend

Dear Patrick,

Your book made me think deeply about my life. There's a radical love that infuses the text, the kind I see in the golden leaves of cottonwoods in New Mexico, leaves once green, fully complacent in their green life, to be jolted by a deeper archetypal calling to their true nature as its gets colder and a reverberation of burning love swells in the center of all life and ebbs and flows out, urging us into new ways of being.

I can't tell you how I love your book, because then it would mean I give you the meaning of life and I don't know that. But I do know when I see my 9-year-old daughter playing piano and trying out new keys to find the sound she's looking for or when I see my 13-year-old son fighting to retain his sweetness in mid-school, when there's so much chaos in the world, so much embittered dam breaks in every person's life, they staunch the bleeding with their call to life as you and your book do.

Your book is an honest revelation that courses from the ground like those acequias in Salinas, like those calls of children at the school bus stop, like the leaves, the burials of gangbangers, the bleak pistols shots in the deep of night.

It seems your book breaks down the separations and calls the convicts, the poor, the addicts, the hopeless, and the mean-spirited to gather and praise life, praise the worthiness of pain and sorrow, and make of it something to bind us all into a grateful crowd of brothers and sisters, unrelenting in our belief that God's love can see us through our own darkest hours.

It's a beautiful book, and one that needs to be in every school and library and, indeed, given to every senator and teacher and congressman and counselor and priest and rabbi and jail guard.

It is a book that allows us to rest our heads for a moment and sigh with relief that we are loved when we have always believed we are not lovable, a book that sets the intellect aside and allows the heart to speak and what it says is: my heart has room for the thousands of Mexican orphans whose parents were killed by cartels; bring the lonely and forsaken and wandering souls lost in their misery of addiction and targeted by racists as inhuman, bring those who exist in silence and I will speak for them, I will cry out for them, and I will be heard from valley to peak coast to coast with our righteous indignation and our song of love.

Ultimately my brother, your book is a field worker's song of love, and every hand that reaches to the plant stalk, every hand that works the furrow, every hand that wipes the sweat from the face, every hand that pinches thorns from flesh, every hand that clasps another to lift him up from his knees is what this book represents.

Thank you for stepping up to the call of life and writing it,

Jimmy Santiago Baca

Editor's Introduction

As the editor of this book series and a colleague of Patrick Reyes, I was moved to write these words of introduction, which, like this book itself, deviate from the norm of dispassionate observer.

When I first met Patrick Reyes he was holding a well-worn machete that he had once used to sever a head of iceberg lettuce from its root in a California field. He passed this machete around a hotel conference table, acknowledging the reality of his community while helping a room full of scholars see farmworkers as the subjects of their education, rather than mere objects within a system.

I sensed his genius then: it is the genius of one who weds head, heart, and body, while not apologizing for speaking in story and holding intuition in utmost regard.

After that day, I was never again able to see "the field" of religion, or theology, or religious education abstractly: from then on "the field" was a real place, a place of toil and soil, of sweat and blood, the site of both dying into compost and sprouting forth into new life.

In this book, Reyes defines "vocational discernment" through the lens of his own embodied childhood and adolescence as a Latino growing up in one of America's most underserved communities, where generational poverty and the ensuing violence continue *in this moment* to threaten life. He survives, and writes to tell the "who, what, why, when, and how" of his journey into adulthood as a scholar, activist, and practical theologian deeply committed to creating tangible hope in his community-of-origin.

Beautifully, the church plays a role in this survival. It is a church depicted through a grandmother whose long, slow hugs heal and who descended from holy people migrating up and down the west coast of this continent before fixed borders. It is a church depicted through rosaries, catechisms, and robed clergy—not as spooky images in a horror movie—but as the very incarnation of attention paid to the "least of these." It is a church depicted through migrant workers organizing late into the night for better working conditions. It is a church alive and churning with the energies of saints and ancestors coaxing hope out of the dark night of our souls and our deepest states of dreaming.

This book is at turns breathtaking for its poetic descriptions and at other turns hard-to-keep-reading because it brings you face-to-face with violence taking place on the playgrounds and basketball courts of our cities. Though Reyes tells his story in thick particularity, it opens windows for us all to be still, imagining vividly the horrors other young people are experiencing *now* as they struggle to survive in households of violence and addiction, gun-infused neighborhoods, and communities rife with bureaucratic initiatives that inflict more violence on the already beaten-down.

This book speaks to young people who may be growing up in spaces similar to the ones Patrick knew. To them it says, "You are called to live. Even when there seems to be no hope, God is calling you to survive."

This book speaks to educators, pastors, community workers, youth ministers, artists, poets, and coaches called to reach out to young people in our most underserved communities, where pain and violence diminish the possibilities of hope. To them it says "Listen to the people you are called to accompany. Follow gravity down, down to the places of greatest pain and hang out there awhile, learning, listening and being with God."

It speaks to all of us who've sat in the classrooms of theological education with a certain element of privilege—be it white privilege, class privilege, or the privilege that comes with a college education— and it says to us: "This place was designed with you in mind: look for, listen to, and prioritize the people whose presence here was never imagined."

I have sat through lectures and read chapter upon chapter of good books that painstakingly define "vocational discernment." Reyes totally recasts this conversation, placing community at its center.

Along the way, he achieves a much loftier goal. He corrects images of God that have too long malformed our religious imaginations. Those malformed images of God thwart our vision of who we are called to be and the future we can create together. Interpreting scripture through his life, he makes dry bones dance, birthing new possibilities for us all through this ancient story.

Following Reyes's lead, I close with a story. When I received my Ph.D. in religious studies, my daughter, then six years old, said, "Mommy you're the kind of doctor who fixes God, right?" I only cringed a little at the implied arrogance of this statement. As a feminist deeply committed to the stories that women and people of color have had to retrieve from traditions of whiteness and patriarchy, I affirm that dominant images of God *do* need fixing.

Patrick Reyes is a doctor of the church who will inspire a movement as we, collectively, rise to the challenge of fixing—not God—but the worn-out, limiting, and actively harmful images of God we've inherited.

Reyes inspires those of us who would support the young leaders called to this movement, teaching us how to show up. And he calls out directly to the next generation of leaders themselves who, like him, are called by God to survive even the most hopeless of situations, turning machetes into teaching tools and breathing new life into our communities.

Dori Baker, Series Editor

Psalm 23:4

A psalm of David.

Even though I walk

through the valley of the shadow of death,

I will fear no evil,

for you are with me;

your rod and your staff,

they comfort me.

Introduction

I was staring down the barrel of a gun that my friend Michael was pointing at my head as he shouted at me:

"We're going to show these mother f—ers what it's like! We're going to make them fear this shit. We know what's up."

Michael, a young Latinx like me, has a bald head like mine, goatee, dark sunglasses, and tattoos covering his neck. A thousand times before he'd pointed that gun, only this time he was pointing it at me.

"They are going to know this isn't a f—ing game. This is about life."

"It is about life," I agreed. "But we don't need to show them a gun for them to know that."

"Padre, what the f— are you talking about? You know better. You know what it's like. This is the only way they'll get it."

"I don't need them to get it. They need to know who we are and what we are doing to heal our wounds."

"But if they don't feel it in their bones, if we don't make them fear God, then it won't matter. They won't know the story. Oh, and don't worry, the gun isn't loaded."

We were in our hotel room at an academic conference in California addressing violence in communities, and my friend Michael had agreed to present with me. But somehow he'd gotten it into his head that the only way to impress the academics was to pull a gun on them. He wasn't actually going to shoot them. Sure, I understood his reasoning. So often academics fail to understand and embody the issues we theorize about. My friend wanted to show them these matters were not just something we could think about abstractly as we sat around and a table. He wanted them to know that this was a matter of life and death.

"My God calls people to life. You pulling a gun on people doesn't do it. Drop it, Michael; we're not going to do it," I said as forcefully as possible.

"Padre, this is all we have to show them," he insisted, now with waning confidence.

"That's bull and you know it."

"What do I have for these people? What do I have to show them? They don't want anything from me. They don't need me. This is all I have."

"That's *bullshit*." I repeated. "Look, we are going to tell our story, and then they'll know. Put the gun away. You can't come if you bring the gun."

"You think they will know about that little girl, or Jesse, or José, or anyone else that we know that is buried because of this violence shit if we don't show them it exists?"

"I think they will know we pulled a gun on them. I think they will see a couple of pissed off ex-bangers and not hear what we have to say."

"That'll make them afraid of us."

"They already are. You know that, right?"

"*¿Cómo?*" he asked incredulously.

"They are afraid of who we are, because of who we are, where we come from, and what we look like. But they also know that if people like you and me show up and we say we have been called to life by our own people, by our own God, that we have our own practices and methods for healing through the violence, that we have the desire and power to put down the guns to work for peace, then they may not have a reason for coming into our neighborhoods to save us poor brown folks, poor violent Latinos and Latinas that can't keep killing ourselves. We aren't just violent ex-gang members or violent *cholos*. You know that, right? Listen, *you* know just as much as every single person in that room today about healing. *You* know more than all of them about organizing our community for healing and transformation. But believe me, if you pull that gun on them, you will just be the thug they're all expecting you to be. *¿Entiendes?*"

"Padre, but…"

"No buts. And if you pull that gun on me again, we're done."

Michael's attempt to bring a gun to our presentation was a response to how we were made to feel powerless. This is how internalized our violence had become and how real our fear was of not having anything to offer this world. People from poor, violent, struggling communities of color like ours understand what it means in John 1:46 when the people ask: "Can anything good come from Nazareth?" In turn, we ask ourselves: "Can anything good come from *our* neighborhood?" After being told so many times that nothing good comes from our community, we sometimes believe it.

This particular academic conference brought together practitioners and scholars to address peacemaking in communities of color. I'd worked with Michael years before in *Nueva Comunidad,* a local and self-built program for healing from the traumatic memories of gang violence, though at the time of this conference I went to school full-time at a university in Boston. Michael and I, even as young adults, would co-facilitate work with teens in the midst of violence in Salinas, California.

That day in the hotel, Michael wasn't suggesting that we actually pull the trigger at the conference session. But he thought that in order to understand the reality of the life-and-death struggle in neighborhoods like ours, academics and leaders of all types needed to be shocked out of their theoretical comfort zones. Though presenting research and best practices for healing communities—specifically, communities of color—is now part of my vocational reality as a scholar/practitioner/administrator/elder, sometimes I still agree with Michael: If this is truly a life and death struggle, why don't we act with the urgency of life and death? Why doesn't our work communicate that lives are on the brink of being snuffed out?

The conditions that made me who I am today, how I can end up in a room with a person who brings a gun to a meeting and yet continue to discern the call to life, is the story of a vocation. It is a story that is incomplete, but I ask you to accompany me on that vocational journey to see how God and others saved me.

Violence has always been part of my narrative. Michael was right that everywhere I go to talk about these issues people want to hear about the guns. They want to hear about how I survived to adulthood. I want to tell them that what I survived is what motivates my vocational discernment, that what I survived makes me ask myself every day: *How am I going to live? Who is calling me to life?* As Michael was pointing out, the sight of the gun quickly strips these questions to their core: *How am I going to live when the world wants me dead? Who is going to call me to live when it means risking their lives to step in front of that gun?*

These are the questions Michael and I—and you, especially if you are from a community of color—faced on a daily basis. These are the questions that prompt vocational discernment.

> *How am I going to live when the world wants me dead?*

Vocational discernment through narrative is never just a personal act. My narrative is predicated on being in relationship with God and with others. Without God moving in a Christian Brother, a grandma, a father, a friend, a partner, and a community—all of whom you will meet in this book—I likely would not be here today. Still, it took years of struggling through and surviving the trauma of life and having networks of love and compassion to call me to life. In order to discern our vocations through narrative practices, we must first acknowledge that each of us is not the only character in the story, not the sole protagonist. We're all part of an ensemble cast, all of us finding ways to live and call others to life.

Vocation in its most literal meaning comes from the Latin *vocatio*, referring to a "call" or "summoning." Christian vocation, then, is responding to the voice of God calling people to new life. This is not something new. In many of the biblical stories, especially those about prophets such as Moses and Deborah and Jeremiah, the voice of God calls people into new life, then calls them to call others to new life. The types of call I will refer to in this book are those times when we are called into flourishing and new life. This book is not about finding your dream job, your first call to ministry, or the like. It is about being called to *live*. Understood like this, vocation is a life journey that we take with the diversity of God's creation, including the environment, animals, and all inhabitants of our world.

The following chapters explore my own vocational journey using the tools of theological reflection and vocational discernment. Each chapter includes pieces of my life story. In the first chapter, I talk about finding God in what Latinx theologians name *lo cotidiano, everyday living,* and what this looks like when the conditions threaten one's life each day. I use the term *Latinx* (rather than Latino or Latina) throughout the text to highlight the diversity of the Latinx experience across gender, sexuality, nationality, place of birth, and local community commitments. I will show how discerning through the everydayness of our lives and our community is part of the Christian vocational call. I narrate stories of growing up in a Latinx farmworking community, but ultimately being called out of my home and into school. My story starts where it might have ended, with me as a young person, abused, nearly killed, and surviving because a Christian stepped in and saved my life.

In chapter 2, I tell you about being caught in the crossfire of a drive-by shooting in our gang-and-violence-infested neighborhood, and how seeing a young girl murdered before my eyes changed my perspective on life and my vocation. It was the courage of my grandmother that challenged me and those involved in our neighborhood gangs to turn to a new, communal way of being. She called us to new life.

In chapter 3, I explore the challenges to living into one's Christian vocational calling. For my community, our vocations start with survival. The world was not built for us, though it was built on the backs of our ancestors, the colonized, the oppressed, the enslaved, and other marginalized people. My narrative wrestles with how the status quo has incredible investment in keeping people like me in their place rather than calling us to new life. The chapter explores how, by asserting life in the face of those who would limit our flourishing, we can better live into the narrative to which God has called us.

Chapter 4 turns to survival as vocation. By looking at how generations have heard the call from God to survive, I hope we can see our own narratives intertwining with the biblical tradition and the history of our ancestors.

Chapters 5 and 6 explore the transformative power of committing to a particular geographic place and a people as part of discerning one's vocation through narrative. By focusing on the setting of one's narrative, we go beyond having an abstract notion of vocation as work, and can imagine our own narratives interacting with others. In *The Long-Legged House,* author, poet, and agrarian Wendell Berry writes:

> A community is the mental and spiritual condition of knowing that the place is shared, and that the people who share the place define and limit the possibilities of each other's lives. [Community] is that knowledge that people have of each other, their concern for each other, their trust in each other, the freedom with which they come and go among themselves. (Berry 2012, 71)

This commitment to the spiritual lives of your neighbors is part of your vocational discernment. Your call to life is not just about you! It's also about your context, your surroundings, and your com-munity. Vocation is both being called home and being called to the larger kin-dom of God, in which we live together and for one another, as opposed to a kingdom of God with rulers and lords, and the underlings who have to do their bidding and work for them. The connections to a community and a people are incredibly important to hearing God's call to life. In chapter 7, I turn to the call of community as part of one's vocation. I will tell the story of my work to build community, both in higher education and in my home community, and show that issues of

> Vocation is both being called home and being called to the larger kin-dom of God, in which we live together and for one another, as opposed to a kingdom of God with rulers and lords, and the underlings who have to do their bidding and work for them.

class, race, education, and many other factors are often determined before we are born, but how we can challenge these conditions in a life-generating way. Through my scholarship, and my administrative and teaching roles in higher education, I have a responsibility to use education to create a place for healing and for people to be fully alive.

Finally, I turn back to scripture. The stories I tell acknowledge God's grace watching over me in the forms of religious leaders, of Grandma Carmen Reyes, of family and community, of the little girl I saw gunned down all those years ago. I will write knowing that the work of being called into new life is not just for me to live, but for me to extend as an invitation to the next generation. In all of my stories, I have altered details and names to protect the lives of those I care about.

> *I should not be alive. But here I am.*

There is no doubt in my mind that the odds were against me being here today. *I should not be alive. But here I am.* I am called to life both by God and by others. I hope that the story of my life inspires others to hear God's voice. For those of you whose bodies remain trapped under the weight of oppression, and for those of you who feel as if the world around you is muting the sound of God, I hope that my story creates the space for you to hear God's voice. For those whose hearts have been hardened by oppressive expressions of Christianity, I hope that you find the freedom to hear God calling you to life and offering the freedom to create a community that will sustain you. As an educator, scholar, survivor, friend, and partner, I have written my story for those who are on the margins and are being held there by violence, so that they might be able to discern God's call in these stories. If you have never been told explicitly that you are called to life, or if you have not yet heard the call of God to life, I pray that my story calls you to life now.

Chapter 1

Called to Live

[In our world, it] is not possible for a child—any child—ever to use his family's language in school. Not to understand this is to misunderstand the public uses of schooling and to trivialize the nature of the intimate life—a family's language.
— Richard Rodriguez, 1982

The first time I heard God call me to my life's work and vocation was the first time God called me to live. Hold my story in care. *For survivors:* My story contains tragic violence. I want to care for those for whom this story may be a trigger or who are in need of healing from violence. Know that you are not alone and that I pray you receive the care you need and deserve.

God, Where Are You?

As a child, I always listened intently for the sound of God. God could have come in any form. Raised in a Latinx Catholic church, I longed to hear God calling me out of my adolescent reality and into a thriving future.

Sometimes, that is what we think vocation is: God calling us out of our present reality and into some divinely purposed and infinitely better future. Unfortunately, life does not always allow this to occur. In fact, God often just calls us to survive. That's how it was for me.

The days were always short when I knew what was waiting for me at home. When my parents split, I was only 12. I remember feeling as though my conscience split. My sense of right and wrong, my grounding,

7

my sense of belonging to a space—to a people—belonging to the Holy, all felt off. It's a deep disconnect many families are experiencing today. As a mixed-race, light brown-skinned, Chicano boy in a gang-infested neighborhood, my identity was difficult for me to navigate. Language barriers in both English and Spanish, historical marginalization, and lack of opportunity in education and livelihood defined every step my father took for our family. Here I was in adolescence, already split in conscience by our society as Latinxs, neither belonging to nor excluded by our community. But now within one of Latinxs' most coveted categories, *familia,* my identity was shattered. I didn't know to whom I belonged. I didn't know where to call home.

I was the oldest of three boys. We are fortunate now to have another younger brother and sister, whom I love dearly. But at the time with just the three boys, I had settled into my life of being the extra parent, the strong brother, the student, and the steady example. I helped raise my two younger brothers both in mind and spirit—despite my parents wishing I wouldn't. I remember my mother telling us less than a month after my parents stopped living together that she was moving a new "man" into the house. I was 12 years old at the time. I said as forcefully as one can at that age that I didn't feel that was right. Everything about this Stranger unsettled me.

"You are just a child. I am the adult. This is what's right."

I wanted so desperately to be heard, seen, and included. I wanted my truth to be recognized. My encounter with the gospel at this point was limited to Catholic Catechism on Sundays, but I knew that Jesus would have included me, a child, just as the stories about Jesus and children in both Mark 10 and Matthew 19 report. I wish Jesus had my back in that moment. Instead, my mother sent me to my room. Children often have wisdom and insight far beyond their years because their eyes are not clouded by rationalizations or passions.

The Stranger moved in the next day.

I had recently been admitted into the local Christian Brothers all-boys school. Every day I returned to the house that my parents had once shared to find the Stranger in it. A Stranger with bad habits. A Stranger whom I now can imagine must have been suffering far more than I ever realized. A Stranger who had yet to hear God's compassionate and loving call to new life, a new way of being in the world. He was a Stranger who brought with him shadows of pain and storms of violence that clouded my future and caused the waves of my past reality to crash around me.

I acclimated to his abuse, knowing when and how to step in, when to incite it, how to redirect it, ways to focus its hateful energy toward an external object, or how to hide from it. As the oldest sibling, as the protector, the model citizen, a "good" Christian, and at the beginning of my adolescent journey into and through the expectations of cultural machismo and manhood, it was my duty to protect my brothers from the pain of this world—a duty I know, now that I am out of my youth, was one that I could never have fully realized.

I felt very fortunate to have an opportunity to go to this Christian Brothers school. Not everyone in my community did. I always enjoyed learning and still do. School provided me an outlet to succeed in what was otherwise an overwhelming and defeating life. I remember saying in a session with a counselor that I shouldn't need help processing the world. What I needed was someone to help me survive what was happening at home. No child should have to process abuse.

One day I came home from school and prepared to do my homework. I pulled out my books, which were carefully wrapped in old brown paper grocery bags, and placed them on the white laminate desk. I heard footsteps coming up the stairs. I turned in the small chair to look through the open doorway. Competing with the sound of the Stranger's footsteps were the shrieks and bumps of my brothers roughhousing in the room adjacent to mine. Then the Stranger's first yell: "Knock it off, or I am coming in there." I remember my brothers quieting down for a moment and the footsteps stopping. I froze in my chair. The whole house was in suspended animation. I sat there staring over my books, hoping that the Stranger wouldn't say or do anything to my brothers, wishing that I could escape this reality of ours.

Seconds passed, and it was not long before my brothers were doing what young boys do—playing again. The Stranger's steps quickened their pace. Now footsteps were at the top of the stairs, so forceful, even with the gray carpet designed to dampen such noise and impact, that they rumbled the entire second floor. As they grew louder and louder still, my brothers instinctively slammed their door. But the Stranger continued to move toward it, eyes bloodshot from his self-abuse earlier. My mother was in her room, telling the Stranger to stop. I remember his gaze and his footsteps turning toward my brothers' bedroom.

When he'd made it near my mother's room, just a few paces away, I scurried to my brothers' bedroom door. Through the hollow white door, I told my brothers to go outside. As they ran down the short hall, the Stranger turned his focus back toward my brothers, who were frantically trying to make it to the stairs, nonetheless laughing as he yelled after them. I don't know if they thought it was actually funny or if they were more aware than I ever gave them credit for, and were laughing nervously to mask their fear.

The Stranger turned toward my mother, "I am going to shut those kids up." There was something about the look in his eye, and the image of his large clenched fists that made me certain: *This time he's coming after them too, not just me.*

Where was God in this moment? Would God have protected my brothers had I not intervened? Would the Stranger really have gone after them if I had not provoked him?

There was no time for such questions all those years ago. Instead, as he turned toward the stairs, I screamed out.

"*HEY, ¡PENDEJO!* You dumb pile of shit! Why don't you leave them alone!"

I screamed out words of profanity, words I will never utter in front of my son, words of lament, words of pain, words that turned the Stranger's attention toward my small adolescent body, a body that wanted nothing more than to do homework. I stood in the door and ripped into the Stranger, naming all of his bad habits, naming all of his shame, lighting the fire in his eyes, and focusing his pain and hate on my small figure. The Stranger stood nearly 6'2" and weighed 220 lbs., and here I was, 4'11" and maybe 105 lbs., daring to challenge him. I was David in the face of Goliath, slinging my rocks. But unlike David, my rocks did not stop the Stranger.

"What did you say to me, you little brown piece of shit?" His racial and ethnic hatred for those he saw as inferior to him was now directed at me—his Latinx other.

"You heard me! Who the f— do you think you are?" I yelled. Then his body lunged at mine.

The impact of a grown man slamming a fist into a child is a pain I never want any child to know. After hitting me once, I fell backward on the floor, dazed. This was not the first time he had hit me, but it was the first time he had hit me like I imagine he would have hit a man his own size. In the past, there had been a limit to the amount of abuse that he had inflicted on me, as if he was saving himself for a better fight, a fight with a worthier opponent. This time there was no limit. The strike was meant to destroy me, to destroy my humanity.

"You think you know better than me, with your books?" The Stranger lifted the books off my desk and threw them judgmentally in my direction.

"I *do* know better," I whimpered as book after book struck my small body. Those were the last words I remember saying.

The Stranger threw my desk chair against the wall. He reached down and lifted me up by the shirt. I tried to kick and punch back. Before I had an opportunity to stand up, his large frame towered over my body. His eyes were the color of hell. As he stood over my body, my body seemed to shrink. My body ached not just from the strikes that came, but from my perception that my arms, legs, body, and head were all collapsing inward. At that moment, my body was the smallest thing on the planet and the Stranger's, standing over me, was the largest. I tried to cover my face and my body, flailing around like a fish out of water, only to be stopped dead cold by the Stranger's right hand reaching down and wrapping its way around my neck like a giant snake preparing to suffocate its victim. The feeling of my body slowly rising against the wall, the force of the constriction, and the strain to the body as it rose are all sensations I do not remember as vividly as the strikes. I only remember rising off the ground, placed up on my cross, my body nearly lifeless.

No child desires a cross; no one wants to suffer; there is no redemption in suffering.

> No child desires a cross; no one wants to suffer; there is no redemption in suffering.

Suspended above the ground, I remember looking for and longing for the eyes of my father. He wasn't there. I searched in vain. I looked all around, avoiding the violent gaze of the Stranger. My father wasn't there. I remember hearing my mother crying, yelling for the Stranger to stop, telling me I was out of control. In a way she was right, for I had no control in that moment. I remember, or perhaps I project back onto that memory, a simple question: *Where is God?* Suspended above the ground, feet dangling and kicking as I breathed my final breaths: *God? Where is my father? God? God…*Then my vision faded to black.

I pause the story here because this is the very point at which I discerned my vocation. If in this moment I can't make sense of what, where, and how God is calling to me, then I am not sure my "vocation" is worth discerning. In this moment, all I wanted to do was live.

This book is about living. It is about hearing God's call in the moment when we are suspended, off the ground, the moment when we have no way of knowing how or when we will get down or whether we will still be breathing when we do. It is about discerning the call to life in the midst of almost certain death.

When was the first time you heard the voice of God calling you into new life? When was it that you first knew your vocation? Did God provide a job description? Did God map out your life journey for you? Did God answer your call when life no longer seemed possible?

God didn't provide me with a job description either, but God did provide mentors, guides, leaders, role models, loved ones, and experiences through whom and through which I could hear God's voice calling me into new life. This book is about how you can discern your vocation through your own narrative with God and God's community.

Books about Christian vocation are often riddled with questionnaires, self-assessments, spiritual gift mapping, contact details for spiritual directors, and so on and so forth. What you will find in this book is guidance about how you can identify your vocation through your own narrative and by discerning God's voice within that narrative.

Exploring the call to Christian vocation through narrative is not new. Christian authors have been using this technique since the time of the early church mothers and fathers, back in the centuries right after Christ. In fact, if you were to read Augustine of Hippo's *Confessions*, written at the end of the fourth century, as an example of how you comes to know God in and through one's own narrative, you would find that Christians have explored their Christian vocation in this manner for almost two thousand years. Augustine famously opens his story with this statement: "My Confessions, in thirteen books, praise the righteous and good God as they speak either of my evil or good, and they are meant to excite people's minds and affections toward God." I likewise hope that my story will inspire a generation of Christian leaders and seekers and transform their faith.

More recently than Augustine, theologians, scholars, philosophers, and church leaders have been sharing their own personal narratives to suggest how one commits to a Christian vocation. Famously, Thomas Merton (1915–1968) wrote in *Seven Story Mountain* about his own coming to know God and his own Christian vocation at the age of twenty-five. In his writing about vocation, Merton explored what it meant to be called by God. His definition has reverberated in my soul since the first time I read it. In a follow-up book called *No Man Is an Island* (1955, reprint 2005), Merton says of vocation, "The difference between the various vocations lies in the different ways in which each one enables men to discover God's life, appreciate it, respond to it, and share it with other men. Each vocation has for its aim the propagation of divine life in the world" (162). Taking my cue from this, my definition of Christian vocation is "God's call to new life for all creation."

You will find in this book tools to help you discern that call through narrative. I offer guidance about how you might discern your own story, tie it to the biblical narrative, and ultimately discern how God is calling you into new life. I do this through narrative. I am a theologian and religious scholar who has lived alongside and with some of the most marginalized people in North America—a Latinx theologian who has strong commitments to honoring my family and my roots. My own discernment of Christian vocation is ongoing. By recognizing in my story those moments when God was calling me to new life, I am able more clearly to see my call as a Christian educator, theologian, husband, father, friend, and the countless number of other identities I am and will continue to be called to. More importantly, I can hear God calling me simply to live.

Others may be called in very particular ways or in very general terms. You may be called to be a teacher, a farmworker, a laborer, a lawyer, a pastor, a theologian, a businessperson, a mother, father, sister, brother, lover, friend, poet, activist, etc., but I believe that before all of that, each and every one of us is called to *live*. Living is our primary vocation. You will read over the course of this book that in many ways it is surprising that I am actually alive. There are countless times when I could have died or my soul could have perished under the weight of violence in my world. For me, in these instances, vocation has meant God calling me to live. Only when I was finally given the freedom and space to discern what living into full human flourishing looks like was I able to discern a call to do or be anything other than just alive. When I had that freedom, I heard God call me to bring life to the marginalized, subjugated, and violated community from which I come.

I found my call as a Christian educator in a pluralistic world, offering programs and support in particular for Latinxs, students of color, and socio-economically disadvantaged students, not simply because this work is needed, though it most certainly is, but rather because that is the context in which I first heard the voice of God. Ever since a Christian educator held out his hand of life to me, I wanted to share the good news through education.

This book is my narrative of how God saved me again and again through the work of the faithful. God called me into new life though these people who were living into their vocations, and in turn that is how

I found my call. You will find here stories of joy, sadness, brokenness, adversity, triumph, and loneliness. You will read of times when God's voice cut clearly through all the noise of our busy world, and times when God seemed to be totally absent to me. Yet through it all, I hope you see that God is constantly calling us into new life, calling us into our own sense of vocation.

In the following pages, I model how narrative can be used to discern vocation—yours and those whose lives you touch. After telling my story and discerning the call to life through the narrative, after reading the biblical text for its insights on vocation, and after looking to the theologians of the church to amplify that meaning, I show how Christian vocation, discerned through personal, biblical, and theological narratives, can be a powerful tool for hearing God's call to new life. David Brooks writes:

> A vocation is a calling... A person with a vocation is not devoted to civil rights, or curing a disease, or writing a great novel, or running a humane company because it meets some cost-benefit analysis. Such people submit to their vocations for reasons deeper and higher than utility and they cling to them all the more fiercely the more difficulties arise. (Brooks 2015, 24–25)

Brooks does not follow his "what a vocation is not" with "this is what it is." Rather, he provides examples of people whose lives reflect a call to vocation. He names those who were called to the life. Not to a cause, or a people, or a place, but to the life involved in all of those places and identities. People called to a life. Brooks continues by saying:

> But if you serve the work—if you perform each task to its utmost perfection—then you will experience the deep satisfaction of craftsmanship and you will end up serving the community more richly than you could have consciously planned. And one sees this in people with a vocation—a certain rapt expression, a hungry desire to perform a dance or run an organization to its utmost perfection. They feel the joy of having their values in deep harmony with their behavior. (Brooks 2015, 25)

People who have found their vocation place their values in deep harmony with their behavior. Think of how often we enter into our own vocational discernment process by asking, "What do I want to do?" rather than asking ourselves first, "How am I using this living, breathing body?" or "How does the way that I am living reflect a certain call to live and breathe?"

When I work with young people, they typically think they're supposed to ask themselves, "What do I want to do?" rather than, "What am I doing with my life? Do my actions reflect my values, and are those values about life? How do I structure my day to reflect my own thriving? My own call to life?"

For Christians with stories similar to my own—and, I would suggest, for many people of color—the first call to life from God that needs to be named here is a survival to adulthood. My first vocational call was exactly that: simply a call to *live*, to *survive*. Providing the basics for one's own life and those immediately around us becomes a calling in and of itself for many of us, especially if we're people of color.

> Providing the basics for one's own life and those immediately around us becomes a calling in and of itself for many of us, especially if we're people of color.

Back to my story with the Stranger. Or perhaps more accurately, the first time I heard God.

The next morning, I woke up sore from the night before. I was still in my clothes from the previous day, but in my bed. I don't remember how I got there. I got out of bed and walked around the room, still trashed from the previous evening.

I looked at my desk and realized I had not done my homework. My books were all tossed about the room where the Stranger had thrown them in judgment. I cracked open the bedroom door to hear who was in the house. The Stranger always left for work early, and he had that morning, too. To the Stranger, there was nothing special about this day or the night before to alter his routine. I went to check on my brothers. Their door was shut and they were asleep. I looked at the clock and saw that there was not much time before school, certainly not enough for me to get my homework done. I made sure my brothers were up and getting ready for school, then, as quickly as I could, I ran to get in the shower. I washed and cleaned myself up. I was drenched in sweat and my body was sore. The hot water and steam from the shower soothed my small body. I sat there hunched over in the shower, taking respite in the warmth of the water and the way it comforted my broken body. Water is Holy. I picked out my clothes and headed down to get in the car to make sure we would get to school on time.

As soon as I got downstairs, my mother stopped me. She took me back upstairs, looked through her closet, pulled out one of her turtle neck t-shirts, and told me to put it on. A macho Chicano doesn't want to wear his mom's turtleneck. I had enough problems with peers mocking me for living on this side of town. She told me I had to wear it under my collared shirt, despite it violating the dress code. Knowing that I would be late for school if I argued, I put on the shirt and got in the car so I could start doing my homework.

The twenty-minute car ride went too fast. I remember asking my brothers whether they were okay, whether they had had breakfast, and told them to have a great day as we approached the parking lot. There was no way I was going to be able to finish my homework before classes. I was heartbroken. I wouldn't be able to be the straight A student I wanted to be. I wouldn't fit in with my classmates. They would know I was different. They would think I didn't belong. As I got out of the car, my bag of books felt especially heavy because of the soreness in my shoulders. I could hardly sling it over my shoulders.

Every morning the principal, a Christian Brother, stood in front of the school and said "good morning" to all the parents. As we pulled into the parking lot, I was so ashamed that I had not finished my homework that I did my best not to make eye contact with him. My face flushed. Would he know I hadn't done my homework? Could I get past him without him seeing me?

"Good morning, Patrick. Can I talk to you?" He must have sensed I hadn't done my homework. I walked nervously in his direction.

"Your shirt isn't dress code."

I remember flushing and thinking, "This is what I am getting in trouble for? This is what this Brother of the church wants to reprimand me for? A shirt? Surely God has better things to do!" I didn't say anything though. I just stood in front of him, head down.

"Look at me, Patrick."

As soon as my eyes lifted enough to see the Brother's face, they filled with tears. I remember the deep shame I felt in my body. "I am sorry," I said again and again, crying hysterically. "I'm sorry. I didn't have time. I need to finish my homework." The crying continued. I remember him looking at me seriously, expressionless.

"Don't apologize...ever. Do you have a piece of paper?"

I pulled out my notebook, which was all messed up from the scuffle the night before, and tore out a blank sheet. He took it. "A pen or pencil?" I handed him a pen. He tore the page in half, wrote on both pieces, and handed them to me. "The first note is for you to carry around saying it is okay for you to be out of dress code. The second note is excusing you from homework for all your classes for at least a week, and I want you to take it to your first period teacher right now and let him know that he is to follow the instructions on the note. You will spend first period with me."

"But..."

Pleading was useless. Confused, I did what he told me to do.

When I arrived at his office for first period, he asked me what happened and why I was wearing a turtleneck. No longer nervous about my homework, I started to cry again. Again he asked me to tell him what was happening at home. I couldn't. I couldn't tell him what had happened. I couldn't because I was afraid of what my story might mean for my safety when I did go home, for what it would mean for my brothers' safety. I cried for what seemed like an entire day. I had no power and no sense that he could save me from the trouble I was in. I was still up against that wall, suspended, with the weight of my family's suffering tugging at my feet as I was dangled by my neck. It's a burden of suffering to which God calls no one.

> I was still up against that wall, suspended, with the weight of my family's suffering tugging at my feet.

He sat with me for what might have been the entire day. After giving me space just to be, to exist, to breathe deeply the safety of the space, he reminded me that school would always be a safe space for me. He said that I would always have a home there at the school and with the Brothers, and that they were dedicated not just to educating me, but to providing a space for my flourishing. He invited me to morning-prayer time, and told me about all the extracurricular activities the school offered. He said that I could be at school as long as my family would allow. He would hold the space for me to be who I needed to be.

Over the course of the next six years, I took him up on all of these offers. I flourished there, and in many ways owe my life to these followers of Jesus. Now, not everyone has such a good experience with religious orders. I think especially of the clergy abuse that is becoming widely known. However, I firmly believe that it was the first time I was aware of God calling me to new life. It was as if I had received a personal invitation into the kingdom of God.

A theologian and mentor of mine, Dr. Frank Rogers, writes, "We are most fully human, most fully ourselves, when we see someone in the truth of his or her experience and are moved to respond with kindness and care" (Rogers 2015, 9). I often wonder what moved this Christian Brother in that moment to see me, in the truth of my pain, beneath the coverings of a turtleneck sweater—a scared, scarred, alone, frightened soul? What brought him to see me—to *truly* see me—as I walked across that parking lot? Was it God? Was it his Christian calling?

There is no doubt in my mind that I am saved. I am saved because at that moment God reached out and called me to life. If Christian vocation is the call by God to God's beloved for new life, then this Brother not only called to me on behalf of God, but also provided me with a space where new life could blossom. This was my first exposure to what Christian vocation is and to a living example of someone who lived into it. It was the first time I had experienced God.

If school were going to be a safe place for me, then I wanted it to be for others too. For God called me to three things that day: The first was to live, to survive to adulthood. This proved more difficult than I would ever imagine, as you will read. The second was to pursue theological education, because this life that the Brother was living saved me. I knew that following this call would fuel my life. I knew this because I witnessed someone living his vocation in this principal's actions of care toward me. The third thing was to hold open a space where people could be their truest selves, to be safe, to be surrounded by the goodness of God's protection. But all of this takes dedication to a way of life that allows for the space to live, to educate, and to hold space where healing can take place.

The Christian Brothers have a long history of educating young men. Blessed Brother Edmund Ignatius Rice (1762–1844 CE) was an Irish Roman Catholic missionary and educator. He was the founder of the Congregation of Christian Brothers and the Presentation Brothers. He was a married man who lost his wife in a tragic accident that also left his daughter disabled. After this tragedy, Blessed Edmund Ignatius Rice left his business and dedicated his life to the vocation of educating and serving the poor. At a time in Ireland when Catholics were not allowed to be educated under the British, Rice dedicated his life to the training of teachers who would teach children, focusing on the poor and marginalized. Eventually, several schools were built and the first few brothers took official religious vows, becoming one of the few Irish and lay-led orders. After his death in 1844, the Christian Brothers carried on, and they do so in my hometown, providing education and sanctuary for those young men who need it. I heard God's voice through this one Brother and the years of sanctuary I was provided by the Brothers. As a result, I knew I should dedicate my life to the human flourishing of my students. The most authentic way I can do that is by simply inviting them into a new way of understanding how we live into God's compassion in *lo cotidiano*—our day-to-day lived realities.

The Brothers take vows of poverty, chastity, and obedience, as well as perseverance in the congregation and teaching the poor. This particular school of mine is "missioned to evangelize and to catechize by fulfilling the four apostolic goals: spreading the gospel message, building a faith community, celebrating the faith, and performing service to those in need." Here was someone living the legacy, mission, and spirit of their vocation in a radical way, in a radical act of compassion. This brother knew he was going to educate young men. I am sure he did not know that morning that he would be called to reach into the life of one of his young students, see the depths of his suffering, and offer not only a compassionate hand but also saving grace in the form of the rhythms of his own Christian vocational calling.

His vocation was played out in a particular way. He invited me to participate in the beauty of his life, not knowing the particular pains I was bringing into his home, into his narrative, and into his vocational journey. He had committed to being in a space, to a mission, to vows, to God, and it manifested itself one morning in the simple act of inviting me to join him on his walk.

Here was a radical act of one's vocation. By radical, I am not meaning politically liberal or advocating on behalf of any one thing or the other. Rather, I mean in the sense that the word *radical* comes from the Latin *radix,* meaning "root" or "having roots." It is through this rootedness in the Christian tradition and in community that he lived into his vocation.

It is clear how this particular Brother's vocation was expressed in and through my narrative. He saved me. God called him into life and he in turn called me into life. When I think about my own vocation as a Latinx, Christian educator, religious scholar, and theologian, it was in that moment that I heard God's voice calling, showing me compassion, and inspiring me to know that this act of grace bestowed on me would also become my vocation. I wanted to extend God's hand further, and through religious education, transform the lives of others. This was the first time I had heard that still, small voice of God, and I wanted to amplify it throughout my life.

When I write and educate today on the margins of the academy, or research those places that are using religion and education to transform the lives of their communities, I am living into that first call from that Brother: a call to walk a life of justice and compassion.

Chapter 2

Valley of Death

Even though I walk through the valley of the shadow of death,
I fear no evil, for You are with me; Your rod and Your staff,
they comfort me.
— *Psalm 23:4, NASB*

As a young father, I want nothing more than my son to be safe. We live in a place where we know our neighbors. I am doing the necessary inward and ongoing work of processing life events that might otherwise create a monster. I create a safe learning environment for him; mitigate the chances of him having an encounter with a *Stranger* like I had; surround him only with those that love him. My partner, not having the same scars as were inflicted in my childhood, reimagines with me what a household might be, challenging norms, while at the same time adopting and living out others. Conditions worthy of human flourishing are needed for deep vocational discernment. However, these conditions are always tenuous, for our world is broken, and sometimes we have to do our discerning through the mess.

Vocational discernment often happens in the midst of violence, or, in the words of David, it happens in "the valley of the shadow of death." This valley provides a different lens to vocational discernment than is usually offered. Discernment is not simply about finding our whole selves, the selves that God has called us to be, or the work we feel called to do. Rather, it is about finding the self that cries out to survive. As Parker Palmer says, "From the beginning, our lives lay down clues to selfhood and vocation, though the clues may be hard to decode. But

21

trying to interpret them is profoundly worthwhile" (Palmer 2000, 15). We are going to try to decode some clues together. We are going to listen to the Holy through our narratives.

Sometimes I want to tell my son that we should just imagine the resurrection and skip over the violence of life and crucifixion. I mean not only the resurrection of Jesus, but of all innocent bodies. Yet the conditions for this sort of imagining are not conducive to the neighborhood in which I grew up. In that neighborhood, that was not our reality. Sometimes we live through the violence of Friday over and over again. As trauma repeats itself, our ability to discern our vocation is drastically altered. Violence places indelible markers in our psychological development that we have to work through in order to hear the voice of God. Geoffrey Canada says it much more directly than most:

> What if I were to tell you that we are approaching one of the most dangerous periods in our history since the Civil War? Rising unemployment, shifting economic priorities, hundreds of thousands of people growing up poor and with no chance of employment, never having held a legal job. A whole generation who serve no useful role in America now and see no hope of a future role for themselves. A new generation, the handgun generation. Growing up under conditions of war. War as a child, war as an adolescent, war as an adult. War never ending. (Canada 2010, viii)

When I was a child, there was no future role for me. My community had been abandoned in the wars of poverty and violence. We were casualties of a war fought by our ancestors. Here is the story of one such war for me. A story that has me reimagining the resurrection of my own life daily and that thrusts me into the work of justice and compassion.

The Christian Brothers did a good job of keeping me out of trouble while I was at school. But of course I wasn't able to spend every waking hour with them. More importantly, the home with the Stranger wasn't the only place that was violent. In fact, it was not long after that event that I no longer had to live with the Stranger, moving in with my father full-time. His home was safe. But the community around it was not always so.

I would go home from the Christian Brothers school, and, like all kids, in my adolescence I had my place of escape. For some that place of escape is their room, a friend's house, or buried deep in technology.

For me, it was always the basketball courts. I would go to the same park every day, and sometimes play until long after dark. There were no lights at this park. There is safety, however, in knowing the contours of the darkness. These conditions formed me.

The problem with this park is that it rested on a boundary line, a border, no more artificial than an international border, but just as real in terms of enforcement. For those from my community with the migrant narrative written into our very DNA, these borders might have been those large walls patrolled by heavy duty machinery and Immigration and Customs Enforcement (ICE) officers. We dared not cross those borders, and when we did, we did so deliberately. Sometimes we crossed because the grocery store, or the gas station, which were essential to our survival, were on the other side. Other times we crossed because we wanted to challenge the "border patrol," to tell them that this is not their land. But this border patrol was not the type of border patrol we are used to hearing politicians talk about, though as a Chicano I maintain that the border patrol of the United States is no less gang-like.

These border patrol agents had uniforms. They had colors. They had weapons. They knew how and when to enforce their rule. And as with all borders, enforcing them was a matter of security for their territory, and more importantly, a way to look after their own community and their own interests. The park also signified a marketplace—not for the exchange of ideas like one would find at a university, but for drugs and other paraphernalia. This park was for "meet-ups." It was also for kids. Every park, every open space, every hidden space, has a purpose on the map. And I knew every spot on this map. My basketball court was usually off-limits to the older teenagers and adults, or so I thought. It took a lot to keep it that way. I had to know every person who came to it, meeting and talking to every party on my side or the other. This was a safe place, a place granted an almost religious immunity.

Now that I had been saved by the Christian Brothers, I shared my story at this park with anyone who would listen. Doing so was infectious. It was church. Like the great Chicharito, I would pray before we played and would often ask God to keep us safe above all things.

For the park was also a place where rival gangs would cross each other. It was *la frontera*. Though she meant it differently, Gloria Anzaldúa gave us the image of the border as being like barbed wire, where two worlds slice across each other. Borders are places where bloodshed occurs regularly. The young men and women of this neighborhood, from an early age, knew this park as a place where the power and control of the barrio was held. Other than that, the park was nothing special.

Situated in a ravine, the park separated a popular middle-class suburb from an older neighborhood in Alisal, a suburb of Salinas. It had a nice path that followed the creek at the bottom of this ravine. Next to the basketball courts was a volleyball pit, and not more than 50 yards from them was a skate park. It was a standard park—benches, trash cans, and families walking and playing with their children. It was also within a stone's throw of my father's house at the time, a house he rented with my stepmom and younger brother and sister.

I would be naïve to think that I did not choose this park over other parks for a certain sense of comfort in knowing my enemy and my friends. Such familiarity makes it easier to be able to see the colors of those who you are not supposed to be near and stay away from them if need be. It is also better to be known in such spaces and able to represent certain things, ideologies, and neighborhoods. I felt a certain degree of safety in knowing where I stood and who stood with me—even if it is an artificially constructed sense of safety.

I came home one afternoon particularly excited. My stepmom was driving up my younger brother and sister to their birth father's home, about an hour away. My grandma had come to stay with my father, whom I was living with by this point in my life. I don't remember why she was there, but when Grandma came around, my whole world changed. It's not just that she was the walking stereotype of an *abuelita* who cooks amazing food, pinches your cheeks, loves you unconditionally, tells you how it is when you need to hear it, and is the only one there when everyone else has abandoned you. She was all that and more. When saints speak, you listen. When they work miracles on the wounds of your heart, you are healed. My grandma represented for the Reyes family this magical meeting place of a deep Catholic religiosity and an ancient sacredness that predated the Spanish people's arrival in the Americas. She had ways of healing the sick of heart that inspire me to this day.

> My grandma represented for the Reyes family this magical meeting place of a deep Catholic religiosity and an ancient sacredness.

That day, when I got home, my father and my grandma weren't at home yet. Not knowing where they were, I did what I did every day—I went to the park.

Perhaps it was because I was feeling especially confident that day that I changed my clothes. I made sure to wear the right park attire—extra wide black cords, cloth belt buckle, white shoes, white undershirt, button down gray and black shirt, rosary hanging in plain sight, and, at the time—those who know me now would laugh at this because of how fully committed my head is to being bald—my hair greased over and held in place. I checked my look in the mirror. Right colors. Cords straight. Kicks clean. Chest puffed out with the cross dangling for all to see. Ready to go represent at the park.

I hopped the large concrete wall that separated my dad's street from the park. I ran down and immediately saw some of my neighborhood friends. These friends did not look like the kids at the Christian Brothers' school. These were the kids of my neighborhood—brown like me, dressed like me, afraid like me, but without a school to fall back on. I had grown up knowing these kids, but they never came over to the house and I never went to theirs. We celebrated our hangout space as our space.

A few of us gathered, exchanged the usual casual chat. They called me the *pocho* priest, because of my obvious lack of loyalty to *la raza* evident in my not knowing enough Spanish, going to the private school, and being religious. I called them names that only we would call each other, and that I won't repeat here. We laughed. They smoked weed one of them had brought to sell. We sat on the park benches and were loud and obnoxious. We annoyed the parents that were in the park with our swearing and smoking, but we were in charge of this space. It was our space, won by knowing and defining our boundaries.

The point of conversation that day, and every day in these environments, was escapism, though we didn't use that word. We did our best to imagine what life was like outside of the valley, outside of the neighborhood. At this point, we all imagined a life outside of the fields of Salinas, some more figuratively than others. I had a leg up in life. My father was a "manager" at one of the plants, working in IT. After 10 years of seeking his degree, he became the first in his family to get his college diploma. He worked full-time, loved his children full-time, and finished school full-time. I remember he worked in a plant while he was in school. I must have been two or three years old. They would roll my little round body down the assembly line. Now, he had made it off the assembly line, and my friends would tell me over and over how I had won the lottery. In many ways I had, and I continue to reap its benefits. Life in these neighborhoods is often a game of chance; odds are never in your favor. Like the lottery, we imagined what we could win. We talked about the cars we would buy, the girls we would date, the places we would go—none of them outside of California, except for a few places in Arizona.

What did we know about the larger world? Let's be clear, the world wasn't exactly inviting us places or giving us things.

We started to play basketball to help pass the time.

I remember having the ball in my hands, and that is when I saw it: A gray sedan with tinted windows, driving about five miles an hour rolls up right next to the park. As the car comes closer and closer to the parking lot that separates the gray car from us, it was as if we all saw it happen at the same time. The driver side window rolled down and out of it emerged a handgun attached to a body we couldn't see. Knowing what would follow, we all hit the ground.

"Bwat! Bwat! Bwat!"

The bullets flew past me. People were screaming. I squeezed the asphalt like it was a blanket. Then I heard the gray car speed away.

All that was left was the screaming.

I stood up, dazed and confused, trying to see what had followed those bullets. I checked my own body, and saw my colors still shining, my shoes still bright white, my hair still greased over. I looked at my friends: they were still in the same colors without a scratch from the violence. There were no other young adults on the playground, and we were the only ones in gang colors. We had been the target.

The screaming continued. Shell-shocked, I looked for something to attach my eyes to, to make sense of this experience.

No more than 10 feet from my own body, a little girl was lying face down on the black top.

> When life has been taken, it is hard to imagine life at all. When the sounds of gun shots and bullets are whizzing around you, it is impossible to hear God calling you to new life.

Vocational discernment is not a phrase that crosses one's mind amidst images like this. When life has been taken, it is hard to imagine life at all. When the sounds of gun shots and bullets are whizzing around you, it is impossible to hear God calling you to new life.

The screaming continued. I cried. My friends cried. We may have been hopped up on machismo when we set out for the park, but in the face of this violence we were paralyzed. We stood there in our gang colors, marked like Cain for death, only someone else's life was taken that day: an innocent child, an innocent young girl who could have lived a long and beautiful life, but instead was face down. Her mother ran over to her body. She attempted to breathe life into her. She said prayers in her native tongue. It is the only way we know how to talk to God in these moments.

"We have to get out of here!" One of my friends yelled.

The mother of the young girl yelled at us. Called us names. Condemned us. Cursed us. "You f—ing kids! You did this," she screamed. The pain in her eyes still scourges my soul. I stared back at her. I knew it was my fault. I looked at the little girl's lifeless body. With real fear and trembling, I continued to look down at her body until the tugging of *mi carnal* moved my feet away from the violence. At first, we ran indiscriminately. Up one block, then another block right back in the direction we had come from. We ran in circles, hid behind bushes, hopped fences, hid in backyards of people we knew and people we didn't. Like Bigger Thomas in Richard Wright's *Native Son,* we ran knowing that the system was out for us. After all of this running, we ended up across the street from the scene of the crime in my father's house. By the time we made it there, there were only two of us left. We were tired and sweaty. And no sooner had we opened the door and gone inside than there was a knock at the front door.

I imagine the police watched us run down the street and followed us to the house. When the officers heard us talking, whining, asking each other if we should open the door, they banged more loudly. "Open the door, *putos*!" I looked through the little peep hole, and saw a white officer was standing there, hand over his gun.

"What do you want?" I yelled back.

"We just need to talk to you about what happened. Open the door now!"

My body told me not to, and, as soon as I cracked the door it was slammed open and we were dragged out to the driveway without any words being exchanged. We were handcuffed and told some words about why we were being "detained." I didn't understand the gringo's English or Spanish, but I just knew we were in trouble for multiple reasons. One reason: That gray sedan was surely still out there. It could be watching us right now, waiting for these cops to let us go. The second reason was that the cops had "declared war on the gangs." The remaining friend, Javier, and I were dressed for war. We had all the colors and markers to signal we were the enemy to these uniformed and armed militia. It was a legitimate war zone, with us experiencing fire from all sides! We were taken out of the house and thrown into the back of his police car.

"You little *vatos* are going to burn for this shit. You know that, right? This will teach you to bang in my neighborhood." He drove us out of my father's neighborhood back to the park. I didn't know police protocol, but none of this seemed right. First I fidgeted in the back seat, then I started screaming in protest, kicking the seat in front of me.

"Don't take us back there! You're gonna get us killed!" I yelled.

"You pieces of shit deserve to die," the policeman responded.

In many ways, it seems my life is always a series of going to and from that park. The place where the little girl was murdered had been cordoned off with yellow tape, but the little girl's body was still on the ground for everyone to see. This was one of those times where the police officers—who didn't look like us, talk like us, or care about us—allowed a little girl to be murdered again, and again, and again. The community watched that girl be murdered every time a cop went over to look at something around the body, or another reporter's van arrived, or worse, when we rolled up with the cops. Handcuffed and colored, we could feel that the community's eyes were on us. It was as if we had actually murdered the girl. It was like a Western: The Marshall had caught the Bad Guys, and was bringing them back to the community to be judged and hanged.

When we arrived, we were approached by a guy in a tie. "You know what happened."

"They were the ones that they were shooting at! They are why my girl is dead," the mother yelled from the other side of the yellow tape.

We were quiet. Here we were back at the scene for everyone to see. They dragged us out in public! Like the mother, they must be blaming us for what happened. *They want us dead,* I remember thinking. After the shooting, we realized the guys in the gray sedan were shooting at us, not at the little girl. The cops might as well have been shooting at us too. If we said who we knew it was, we were dead. Perhaps we were dead anyway.

The police in our neighborhood never seemed to understand the politics they played with brown bodies. To them we are all equally guilty. It was as if we are all dark-skinned demons, creating a perpetual hell where we torture our own kind, and disrupt the white haven they created. We needed cops who engaged our community in positive ways. Who came to our backyard parties. Who visited our homes. Who knew our names and our families. Cops like that would have changed our neighborhood. We didn't have that, though. Instead, we had the "Gang Task Force" declaring war on our neighborhood, our community, and our people.

This specially assembled group of individuals rolled up on the park like they were in a superhero movie. A specially created super-trooper unit, this group was designed for the sole purpose of fighting the "thugs" on the street. To borrow from Frantz Fanon's famous investigation, this group consisted mainly of brown-skinned, white-masked individuals (Fanon, 2008). They looked like us, but wanted to prove to white society they were on their side. They were the "good" browns, who could beat the other browns into submission because they knew how to think like us, walk like us, talk like us, drink like us; shit, they even grew up and lived on our side of town. Why couldn't we, the violent and incredulous youth, just be more like them—people who took orders from those who created these borders with economic and systemic violence, the same policies and laws that created these battlegrounds in the first place? But they didn't understand that. For them and the local lawmakers, our lives and our communities were the set of a superhero movie, and we were the villains they were going to fight and defeat.

One large brown-skinned white mask came over to me. He was probably six feet tall, full-body armor covering him, dark glasses. He came and stood right over the top of me. Pushed me around.

"Who shot? I won't mess you up if you tell me." He pushed and shoved me like he had some power over me or my friends. And he did. I had no control of my body anymore. He shoved me toward the little girl's body.

Grabbing me behind the neck, he focused my attention on the body, "You did this. You know that right? You going to tell us who took the shots?"

I threw up all over my clean white shoes and started to cry. "You going to cry, you little b—h?" he said. "You protecting your homies? Or are you scared of what they are going to do to you? You scared of what I am going to do you?" He didn't understand power. He just tried to play like he did. He thought that our fear of the pain he could create for us would force us to talk to him. He thought he was in control of our bodies, of our neighborhood, and of our lives.

But we didn't say anything to him. Why would we? He only wanted us to confess that it was our fault that the little girl was dead. It was. But not just us. He was guilty too! And the people in the gray sedan. Why

> We are all guilty in the death of innocents.

didn't he see that? We are all guilty in the death of innocents. Some of us just feel it more than others.

I still carry that mother's tears and cries with me.

After failed attempts to get us to talk, and after retraumatizing us by forcing us to return to that place of incredible violence, the cops allowed us to go home. We were told that if we'd seen anything or knew anything we needed to call the police immediately. When they followed up with us a few weeks later, we of course told them everything we could and that they already had from their eye-witnessed reports. There was nothing surprising about who and where the shooting came from to anyone in the community. I can only imagine we were let go that afternoon because at little girl's mother or a passerby knew we were the ones they were shooting at. I don't know for certain though. I was just relieved to go.

It was dark outside. I walked to Javier's house with him. Once he was inside, I ran home. I ran home hoping no one would see me. As best I could, I hopped fences all the way home trying to avoid the roads. I am sure that evening at least one phone call was made to the police about the "leap-frogging, fence-jumping Mexican."

I made it back and my father and grandma were both home. I ran to give my grandma a hug. I cried my heart out. "Oh, mijo." She just held me. She commented on how sweaty and stinky I was. You can imagine the amount of hurt and pain I brought into this house, not just because of this experience, but because of events I described earlier. Layer these oppressions with the socio-economic marginalization of my people, and the voice of God in me was all but gone. It was not even a whisper at this point.

I held on to Grandma, not because she could make all of this pain go away, but because she was one of the few people in the world to whom we didn't have to explain our pain. She could hear the story in how hard I squeezed her. She could tell me the narrative of all that I had encountered that afternoon by tending to every tear that fell from my face. She knew the pain. She didn't tell me until much later how she knew. At that moment, she just held me. She pulled me close and said, "We will make this right." Little did I know how sincere she was about making it right.

After she went back to her own home in Bakersfield, California, at her request I did everything I could to find people who shared my experiences. I plugged in to the National Coalition Building Institute, thanks to the wisdom of a religion teacher at school. I started going to local youth meet-ups in the neighborhood. There were churches, community centers, schools, and even the local library that were all building programming to address the violence.

I started spending my time on and off campus organizing and staying involved in local community events to combat the violence in my neighborhood. Also, like any teenage boy, I fell deeply in and out of love. I won't make light of this experience. Though I was too traumatized to be in an emotionally stable relationship at the age of 15 or 16, I am ever-grateful for the care and compassion of my first love and her family. They provided a refuge when I had few places to go.

In my free time, I would walk down to the local high school and meet with those students I knew from the surrounding neighborhoods, to play basketball and to continue to talk to my peers about stopping the violence in my neighborhood. But such places, though created by well-meaning people, are not permanent structures. While I am grateful for the homes I was allowed into, they did not provide the structure necessary to keep me safe.

I remember calling my grandma some time later. "Grandma, I can't stop thinking about that little girl. You know, they haven't caught the guy."

"Mijo, things don't have to be this way. I will pray that the angels watch over you as you figure this out."

"What am I supposed to do?"

She told me I had a responsibility to change what was happening. I believe this was the first time I heard God speaking directly to me through my grandma. That call came to me in her words about responsibility to my community, a responsibility I am still consistently falling short on, but it was a call for me to be with my people.

> She told me I had a responsibility to change what was happening. I believe this was the first time I heard God speaking directly to me through my grandma.

She had me call the local priest, whom I had known since I was younger, and a few other local leaders. She told me that together we could organize to change this situation. But after gathering a group of about five, this group of white adults treated me as if I was a fly on the wall. All I could do was listen to adults discuss what they declared was a youth problem, one which they gave the youth no agency to solve.

They proposed solutions. Let me go on record saying that these were the worst solutions one could possibly imagine coming from a group of well-meaning adults. This is not to say that all white liberals come up with such horrible plans to "help" the poor, disenfranchised, abused, and tortured black and brown bodies, but these ideas were some of the worst.

One idea included bringing in "good" kids, so that we could be "exposed" to good examples in our age group. If you don't know why this is a bad idea, you need to spend more time with black and brown youth. Another idea was to bus us to what they called "rehab facilities" ("but," they added, "we need to come up with a better name"). These trips included things like "scared straight programs" at the nearby Soledad State Prison and Salinas Valley State Prison, two maximum security prisons, homes at one point to people such as Charles Manson, Efren Saldivar, Juan Corona, and Bunchy Carter. They proposed taking us to go to see our "future home" if we continued down the path of violence. Another trip suggested was to the local church, to get lessons about how to live a good life. When I tried to explain how incredibly bad these ideas were, and that, by ignoring the underlying issues, and by leaving our neighborhood in poverty and with a lack of access to goods and services, they were perpetuating violence against us, the group of adults just told me to be quiet.

When I suggested that maybe they should invest in grocery stores, school programs, libraries, and community centers, they returned with the usual adult response: "We know better." Here I was again, a youth, saying that the conditions that these adults were helping to create and sustain were the very conditions in which God's call to life was being drowned out. Let's not forget that our side of town was zoned for multi-housing, but their side was zoned for single-family lots. They designed this hell hole. On our side, overcrowded schools and fewer parks. On their side, lots of good schools and spacious parks. But apparently children never know what's best. At least their plans could save one or two of us from our devilish ways and heathen cultures. *Psh.*

Eventually a larger group came together to build a community coalition that wrote a document that addressed the many issues affecting our community. The youth were not included in creating that document either. We didn't receive recognition for our own gatherings or our own ability to discern life in this violent landscape. We didn't even get a byline for our input on what the community might need. Instead, we saw adults professionalizing our problems, earning salaries to discuss our problems, proposing solutions to those problems, and then blaming us when those solutions—which were bogus from the start—didn't make an immediate impact on our community. We weren't compensated for the work we did in our community, but I can assure you we were the ones making a difference in the community.

We marched; we protested; and even though we couldn't vote we worked to elect local officials that represented our community. We gathered together to remember all those who had died or were affected by the violence. This was traumatic for us, to relive *la lucha* every day. But we survived. We attempted to find ways to live through the violence and better our community. What about the departed?

A question that still haunts my work today is: What about the little girl and her family? Did they receive real justice? What justice might be had for the undocumented? I assumed the family were migrant workers. I don't know what happened to them after the services were announced in the paper. I never saw or heard from them, and the media often forgets the undocumented. They don't care about the undocumented; they don't care about the little brown girl who was killed. Had she been a white girl with blue eyes, there would have been cameras in our community for days. Instead, this small girl with jet-black hair, brown eyes, and brown skin was lost to us. But could there still be justice in another way? Could there be forgiveness? Spirits often leave this world, but rarely do they leave our communities.

A few months after her murder, no one had made an arrest. Let me be clear about a few things. Death was right in front of our eyes. We, as those who had to bear witness to an innocent life taken from us, were treated as if we were people holding smoking guns. The police had taken statements. They had mined our community for information. But the criminal justice system treated our neighborhood as if we brought this on ourselves. We were all guilty. This is terrifying for young people of color in communities like ours. To be afraid of the justice system, to be afraid of the neighborhood you are living in, to be navigating on this thin line between life and death is not just a matter of cooperation with the police or doing the right thing. We knew, just as they did, who did what and where they lived. We asked the question, as I am sure you are now, why didn't the police make an arrest? This was a question we asked in our homes, and for those of us who were closest to the violence, the number of possible reasons scared us. What scared us more, though, was that someone out there still wanted us dead.

If we were going to die, would anyone care? Would we be forgotten? Because of who we were and what we looked like, would anyone mourn our death? Like Tupac said all those years ago in his song "Life Goes

On" about the lives of young people of color, "Nobody cries when we die." For a world that seeks our destruction and death, would anyone care if we were gunned down? If there was no justice for an innocent girl, why would the system care about us? If it seemed as if God was absent in that moment, why would God be present in our moment of death? Nobody cries when we die.

Javier (the friend with whom I hopped fences) was over one day and we were talking about the work we were doing in the community and how we were both terrified that we were still marked—that one day that gray car would come back. We talked about what death might be like and what we might have to do to prepare for it. I can't remember why my grandma was with us, but she was that day. It might have even been the last time she came up to Salinas from Bakersfield before my high school graduation. Javier and I were sitting at my father's kitchen table, reassuring each other that "he" wasn't coming to get us.

"Mijo, come here." My grandma was standing by the door. "You know who it was?" I told her I didn't know. She gave me the look that grandmas give their kids before they bring the wrath of God into the room. "You know?" I shook my head again. Javier must have given it away, because he was squirming in his chair.

She dragged Javier and me out to Javier's car. And by drag, I mean she literally grabbed our shirts and pulled us in the direction that her faith was guiding her. She told my friend to drive; I didn't have a car at this point.

"Take me there," she said.

"What?" He asked, with the high-pitched screech of puberty.

"You heard me!"

We were both terrified. Not long ago, this gray sedan had rolled up on us, marked us, and taken shots at us. Now my grandma was driving us across a border, a border we had only begun to organize to make safer, but in many ways hadn't negotiated our own lives around since that experience. Javier put the car in reverse, backed out of the driveway, and started to drive out and around the corner.

We passed the park and then the school. We drove for about 20 minutes. It was a long drive to the edge of town, just across from a small community library. I honestly could not believe what was happening: Javier was actually driving us there! When we got to the street the person lived on, we pulled up and stopped at the end.

"Please don't make us do this!" Javier said.

"Is this where he lives?"

"Down there."

We pulled up to the person's house. No car. Maybe he wasn't home. She immediately got out of the car. I remember nearly peeing myself and thinking, *What is she doing? What is happening? Is this where I see my grandma die and then me right after?*

My grandma's full-time job, as I understood it, was to track down students who didn't come to high school. Considering she did this for her own six kids, plus her nieces, nephews, and grandchildren who lived with her, "rolling up" on someone who had "lost their way" was her living into her vocation and, in many ways, is what qualifies her for sainthood. This was a little different though. While this person may have skipped class, my concern was not whether he would continue his education. It was whether or not he was going to kill us.

She got out of the car and walked down the street. Javier and I were careful to keep our distance, always ready to run.

"This his house?" she asked.

Javier and I both nodded.

She walked up the driveway to the front door and knocked on it. The door cracked open.

"What the fuck do you want?"

"You know what you did?"

"I don't know what you are talking about *vieja*, but you better move your ass off my doorstep."

"You know them?"

His gaze turned up and looked at us. We made eye contact. The connection happened at a primal level. If this had been the wild with just that look passing between us, I would have known where I was in the food chain—right at the bottom. I wanted to run, but I was paralyzed—stuck in this moment between life and death. The cop pointing us out in the middle of the park was one thing, but being put on the spot by my grandma made her a target as well! At least when the cop did it, he didn't have the slightest clue about his imagined immunity from the violence. "You a cop? You sure as hell don't look like one. Hey, you two, you know what's coming, don't you?" This was obviously a rhetorical question.

"Look at me!" Grandma commanded him.

He turned his gaze back to my grandma.

"Turn yourself in," she said.

He stared at her for a moment and then slammed the door.

My grandma turned around and walked toward us. "Come on, let's go. Get in the car." My grandma's pace had quickened. She knew something was coming. The front door opened again.

"That's right." He stood once again on his doorstep—with what I assumed was his gun, perhaps even the same one he'd used earlier. We didn't stay to find out.

On the car ride back to the house, I sat nervously in the back seat. I stared out the back window. Paranoid, I thought he would follow us home. My grandma said, "Mijo, it's okay to be scared, but he is going to do the right thing." I remember thinking that she had no idea what the right thing was. The "right thing," in *our* neighborhood, was for him to get in his car and wait until there were plenty of witnesses, because no one would report you anyway, and shoot us in broad daylight to send a message.

The car ride took forever. I didn't trust my grandma's judgment. She had just gotten us all killed. When we got back to the house, she walked in and got ready for my father to return with my brothers. She began making dinner. It was as if nothing happened. Javier dropped us off and then immediately drove home.

We were pushed into a reality I couldn't imagine. My reality was something more attuned to Joshua or Kings. These biblical books, while they tell some stories about faithful people doing the right thing, actually tell a whole bunch of stories about violent groups of people fighting for the right to exist and occupy territory. Joshua, for example, serves as one of Moses commanders, and is sent out to investigate the land of Canaan, and then, ultimately, to lead the conquest of the lands.

Perhaps this is why early on in the book of Joshua is: "Have I not commanded you? Be strong and courageous! Do not tremble or be dismayed, for the LORD your God is with you wherever you go" (Josh. 1:9, NASB). We walk in war zones. Not just in Salinas, but all over the country: in St. Louis, Baltimore, Houston, Ferguson, Chicago, Memphis, Camden, Tulsa, Detroit, West Oakland, Los Angeles, Charleston, Sacramento, Boston, Washington, D.C., Orlando. For these, and so many more communities, there are areas where, when you walk out your door, you step into a war zone. The temptation, though, is to be like Joshua and to take a community as your land.

After all, we are oppressed and deserve freedom, right? This is what we think we hear God calling us to do. This is what I knew that man would do: come and claim his land. This is what I was very tempted to do, when I wasn't peeing myself, as a teenage boy full of violent, traumatic hauntings and raging hormones. I was going to assert myself in this space. Sure, I could have claimed that God called me to get a piece, put on my *"macho cholo"* costume with the color of my block, represent, and get gunned down protecting my space in historic fashion. This was part of the narrative to which many in my neighborhood thought God was calling them. These are not the ideal conditions for complete human flourishing, in which we can take the time and space we need to discern our own vocational commitments. I never once stopped that day to ask, "Who is God calling me to be in this moment?" I merely thought about survival. This is a powerful recognition, because these are the conditions in which God's faint call can either be heard or disregarded. The call to survival is a call that doesn't fit neatly into these two categories. Sometimes the voice is so faint or muddled in violence, we have a hard time recognizing its sound at all. These are conditions in which witnessing another way can be profound, because, at its core, it is a call simply to live.

> I never once stopped that day to ask, "Who is God calling me to be in this moment?" I merely thought about survival.

I see navigating my Christian call through this lens—as a contested and embattled landscape set out before me in which I must do my best to hear God's call. For so many in our communities, this is not a choice. These are the conditions set before us, and, for many, God's voice is drowned out by the violence and abuse. I often think about how Moses was called. Moses was taking care of the sheep and goats when God called to Moses and said:

> The Lord said, "I have indeed seen the misery of my people in Egypt. I have heard them crying out because of their slave drivers, and I am concerned about their suffering. So I have come down to rescue them from the hand of the Egyptians and to bring them up out of that land into a good and spacious land, a land flowing with milk and honey—the home of the Canaanites, Hittites, Amorites, Perizzites, Hivites and Jebusites. And now the cry of the Israelites has reached me, and I have seen the way the Egyptians are oppressing them. So now, go. I am sending you to Pharaoh to bring my people the Israelites out of Egypt." (Ex. 3:7–10, NIV)

My response to my grandma was similar to Moses's response to God—apprehension, lack of confidence, and forecasting a future of inability to carry out what she was asking of me. Yet my grandma, like God, was with me. She showed me the way to that killer's front door. Now she was calling to me and telling me it was my responsibility to do what I could for my community, to walk to every door of every killer and tell them *basta!*

As we know from the Torah, God does not just call and make things right; God calls and then we have work to do. Moses was called to far more than I was: to talk to Pharaoh, survive ten plagues, escape from slavery and an ensuing attack, and venture through the wilderness for 40 years with a grumbling people. Through all of this hardship, those who followed Moses were called to be faithful. Moses led God's people of out Egypt and through the desert, but he didn't do so alone. He had Miriam and Aaron, both performing their own tasks under God. Miriam in particular acted on behalf of a community while living under a patriarchy that was not ready for women leaders. If you remember the story, Miriam is the older sister of Moses and Aaron. At the request of Yocheved, their mother, Miriam hides her baby brother Moses by the side of the river in order for Moses to survive the mandated killing of all infant Hebrew boys. She then suggests to the princess who finds Moses that she should take on a nurse and recommends Yocheved.

In our neighborhood, brown boys are destined not to survive to adulthood. Systemic oppression, poverty, and lack of access to basic human needs, such as food, education, and work, ensure that the generation of infants will never make it to adulthood. We need more Miriams who can navigate these violent systems. We need more Grandma Reyeses who call us to life.

> In our neighborhood, brown boys are destined not to survive to adulthood. Systemic oppression, poverty, and lack of access to basic human needs, such as food, education, and work, ensure that the generation of infants will never make it to adulthood. We need more Miriams who can navigate these violent systems. We need more Grandma Reyeses who call us to life.

Miriam returns to the story of Exodus when she leads the Hebrews across the Red Sea. This part of the narrative is considered to be one of the oldest written parts of the biblical accounts. In the book of Numbers, she and her brother say about Moses, "Has the Lord spoken only through Moses?" they asked. "Hasn't he also spoken through us?" And the Lord heard this" (12:2,

NIV). While she was indeed struck by God and then cured for these supposedly presumptuous words, there is so much to be recovered in her defiance of patriarchy. And even when she remained outside of the community for seven days with her illness, the Midrash teaches us that she taught women how to survive and thrive in harsh conditions and that there was much to learn from the experience of looking into the camp and being an outsider. For this, she is heralded alongside her brothers: "I brought you up out of Egypt and redeemed you from the land of slavery. I sent Moses to lead you, also Aaron and Miriam." (Mic. 6:4, NIV).

I recover the story of Miriam here not simply because she sang and danced people out of slavery, but because throughout her life she is depicted in this brave role. At a young age, she saved the voiceless and suggested to the powers that be that others should care for the marginalized. She played a prophetic role dancing out in front of the Hebrews, carrying the people's spirit through the wilderness. While she is named a prophetess, and while prophets' teachings are typically recorded, what is curious is that none of her teachings are recorded in this direct way. Both problematic and beautiful as her teachings were her actions—just like Grandma's.

When Moses went up Mt. Sinai and his brother Aaron was collecting gold from the people out of which to make the golden calf, where was Miriam? She was teaching! She visited the women during meals and cared for them. As Carol Ochs names,

> According to our new Midrash, Miriam gave her first teaching at this decisive time. In Moses's prolonged absence, the people grew restive and frightened, and the men planned for war. But the children still had to be cared for and the meals prepared. Miriam visited the women one at a time, as they cooked and stirred, rocked their children and comforted them, and she pointed out, "revelation is taking place right now as you cook and comfort, tend the fires, and nurse the young." (Ochs, 495-496).

Miriam is the first to teach that our experience of revelation is not outside daily experience! In my Latinx theological tradition, we talk about this as God being revealed in *lo cotidiano*. Miriam comes to represent the epitome of a different kind of vocation. She is someone who was living on the margins, was kept at the margins, and yet found ways to help her community survive. Carol Ochs continues that "Miriam helped the others see that...our lives shape and instruct us, and we have all had experiences of revelation and redemption" (Ochs, 501). Miriam's call from God is to help the community survive through all of the hardships of being on the run, being hunted by former masters, and forging a new identity in the wilderness. The young brothers and sisters in my neighborhood all needed this sort of guidance and vocational direction. I needed this guidance. Some of us had it, and some of us didn't. But our Miriam—Grandma Reyes— danced out in front of us, fed our spirits, fed us meals, and cared for our weary bodies and souls.

This model of vocational discernment does not lend itself to traditional vocational discernment literature, which often resembles *Don Quix*ote more than anything tied to realities that marginalized communities experience. Because Miriam does not hail from the dominant cultural paradigm, she is marginalized. Miriam represents for our community those women like my grandma who lead the community in our survival. Miriam is like the mothers that worked with us and said *¡basta!* to the violence. She is like those women who educated, trained, and led us into a new way of life.

Despite having this support, I must admit that the promised land looked really far off when I was initially called. And, like the Hebrew's promised land, it was a contested space. Someone already lived there. Gangs had already carved out which streets belonged to whom, and I can assure you they did not set aside a street for peacemakers. There could not be a more perfect analogy for the neighborhoods and how we operate in this world. There is no promised land where you can build peace from scratch. There is no space where people from my community can live where space is not contested. There will always be someone—a neighbor, an other, an enemy—whom we have to encounter. Grandma taught me how to navigate this territory with courage.

God calls us to work on behalf of our communities in ways to which only we have access. Not everyone in Moses's community had access to Pharaoh, just like not everyone in my community had access to the resources, education, and community help that I did. From that point on, I found that being strong and courageous had nothing to do with how powerful your army or crew was. It was about the faith you display in God and others to ensure your own and your neighbor's survival. This is the cornerstone of discerning one's vocation in this context: survival.

To all the *inocentes*, that young girl, her family, Grandma Carmen Reyes—*presente*.

Chapter 3

The Game Is Rigged

> The paradox for a working-class writer is that we are never more exiled from our real homes, from the blood kin we have honored in our pages, than when we have drifted away from them on that little white raft called the page.
> —Sandra Cisneros, *A House of My Own*

As I write this chapter, the community from which I come is considered the second-least-educated city in the United States, and is setting records for violence due to gangs. The "most violent year on record," they are suggesting. Less than 0.01 percent of the community I come from had a graduate degree in any discipline, and my father was the first in his family to receive a bachelor's degree. We often talk about the idealization of education as a way out of our home communities, and that is exactly what it is for those few of us who were able to attain it. No sooner had my father received his education than he was back in the agricultural community, surrounded by those who look predominantly like us—brown, poor, undereducated. My mother's family was the exact opposite: Eastern European immigrant. White. They knew better than the rest of us. My grandmother on my mother's side once called my father "lazy," "good for Mexican work." She told me right after I finished my doctorate: "I can't believe you were able to do this. Your father is so lazy and stupid. And you are lucky that you didn't end up like him with your Mexican brain." In a sense, my positive sensibilities said, "Okay, she gets the Chicano experience and my family's experience" and I would chuckle at how she didn't realize how it was exactly because of my father and my "Mexican brain" that

I was able to do what I did. Her comments came right after she told me that my dad should never have been in the United States in the first place living the American dream. Apparently she thought that was an endearing remark. *Que?* It was not endearing. It was a racist remark with which many of us are all too familiar. She was a first generation immigrant herself, and yet had privileged her experience because the narrative of our society supports her being here, not us.

As a child of a multiple cultural markers acting on my body, not a day went by that I wasn't reminded that I was brown. I was reminded verbally by those in my community who identified as white that I would never inherit the riches of our fields. I was reminded first by hunger pangs, because at times we didn't have much money, especially when staying with my father. We weren't poor, but we certainly did not have an excess of goods.

I remember inviting a group of kids from my Christian Brothers' high school over to my house to stay the night, and all but one said they weren't allowed on my side of town, except for donating presents during the holidays. These are good Christian families? I remember my entire first year in junior high school; my father gave me two dollars a day for lunch. This afforded me a bagel and a drink – $1.75. I saved up the remaining quarters so that on Fridays I could buy something special with my extra $1.25.

My education and vocational call were plagued by white colonizers, in many ways still are, and even were back in those school lunch days. These new liberal colonizers are those who—for both benevolent and malevolent reasons—not only feel entitled to this world but feel entitled to take what we have. We, on the other hand, have been taught to share because others are hungry. When someone asked for money, I gave it. I remember giving my money to one of my classmates. On those days, I didn't eat. "How much money can you give me?" he would ask. I would unfold my black Velcro, tri-fold wallet and show him my two single dollar bills.

Can young people learn when there is nothing in their stomachs? Can young people socialize during extracurricular or sports when they are hungry? I wasn't giving to the poor. I was giving to the rich. Why? Because they asked. When the powerful ask, it is easier to say yes than put up your fists and fight. This is what we were taught and this is how internalized racism works. We have to make choices: Do we just give because we are all conditioned that certain people are supposed to live full lives, with more of the world's resources? Do we stand and fight? Or, do we do as my grandma taught us and give because we can? If I had fought for my two dollars every time it was "asked" for, my face would look very different than it does today.

This condition continues today, and can be seen by how much less people of color are paid than their white counterparts. I was once told by someone with fewer qualifications, less experience, fewer degrees, and let's be clear, a poorer work ethic and less aptitude, that he *deserved* to make twice as much as me because people were paying for his "vision." I didn't ask for this explanation. It was just offered in the course of a workday. Colonial thinking undergirds our society. It threatens our call to life.

When I moved in with my father full-time, he moved around a lot because of work. One place we lived was this small condo on the edge of town. What you have to understand about Salinas is that it is split down the middle by Highway 101. Whites and wealthy people of color on one side, poor blacks and browns on the other. While my classmates lived in mansions on the south side, or in the valley between Salinas and Monterey, we lived in this tiny one-and-a-half-bedroom condo on the edge of town. In this condo, which we lived in before the house described in the previous chapter, my two brothers and I shared a bed that touched the walls on all sides because the room was so small. We slept head to toe. My father did everything he could to make this place home. We had a small patch of grass in the shared quad that became our personal Wiffle ball stadium. He bought us a dog. We did our best to enjoy the tight quarters. Homemaking is not an easy business, and I know it was not easy for my father.

This was also the first place I struggled with my education. Prior to living here, I went to public school, and it wasn't difficult for me to do well at school. At the Christian Brothers' school, I was immersed in subjects that tested both my ability to learn and to imagine. My first year, in particular, I was challenged about my writing, knowledge of history, religion, and algebra. Mathematics was easy for me—busy work for the most part—but the humanities I found more difficult to grasp. I was not, and still am not, the best writer—a fact that professors seem to have enjoyed pointing out. *Clear, simple, appropriate*: These were the qualities they were looking for. My writing reflected my life: *messy, complicated, indecent*.

There were logical inconsistencies that I would point out regularly to our well-meaning teachers, which only prompted one teacher to call me a "smart ass" repeatedly. These inconsistencies included history lessons that told the story of America from the East to the West. The Mayflower landed on the East Coast, and Americans moved west.

> The Mayflower landed on the East Coast, and Americans moved west. People who were here already were a disruption to this narrative. It was as if speaking about the Southwest and the colonial and mission history was something that had happened out of time and space.

People who were here already were a disruption to this narrative. It was as if speaking about the Southwest and the colonial and mission history was something that had happened out of time and space. The priest Junipero Serra was celebrated; missions were visited; the Native groups of California forgotten. I pointed out the violence perpetuated by the Church in our home state as a glaringly obvious case study. This was refuted as "a different history." *Tonto.*

I remember our teacher of religion, brilliant and wonderful man that he was, explaining to a classroom full of pubescent boys that masturbation was a sin and we would go blind if we did it too much; that natural family planning was the only way to have sex; and that the Bible always taught what was true and good. If the rule stood for his first point that we would all indeed go "blind" as a result of our sins, then our school should have been buying us books in braille. If natural family planning was the only way to have sex, then we had all better be prepared to be fathers of nine children like him. If the Bible always taught what was true and good, I didn't know what to do, logically speaking, with a huge catechism, countless number of prayers that I had to memorize, and perhaps more importantly, what to do with passages in scripture that required me to wrestle with or reject bringing antiquated ways of being in community to today's contemporary world. I simply wasn't going to stone or murder anyone, for any reason. Bullets, as you can imagine, were the modern-day stoning. People who did not quite fit in were gunned down. There was no way I was going to believe in a God that demanded that sort of violence.

This education demanded that we maintain and support the status quo. It was developed so that we would bank massive amounts of information, memorize it, and rehearse it for the powers that be. The process was highly selective. The entrance exams we took prior to entering seventh grade and just before high school would determine the different places people would go. It wasn't just that everyone was smart, but the difference between the smart students and the "regular" students should have been obvious, given one's socio-economic background. When looking at how the classes were made up, those who came from families of incredible means and good primary school environments were in the smart classes. Those who came from the other side of Highway 101 predominantly came from underperforming schools and were in the remedial classes.

This created two classes (literally two in our school's case) of students: those who had access and those who didn't. My question was and continues to be: Why? Why do we as a society allow such things? Why does God have to call for some of us to survive? And seems to just provide for others? And even though surviving looks very different for everyone, why is this a starting place for some and not for others? In my case, you have already heard that surviving to adulthood was my aim. I survived abuse. I survived gang violence. But what about education? Was this something I would also have to "survive"?

I remember playing baseball during the junior high years, and no one on my team went to the Christian Brothers' school except for one who transferred in late. Trying to keep up with my classmates and my work, I would add a book to my baseball bag, whether to read for fun or to finish up last-minute homework when we weren't practicing. There is a paradox in the Latinx community concerning education. There is both a certain pride and fear of education. Parents and elders view education as the pathway to success. We are also a community that lives in the rhythms of now. Those rhythms make way for the regular passages of life. Sports are one of these passages. When we played sports, we competed with our family, friends, and those other neighborhoods that kept us in poverty. We were fighting the systems that kept us in place, though this wasn't explicit. If our neighborhood or high school team could beat the "rich" kids, then our whole community won.

My baseball team was always first or second in our league, our only real competition being the team of my school classmates. They were a white, privileged team, with an ex-major leaguer's nephew on the team. They had all the cool equipment. Their field was nicer. Our field was behind the rodeo, and we would regularly watch the *caballos bailadores* practice. We were that working-class team from the children's movie. Our coaches were intense Latinos who had hard, working-class jobs driving delivery trucks and doing sanitation work. We were the working-class Mexicans, playing the rich whites.

We were nearing the end of the season. We were in first place going into one of these final games against my classmates. I remember talking to them before the game, exchanging the usual cusswords and teasing. Naturally, I wanted to play well against them. I also had an academic decathlon meeting that weekend. I was so proud to be on that decathlon team. My brain mattered to the teacher who selected me. This was a big deal for me. I did the speech competition and participated in the larger subject matter quizzes. One of the subjects was literature, specifically C.S. Lewis's *The Chronicles of Narnia*. Between innings, rather than stand up on the fence like my teammates, I sat there and read *The Magician's Nephew*. Captivated by the creation myth of Narnia, I flipped the pages faster than the innings passed by. Going into the final inning, we were down by one run with a runner on second. It was my turn up. My coach, who was particularly perturbed at my lack of engagement with the game thus far, pulled me aside: "You are going to focus on the game, right?" I remember looking at him, confused. What else was I going to do when I got up to the plate? I wasn't the best player on the team, but I wasn't the worst, so it wasn't like he was worried that I would be that kid who didn't know how to swing the bat in the first place.

The pitcher was a classmate. He teased me regularly. For our age, he was big and I was small. I had been to his house for a basketball get-together earlier in the year: a mansion with a large barn out back, full of toys and go-carts. He had a full glass backboard and a stand-alone basketball court. He had the biggest bedroom I had ever seen. A huge TV, video games, a large oak desk, tons of books—and it all fit in his room! I had no furniture, shared a bed with my brothers— but I did have all the books I wanted. They just came from the library! His cleats were the newest Griffeys. Mine were purchased two years earlier and curled my big toe. His entire family was there. My father was racing home from work, picking up my brothers, getting them dinner, and then picking me up after the game.

My classmate smiled and laughed at me as I got in the box. He turned to his coach (who coached us both in basketball), and said, "It's just Pat." That's right, it was... just...Pat... One of those other nobodies they could forget about.

There was a runner standing on second. A base hit would bring him home. With two outs, it was a big at bat.

He delivered the first pitch. I didn't swing. It was called a strike. I looked down at the coach, who was yelling at the umpire for it being "low and outside." I remember thinking, "Man, is he really mad? I should probably get a hit." The second pitch came down. I hit a screamer down the third base line. Chalk was flying up everywhere. I left the box. The ball was still rolling down and out into the outfield. We were going to tie! As I reached first, the runner from second was rounding third to come home at a pace slow enough that our entire team was screaming and yelling for him to hurry because we were going to tie the game. But the umpire yelled, "Foul ball!" I jogged across the diamond and back to the batter's box. As I approached the box, my coach was out of our dugout and yelling at the umpire. He ran at the umpire, fists clenched together, screaming profanities. He pressed his face close against the umpire's facemask. The umpire just stood there as my coach called him names and yelled. Once I made it over to the plate, I pushed my way between them.

"What is wrong with you?" I yelled at my coach.

His eyes, full of rage, turned to me. "Don't you want to win!?" I just walked him back to the dugout as he yelled and protested the game and the umpire. Once we were all the way back at the dugout, my little hand still on this grown man's chest, he looked down at me again and said, "Don't you want to win? Or, do you want to just read your f—g books, you little f—?"

Well, that made up my mind. I went up to the plate, rested the bat on my shoulder and watched two pitches go by as balls. I yelled at my classmate to throw a strike. The next one went by and I moved not a single muscle. The game was over. My coach ran into the dugout, pulled *The Magician's Nephew* from my bag, ran out to the field, tossed it up in the air, and hit it with a baseball bat. It didn't go far, but far enough that the small paperback split open like a bird in flight.

For the remainder of the season, the team had special "Pick on Pat" days. My teammates would get high before practice, and then, at the prompting of the coach, would take my books out of my bag and throw them. I always chased down the books, which only added to the teasing. These "Pick on Pat" days were as formative as the formal education I received at school. It signaled to me that internalized racism had taken a serious hold on my coaches, my teammates, and my community. To want to read, when the rhythm of life suggested that you should be playing sports and basking in the glory of youth, was to deviate from the norm. It wasn't just the white students at school taking my cash, it was my own community reminding me of our subordinate place. We are an embodied people.

> We are an embodied people. Working class. Rough hands. Brown athletes who win at sports. We couldn't and shouldn't win in the classroom or in professional life. I couldn't be too different or challenge these metanarratives. This is how internalized racism works. It reinforces our way of being in the world, our class, our limits.

Working class. Rough hands. Brown athletes who win at sports. We couldn't and shouldn't win in the classroom or in professional life. I couldn't be too different or challenge these metanarratives. This is how internalized racism works. It reinforces our way of being in the world, our class, our limits. We were working class; to operate otherwise was a challenge to our fragile equilibrium and our own control of what we could be good at. We could never win an academic decathlon, but we could beat them at baseball. We certainly couldn't be good at both.

> In these moments I heard God's voice faintly. These environments, coupled with the violence at home and in my home community, can drown out any signs of life.

In these moments I heard God's voice faintly. These environments, coupled with the violence at home and in my home community, can drown out any signs of life. To survive day-to-day, to break the bonds of this insidious violence enacted on our very spirits, takes an incredible amount of support from the community and those outside of it. But the support is often not there, simply because people have to invest their time, energy, and love in the now. Like the people to whom the biblical prophets spoke, many of us have come to believe it is easier just to give in to the status quo.

And let's be clear: I couldn't win at the decathlon, just as I would never win at becoming an owner or manager at one of the agricultural businesses my classmates were sure to inherit. In many ways, the baseball game was simply the future managers of our town playing the future help. The importance of education, however, is not to win or lose—though, maybe it was that for previous generations. This would be synonymous with the "upward" mobility myth, in which brown kids get a college education and then are promoted out of their class. This was my father's story. But this was allowing the game to win. We were just learning how to play a little better. As my father recently told me, "I think I have only had white men as bosses; and I haven't been promoted in 15 years." He may have made it "out," but he will always be reminded that he was supposed to work manual labor jobs.

The education I received back then was instrumental in equipping my mind to know two things: One, I could play this game. I could operate in both spaces and have the skills to play the game—maybe not win, but at least compete. Two, the game was rigged. Whether it was baseball, a decathlon, education, work, surviving the playground, or operating in society, the game is actively wired to support a specific group of people—and, let's be clear, working-class Chicanxs, Mexican-

Americans, Latinxs, and people of color in general are not part of this group. I wanted to work to help others to know the game that was being played, learn the rules, and learn how to survive the game others are playing with our brown bodies.

If the game is rigged, try to discern God's voice when society has determined who, what, when, where, and how you will be. This education—or, better, the formation of young people—is especially pernicious as you discern your vocation in a formalized way. God's call can be drowned out by all these factors. However, the game doesn't end in junior high school! It continues throughout our lives. Even when we follow God's call, people of color still operate in a rigged game.

However, the game doesn't end in junior high school! It continues throughout our lives.

Fast forward to a decade later, and I was doing everything I could to fit in at seminary in the city of Boston, including preparing for my call to ministry. The only reason I had even considered Boston as a place to learn how to follow my desire to serve God and my community was that a local preacher had gone to the School of Theology at Boston University. One night, while I was on break from working the night shift from 9 p.m. to 6 a.m. with the women in the packing sheds, this local preacher came to tell me I had enormous potential, and I should consider going to the "school of the prophets" and alma mater of Dr. Martin Luther King Jr. This message of going away to learn was reinforced by one of the women on my assembly line, where we filled vegetable party platters. She told me, "We need an educator and a priest. You are wasting that brain of yours, mijo." Because of these two women, I decided to begin looking into graduate schools.

When I arrived in New England, after several hundred years of my ancestors staying west and only traveling to and from Mexico, I experienced culture shock, to say the least. "Fitting in" looks a little different for me, as one can imagine. I bought a child's BMX bike and rode it for five miles along Highway 1 north of Boston to make it to work at a local Home Depot. Here I was: first in my family to leave California, second to get a degree in the first place, first in my community and family to go to graduate school, first person I'd met outside of the local priests, doctors, and lawyers that would pursue graduate education. To review, less than 0.01 percent of my community had a graduate degree in any field, and those I knew who did, they were the Religious. That preacher who told me about my first graduate school was the first person to suggest that was even an option for me! I was following not only the lead of my elders, but honoring my grandma, who loved that I wanted to be a religious educator and leader, and honoring that Christian Brother, who, years before, had saved my life.

I spent most of my hours for a year working at the Home Depot north of the city, riding my bike along this six-lane, open highway, to save up for the upcoming school year. There was a Barnes and Noble across the parking lot from work, so every lunch I would go over there to devour as many books as I could to "prepare" myself for my academic journey. I read classics such as Khalil Gibran's *The Prophet,* a large C.S. Lewis reader, some books by popular contemporary Christian authors such as Shane Claiborne, Rob Bell, T.D. Jakes, and Brian McClaren, plus my Catholic loves, such as Dorothy Day and Flannery O'Connor. I have always found O'Connor's "The Lame Shall Enter First," a great challenge to my own theological musings.

The Barnes and Noble didn't have books in religion written by Latinxs at this point, but I did manage to make it over and read Junot Díaz for the first time and immerse myself in my favorite Latin American authors, such as Gabriel García Márquez, Isabelle Allende, and Jorge Luis Borges. Though I was focusing on reading as much theology, church history, and Bible as I could fit into my lunch hour, thinking that these texts were the canon for Christianity, I had not at this time been taught that this was a limited, white, progressive Christianity. I would not only have to know this bibliography but also my own if I wanted to help make a change in the way people think about religious education. This wasn't on my mind as I prepared to start my education. At this point, I just wanted to fit in. Symbolically, I was still filling my baseball bag with books for the decathlon.

If you were to poll some of my peers in seminary, removing the fiction and Latinx authors from what I was reading in that Barnes and Nobles store, the other texts certainly made the canon—if you also added a lot of denser, lily-white theologians who liked to talk about the power of God or God's "becoming." I should have known going into graduate school that what was on the shelf of that Barnes and Nobles in the Christian section was indeed the popular stuff for devout Christians, but that it was not sufficiently academic for those who were raised on these books and had moved to more "challenging" texts. It was never the canon for me. A student of color is tasked with knowing multiple bibliographies. We have to know the bibliographies of our own histories, our own narratives, for the purpose of survival and passing the sacred wisdom and stories of our community down from generation to generation. And if we want to eat, we must know the bibliography of those who determine what is necessary to know. Surviving in these spaces is a call to consume knowledge as if we are starving, and this is precisely because many of us are—sometimes literally. And sometimes starving for something, someone, or God to call us to life.

After saving for nearly a year, riding my bike along that busy highway, I finally started classes. I remember that first day. I got dressed up: khaki pants, nice button-down shirt, and tie. I filled my binder up with all the things I might need,

> A student of color is tasked with knowing multiple bibliographies. We have to know the bibliographies of our own histories, our own narratives, for the purpose of survival and passing the sacred wisdom and stories of our community down from generation to generation. And if we want to eat, we must know the bibliography of those who determine what is necessary to know.

just like high school. There was one other gentleman who dressed like me that day, also a person of color—the only other person of color in our class. We walked together, not saying much, just taking it all in. I learned firsthand how I hadn't come quite fully prepared to engage this academic world when one professor who was part of the welcome lecture pointed out that I should get a laptop like everyone else. Nice suggestion, but my bank account had negative numbers at the time.

My classmates all introduced themselves and gave themselves clear labels that I am sure they thought "placed" them in this academic environment: "I am going to bridge the gap between church and academy"; "I am already a religious educator, this is just a step to my Ph.D."; "I have already been to seminary for a year, so I am a second year and know most of this"; "I plan on helping the poor and vulnerable"; and so on. White students were either considering what they were doing as a stepping-stone to greater things or getting an education to prepare them to "save" the world. I didn't know where I was. It was like I had stepped into Narnia. Here I was, a young, California Chicano activist, from a working-class background, currently working side jobs in construction to pay for this education, having worked the fields and in packing sheds, having negotiated cease fires and peace treaties with gangs—though we didn't call it that—in arguably one of the most violent neighborhoods in the country, and I introduce myself as: "Pat and I am here to learn." I wanted to fit in. All that I had lived through before I arrived wasn't relevant. They were all studying to go out and do the work that I had already been doing before coming in to my seminary experience, but I didn't know that. I just wanted to stand alongside these incredibly brilliant students and be recognized for my academic ability. I didn't want to be or become their story. I kept my experiences hidden from all but two people during my entire three years at seminary—for one simple reason: I wasn't going to be another "saved" story. I wasn't going to be saved by my peers, my professors, or the institution because of my background. I was going to prove to myself and to my classmates that we were equals—though, as I said before, the game is rigged.

I learned this very early. This was not the first time classmates or scholars had tried to tell me they were smarter, more qualified, or better equipped than me to do theology, peacemaking, teaching, scholarship, etc. Nor was it the last. It still happens today. And in many ways, it is true. When we had study sessions or talked about how tests or papers had gone, it was never a surprise to me that I would do well after studying, but, for the most part, I was reading texts for the first time. I don't blame my classmates for the perception that I was lacking a certain "background" in theology. There were a few who knew about my academic background coming in, who knew I had "potential." However, for the most part, my classmates behaved as if they knew the system was rigged in their favor. They were supposed to do well. I was supposed to be thankful for being there. This idea was shared by some faculty. And at times, I believed it too.

This notion came to a head just a few weeks into my seminary experience. I was working nights at an apartment complex hanging sheet rock. It was a nice, luxury apartment building. I had met one of the contractors when I was working at Home Depot, and he needed someone to hang "rock" to catch up to his deadline. Needing the money, because rent and school were quickly draining what I had saved, I took the job. So for about two months going into my first semester, I would work three to four nights during the week, hanging rock. For those who haven't hung rock before, these 4' x 8' sheets produce a white powder that dusts your body. If you were sanding or taping "mud," which is also an off-white color, it would also cover your body in this white substance. The boards each weigh just over fifty pounds. Hanging walls wasn't too difficult, but ceilings meant lifting these boards above your head and tacking them with your off-hand, which held a screw gun or hammer adding a few extra pounds to hold. I worked with a man from Mexico, who said this was his third job to support his family with four kids. We worked hard, trying to earn as much money as we could.

After working all night lifting these boards, I would get in a few hours of sleep—usually in my dirty work clothes—and then travel into school. I took a bus and two trains to make it to campus, and it usually took me about an hour and a half. One afternoon, I got a call from the contractor saying that we had to beat the inspector the following day and that he would pay me by the piece if I could work that night. This was a chance for a lot of money. So I took the job and we worked all through the night. No sleep before class. It was also a mid-term. I had prepared a bit, but I hadn't dedicated many hours to the subject. I came into class, covered in that white powder. In many ways, being covered in white powder was fitting considering I just wanted to be respected and listened to like my white classmates. I sat down and started taking my test. I felt I was doing okay, until about halfway through the class the professor asked to see me outside. I stood up and went outside with the professor.

"If you are going to be a grad student, you need to act like one or you probably shouldn't be here."

"What?"

"Look at you. You smell. You are covered in who knows what. You don't dress appropriately." I admit my work boots, pants, and flex cap that was covered in sweat was not my best look. "You aren't doing well on your exams. And you are distracting to my more serious students."

"Well…"

"No. You know, grad school isn't for everyone."

"I didn't even get a chance to disappoint you. Can I at least finish my test?"

"If you think you can finish the exam, sure, you can finish in the hall."

The professor brought my exam out to me in the hall and I finished the test. When I had finished, rattled and confused about what had just happened, I went to turn in the exam. I looked at the professor, who began grading it right in front of me. Her red pen was flying. I didn't do well on that exam. "Like I said, grad school isn't for everyone. Certain people just aren't meant to be here." She handed back the graded exam.

I walked out of the class, determined to show her. Now let's be clear: This is not some feel-good movie plot. I didn't "show her" or get an A. I did as well as I possibly could, but I was not getting an A in that class. The game is rigged. I did very well on every exam and assignment after that point, but I was not one of the students who was predetermined to do well. And this made very little difference to everyone else in the class. Not a single one of the other students said anything to me or to the professor. They complained to the dean about the professor when they also didn't do well on the exams, but no one talked about that moment. I don't know if they didn't see it or they couldn't see it. Perhaps understanding institutionalized racism is a skill that can't be taught? My classmates were some of the most enlightened, well-meaning, educated, and progressively minded folks I knew. If I had told them this story was about someone else, they would have actively protested the professor and the institution, but with their eyes on their own exams, the conditions were perfect for me to be singled out. This is how the system works.

> I wanted to fit in. I wanted to serve in ministry. But the game is rigged. It is rigged to exclude those who navigate multiple worlds. It is rigged to keep out of the scholarly world the person who can identify with the biblical narrative on an embodied level.

I wanted to fit in. I wanted to serve in ministry. But the game is rigged. It is rigged to exclude those who navigate multiple worlds. It is rigged to keep out of the scholarly world the person who can identify with the biblical narrative on an embodied level. It actively seeks to re-create what it already is, and, in my case, that apparently meant being white, privileged, educated, and dressed appropriately.

This was "Pick on Pat" days reimagined, but with serious con-sequences. This was actively working against the kin-dom. This was another version of my coach taking that book out of my bag and hitting it into the outfield, all to remind me that my place wasn't here, wasn't among the more serious students.

This was and is a form of Christian education. You may read it as "not Christian", but this was Christian education. Christians in America have been labeling who is in and out in my land since the Spanish first landed. This was the continuation of colonial thinking. It was where the educated church decided who mattered and who was disposable.

> Christians in America have been labeling who is in and out in my land since the Spanish first landed.

It was and is a labeling of who deserves this education and who does not. Moments like these keep less resilient students from finishing, and I might have fallen into that category.

I returned to California that winter break after the first semester to work. I got a job at the agricultural company my father worked at, making 10 bucks an hour. I did whatever needed to be done—sometimes administration help, sometimes working in the sheds.

When I went back to school, I cut back my course load. I called home and told people I wasn't going back to school after I came home for good that summer.

The spring semester went by with a continued sense of isolation. I signed up for a class that would help me with my public speaking, thinking that when I returned to the community I would go back into community organizing on the side, maybe even teach a little. However, I wasn't allowed in the class, because I didn't have the right "biblical background." The semester cruised along and the day the last class was done, I took a cab and two bags to the airport. The system had won.

I started work that summer in quality assurance. This meant inspecting the loads of produce as they came in out of the fields, and, occasionally, working inside the plant to inspect the lines for sanitation. This job required sitting in a trailer, sometimes with one other person, but mostly alone, counting broccoli florets, tomatoes, carrots, cauliflower, etc., and placing numbers into a spreadsheet that would determine whether or not the percentage of below-par produce was sufficiently negligible.

The majority of the workers inside the shed and the truck drivers were people I knew. Unlike my experience in New England, this community spoke almost exclusively Spanish. Given that a lot of my job was talking to my co-workers about the produce, or where it came from, or about their lives, I did my best to strengthen my limited language skills in my second tongue. Though they liked me, they loved their cute *"pochito"* for his general happiness. I was content to be home.

Every day I got ready in the break room, surrounded by community members who either worked with the union or for the company. For all of us, this was more of a home than it was a place of work. We saw each other more than many of us saw our own families. And like many of the migrant workers who came and worked seasonally, this was the second time I had worked at this plant. The first time I had worked the night shift packing vegetables into those party trays that appear at every birthday party, baby shower, and family gathering— the ones with the dip in the middle. I got that job to help pay for my undergraduate education. Here I was again, though in this case it was to pay for the year of costs I had just incurred because I felt it necessary to quit my construction job and take out loans so I could "fit in" with the more serious students. This was something not seen in the plant. If you had a college education, you were able to work inside. I was in the plant.

In the plant, we worked for each other. Every worker was tied to the others. We shared meals at lunch and took our wages home to families that collectively shared the income to make sure that everyone's rent was paid and everyone had food on the table. After coming home from that first year in seminary, I shared a room with my youngest brother, who was still in high school at the time. I would work all day, come home, and read books or tease my siblings. After a year in grad school, I couldn't tell them that the experience felt like a violent exposure to a world that we didn't have to know nor had been invited to, and that I preferred to be here. I understood how tempting it was all those years ago with my coaches trying to get me to focus on playing baseball. It was an experience of deep shame, because they probably also had been told by someone along the way that they were "not serious enough" or a "distraction" to everyone else. We bear this shame as part of our own vocational journey.

Bell Hooks suggests in *Teaching Community: A Pedagogy of Hope* that there is "practical wisdom about what we do and can continue to do to make the classroom a place that is life-sustaining and mind-expanding, a place of liberating mutuality where teacher and student join together work in partnership" (2003, xv). The classroom for Hooks is not unlike our homes. It is not only supposed to build us up out of this shame, but also to help us understands the reality of it. She says:

> Competitive education rarely works for students who have been socialized to value working for the good of the community. It rends them, tearing them apart. They experience levels of disconnection and fragmentation that destroy all pleasure in learning. (2003, 49)

When I first read Bell Hooks that summer, it was as if someone had reached into my experience and affirmed this feeling of the shame I had experienced for my entire education. The answer was simple: In the education system that pitted me against their chosen champions, or at least the students the education system was designed for—white, affluent, children of the educated—I was never going to win or even do well. There was too much at stake for white supremacy. Reading Hooks was life-giving in that someone else knew that my education was destroying me. There were people who understood the damage this education does to young people of color.

Reading hooks was life-giving in that someone else knew that my education was destroying me.
There were people who understood the damage this education does to young people of color.

This failure to compete—or more realistically, if dramatically, the failure to thrive—resembles the experience that bell hooks speaks to when she says "messing up, performing poorly eases the anxiety" (2003, 100), and causes "individual students of color, and other marginalized students [to be] consumed by feelings of rage" (2003, 101). I was not only trying to ease my anxiety by working a job I was supposed to work, but I was pissed. I was pissed that I'd spent all this money on an education that wouldn't get me anywhere, wouldn't allow me to do ministry, that rejected me and my ancestor's history. I was taught this lesson as early as the fourth grade, but had not realized it until that first year in seminary. Not only was it easy for me to perform only adequately in school, it was also all my professors expected of me.

In fourth grade, I had a progressive, democratic educator. He was creative in all things that he did. Math was taught using a deck of cards; critical thinking came in the form of daily puzzles for homework; analytical and decision-making skills were taught through chess; ecology taught through tending a small plot of soil for school, where we had the freedom to do what we wanted to with it; there were only four fourth graders and the rest were fifth graders, and excelling in the classroom in any area meant the reward of helping along classmates who were having difficulties with certain lessons. During one of the language lessons, which required we read passages to others, write short stories, or critique sentences, I had finished my work early. Thinking that I was going to get to help one of the other students with his or her work, I asked who would be my partner. I was paired with a student who did not speak English. This pairing lasted throughout the year, and every other day for half an hour to an hour, instead of doing my usual language lessons I would go outside to the field and talk or read with the student. After a year of this dialogue, both of our language skills got better—his in English, mine in Spanish.

I learned that the value of learning from a friend far outweighs the value of the grade. The exchange between friends and community members who needed each other was more formative vocationally than those moments in seminary—mostly because my seminary cohort didn't need me. They wanted my story, but didn't want the voice and body that came with it. They wanted me to be the narrative, while they got to be the theory. I had a grounding, though: I had deep roots in my community. I was able to reach back to those in my community and ask for help and guidance.

I remember talking to Javier during the summer between my first and second year of seminary. He told me I inspired him. He was going to be a professor. When I told him it was a violent experience at grad school, he simply looked at me and said, "Patricio, hasn't it always been?" Indeed.

Howard Thurman wrote:

> It seems that, hundreds of years ago, what is now the desert was a dank, luxurious growth. As the desert appeared, the vegetation was destroyed until, at last, there was nothing left of the past glory except an oasis here and there. But not all vegetation disappeared; for there were a few trees that had sent their roots so far down into the heart of the earth in quest of moisture and food that they discovered deep flowing rivers full of concentrated chemicals. Here the roots are fed so effectively that the trees far above on the surface of the earth are able to stand anything that can happen to them at the hands of desert heat and blowing sand. This is the secret of those whose lives are fed by deep inner resources of life. To him who is sure of God, He becomes for him the answer to life's greatest demands and, indeed, to its most searching and withering vicissitudes. (Thurman 1984, 98)

With my community, I could drive my roots down deep. I could be fed by being with them. Because of this passage in Thurman, the desert or wilderness has become an important metaphor for how I think about my own Christian education. Seminary brought to the fore authors and writings by those such as Delores Williams, George Tinker, the biblical authors, Zamyatin, Kurt Vonnegut, Gustavo Gutiérrez, Virgilio Elizondo, Michael Foucault, Ada María Isasi-Díaz, Justo Gonzalez, James Cone, Edward Said, Albert Memmi, Craig Dykstra, Rosemary Radford Ruether, Elizabeth Johnson, Paul Tillich, Juan Luis Segundo, Mayra Rivera, Frantz Fanon, Enrique Dussel, etc., and my own love for countless other novels and literary works (though these largely existed outside of the canon). The wilderness and desert have served as a symbol of where society happens, where the "more serious students live." It is also a place where one survives to escape the oppression and joys of civilization. It is the place where one goes to center. It is the place where one goes to find one's humanity. Even in popular fiction today, we still romanticize the wilderness. For example, *The Shack*—a popular fiction title that seeks to examine how one views God in the face of trauma—uses the wilderness as a place where people are living, surviving, and finding themselves and God. It is where people experience isolation and yet a profound sense of togetherness with others and God. The desert is the place where outlaws in Westerns go to live and where the biblical prophets go to find God. It is also a place where our deep roots keep us alive.

Deserts for the Latinx people, for *my* Latinx people, are often places of violence. It is the borderland, the dangerous passage, the empty space between what we know and what we hope to find. For my grandparent's family, it was the place where they wandered trying to find grass for their sheep, and where agricultural developers brought jobs and seasonal poverty simultaneously. We worked in food deserts. Though surrounded by food, we went hungry. There was no manna. However, what we did have was those deep roots, and they kept us connected to life-giving resources.

In the passage above, Thurman reflects this survival in the desert, through trees sinking their roots deep in the ground looking for that life-giving water. If we are trees in the wilderness/desert, where all life is being evaporated from the surface and yet is plentiful deep below the surface, we too must sink our roots deep down into the ground to find life, to find God, to find ourselves. For my own understanding, this can mean a variety of things. At times it seemed to be a barren wasteland of all that is glorious and wonderful—the connection between God and Others. There have been times during my education when I spent more time with books and people who said they knew of God but who knew nothing and cared little about the reality in which God speaks to me and my community. They said loudly that all theology is contextual, yet they failed to go to a context or think about the context they were creating in the classroom. In that environment, the theological landscape became barren and I was a lone tree, sinking my roots deep into the ground in search of water, in search of connection. This idea of grounding ourselves in the desert is important, especially for those times when we are most alone. It is often when we are most alone that we have a feeling of death surrounding us. Once we take hold of our fear, we are able to embrace a good death. As Howard Thurman says:

> A good death is made up of the same elements as a good life.
> A good life is what a man does with the details of living if he
> sees his life as an instrument, a deliberate instrument in the
> hands of Life, that transcends all boundaries and all horizons.
> It is this beyond dimension that saves the individual life from

being swallowed by the tyranny of present needs, present hungers, and present threats. (Thurman 1984, 71)

By getting out of my hometown, I transcended death. I survived shootings. Let me repeat that for an audience who may not know what growing up in a community that suffers under the plague of violence. Shootings happen regularly. Drive-bys. Shootings in the park down the street. Shootings at schools. We may not always hear the bullets as I did the day on the playground, but we certainly felt the impact every time someone pulled the trigger. I escaped the insidious violence of my neighborhood. Those struggles I knew. I knew how to survive in that context. At seminary, I was "dying" that first year. Dying an existential death. I wanted to live a good life, but had not been helped to find it nor had the ability myself to hear God calling me in those halls and classrooms. I was locked in the classroom, being told that God spoke in particular ways and to particular people—perhaps I wasn't one of them. I sank my roots down deep, only to find out that my roots were not welcome at the well-spring of life.

Imagine again Thurman's image of the tree in the desert. It would have never worked for me. I sank my roots deeper and deeper into the soil, only to find that the water was being used by the other trees around me. It was water for them, not for me. I sank my roots deeper still, reading more and more outside of the required reading, acquiring the discipline needed to read a book every other day, a practice I still mostly keep. But this wasn't my location. It didn't give me access, life, or a community. Then I realized almost immediately that I was not that kind of tree. My roots are not in this soil! The metaphor did not work for me! So I found another.

The Coastal redwoods—Sequoias—in California are some of the largest trees on the planet, the largest of which, known as the Lost Monarch, is 320 feet high and over 26 feet wide at the trunk. The redwood forest was no more than a couple of hours' drive from where I grew up. I remember going there in elementary school for field trips and public school science camp. It was not the height of the trees that impressed me, but how the trees maintain this height. At science camp I learned that, rather than Thurman's tree in the desert whose roots go deep in order to find water and survive, the Giant Sequoias' roots go relatively shallow for their height. For most redwoods, their roots go only a few feet deep, but spread out far along the surface. Even if the tree were to spread its roots out horizontally as far as its height, it would not be able to support itself. It would collapse under its own weight and height. In order to stand as the tallest trees in the world, the coastal redwoods interlock their roots with other members of their same family in order to stand. Their roots are shallow, but they intertwine with the roots of their brothers and sisters. For every family of trees, there is a mother at the center from which all trees branch out. For me, this mother tree was my grandma. From her, all of us intertwined our roots. With her, we could all stand tall and build a forest of the tallest trees in the world.

This networking of strength was a more appropriate analogy than Thurman's for me to think about how we need to repair and restructure our world both for the work I was called by God to do in the world and for the type of support I needed in my education. Our roots need to be intertwined and connected with our families and communities if we are to survive. In order for me to grow to be the tallest tree in the world, to achieve my full potential and to survive, I needed to ground myself in the other trees around me, which I also needed to be tall to hold us up as equals. There was no lone tree sinking its roots down deep, thriving on its own, though this is what theological education at the graduate level is designed for, as Bell Hooks noted of competitive education.

What I needed was the connectedness in which scholars of color can thrive, survive, and heal. It is *teología en conjunto*. It is this connectedness that allows the coastal redwoods to survive fires, dry years, infestations, and diseases that would otherwise tear them down. It is through this connectedness that we can discern and hear God calling us to be our most authentic selves. It is through this connectedness that we are about to hear God's call in and through the trees.

At the time that I was considering not going back to graduate school, I went on a hike with a dear friend named Julio. Of all the people I connected with over the years, Julio seemed to evoke wisdom every time he spoke. Though he and I shared similar experiences and he knew my own struggles, his family faced more hardships than my own. His parents worked in the fields and he was far closer to the violence of our community than I was. When we became close during undergraduate studies, he was pulled back into the life we had hoped to escape.

My father and my grandma did some incredible "root" work. They ensured that my roots had the opportunity to intertwine with others that they knew would hold me up, and they untwined me from those roots that would do me harm. Julio's roots were still intimately tied to our *entire* community. His parents also did incredible root work, but *la lucha* was different for him. He had fewer resources, mentors, and communities outside of our neighborhood. His community and his roots were far more entangled in the web of violence of our community.

Part of his network of support were drug traffickers. While I had substance abusers in my family, buying and selling massive amounts of drugs was not part of my narrative.

When Julio and I lived together during undergrad, we had a conversation in which I said that if I found out that the drug game had made it back into our new life, he and I may have to part ways. Not soon after, he received a request from a family member to start bringing drugs north, trafficking them in his car. Julio confided in me the request. I simply said I couldn't jeopardize my future, not even to have the discussion, and I walked away from that friendship. I knew that if I allowed myself to get too close, those pernicious roots would pull me back into a neighborhood that had raised me.

Our friendship was strained for some time after that. Some of our mutual friends felt it was dramatic, some felt it was necessary, but, more than that, we were both hurt by my decision. I was hurt, because I had not shown compassion and felt betrayed that this was still something we had to wrestle with as a community. I knew why he made the decision he had. He was trying to survive. We both were. The pressure we get from those roots that are trying to survive, trying to "make it" in their own way, will always pull at those of us from these contexts. We are labeled *"traido"* to la raza, to the barrio, to the gang, when we move away, get an education, or choose to embrace another way of life. Living authentically in this tension is not about what is morally right or wrong, but about survival. Our roots determine what our ability is to survive. I did not have the courage to call Julio for many years after that, until that first summer home from seminary.

This was the friend I invited to go on a hike among the redwoods. As we walked underneath these giant trees and through the thick central coast fog, I asked him to forgive me, and that I was coming home. I had decided to stay in Salinas, and work in the vegetable packing sheds. God, I told him, was calling me home. I told him that I had screwed up by demanding so much of him. I wanted to be home. I would just keep my job in the packing shed, possibly work on becoming a teacher, and continue to work for change from the margins.

But once again God chose to call us both to new life.

"No," he told me. "No. That is bullshit and not fair. It was messed up the way things went down, but this is bullshit. You don't think I wouldn't want to be in your shoes? You don't think that I wouldn't want to have that opportunity. F—that. If you come home, I won't forgive you. I'm not sure if you did the right thing back then, but I know I am not selling drugs now. And I do know this is the wrong thing for you to do."

I didn't know what to say. I stopped under the incredible height of those trees. "What do I do then?"

"Go back. Don't let those *putos* get to you. They don't know you. They don't know what we have been through! They don't own you. They don't know what it takes to get out of here. They don't know what you have done. You got an opportunity. Don't be a dumbass."

Our roots interlock with the roots of others to sustain us in the work. I thanked Julio at the end of the walk. I truly believe it was God talking through him. It was God's voice speaking through the heartbeat of my community. When I returned, I heard God calling me once more. I was not only going to do well in school, but every project of mine from there on out was going to be oriented around the healing and liberation of my community. Theological education felt different from then on. I wasn't going to let them get to me. It was Christian educators, family members, and friends who shared my experience and who saved my life, and I was going to honor them by taking what I needed from this experience. I now started to see myself as an elder, working toward healing and liberation, using the education system to glean every possible insight and credential myself to do the work of God. God called me to new life. God called me to survive. If my ancestors could survive for generations in the wilderness, I could learn how they did so by turning to the texts and stories that sustained them.

Chapter 4

In the Wilderness

But I had survived my formative world and all its trappings...
Time to start a revolution, or I could wind up in rags, sleeping
on heating grates, permanently retired to the dreamworlds I
had conjured up since childhood.
—Ta-Nehisi Coates, *The Beautiful Struggle*

Part of growing into our vocation is recognizing that call to life and living into it. Ta-Nehisi Coates reminds us that living into one's values is also living into our own survival narratives and to begin dreaming about the work ahead. I have said repeatedly throughout this text that vocational discernment is about learning to hear the cry for us to live. God also provides guides in sacred texts. There is something sacred about this call, something grounded in our tradition. Study of the texts grounds us in the wisdom of our tradition, but this must be done alongside the stories of our ancestors. The biblical text must continue to live and walk alongside our ancestors, our elders, us, and the next generation. As Orlando Espín notes, it is "traditioning" the next generation to know the histories, theologies, and traditions of the past, so that we may communally create a new future (1997).

By turning to a biblical story with characters who are dispossessed, oppressed, survivors, and are called by God into new life, we view through a window this call to life. For many of the abused and forsaken, this is the first glimpse we see of life out of the mud. Connecting the biblical story with one's personal narrative teaches us to listen to how

God calls us into new being. We also learn through the scripture that these calls are not always accepted or heard by our communities. Though the world, society, and some in our own communities may not accept our call to life, there are those who hear God's call to life. They are the beloved who opened my heart to the theological insights provided by scripture. Without my grandma, the Christian Brothers, my father, my friends, and the roots of my experience, I would not have heard the call to life. But here I am. In order for me to open up to these learnings, I needed to hear the cry for life from my ancestors.

Those who call us to new life have also survived. We who are called to transmit the traditions of survival are also typically the ones who tell the stories of life; we are called to call others to life. However, our world does not allow enough room for our ancestors to walk freely among us. Those with their own stories of survival and caring for the next generation often are lost, forgotten, or buried—lost because colonial histories have acted violently on our histories, erasing our bodies from history, or lost because their stories were not viewed in such a way as to reflected their beauty, their courage, and their own strength to survive their times. So often, the stories of our ancestors are treated as mere side characters or plots to the dominant narratives. I admit in my own storytelling above that people such as my grandma interjected themselves in my life and saved me from certain death. My grandma's longer story and family heritage inform the stories about her supporting me in times of need. Without her survival, without her own support narrative, there is no walking up to that man's house. She got the courage from a lifetime of experience and learning how to avoid certain death, while still courageously looking death in the eye. Without that deep history, she would not have continued to support me in my studies. She would not have known how powerful were the long hugs during which we didn't have to say anything about what we were feeling in our souls, because she had survived deep pains and was passing the wisdom of survival from one generation to the next.

My grandma descended from holy people, or at least that is how my father tells the story. Her ancestors lived and worked the Central Valley, long before the Spanish arrived; some were there when it

> My grandma descended from holy people, or at least that is how my father tells the story.

was still Mexico, some going to and from present-day Mexico. She was one of many children of shepherds and farmworkers. They would travel wherever the harvest was or where the grass would grow for the sheep. From California to Mexico, they lived and worked off the land.

This migratory pattern was how she and her family survived. As the youngest of her family, everyone wanted to keep her safe from the hard life of farm labor. She was supposed to have "soft hands," as my great aunt used to say, another angel I know who is looking over us.

She met my grandpa, who had come from Mexico to Texas to California with his father and siblings. He told me his mother had died young, and that she was a native woman. He didn't remember much of his childhood, except that his father would gather all of his children in a cart and walk them to the potato fields, where they would sit and play all day and wait for him to finish work. Grandpa would tell endless stories about times in the field. His dad also later worked on the railroads. I have a small pocket watch from my grandma's father from his time working the railroad company, which has been passed on from generation to generation. The watch represents a parent's attempt to make a new generation's life a little better than the last. My grandma and grandpa didn't talk much about her father working that job, perhaps because sitting under the blazing sun is far more memorable than his dad leaving for the day to work at the rail yard. From all of my ancestors, I learned the importance of making life better for the next generation.

My grandpa was several years older than my grandma. I remember asking why they got married. She said she liked the way he danced. He was a charming, good-looking, fair-skinned Mexican man. He served in the army both as a bugler and as a driver to a major whose name escapes me. He remembered his time in the service as the first time the "white guy told him to wait in the car." When he returned home from his military service, he found work at the local bar. On a bartender's salary, he managed for a number of years to provide enough income to have at least 12 people living under the same two-bedroom roof.

> I came to love him very much, but there are traumas buried deep inside the house in which my father grew up that I will never fully know.

He was also an abusive drunk, an admission he made to me very early in my time living with my grandparents. I came to love him very much, but there are traumas buried deep inside the house in which my father grew up that I will never fully know. I only know what my grandpa and, to some extent, my father would tell me. This is what I mean by saying that we didn't have to tell Grandma our pain. She had multiple markers on her body as well. She knew how to survive and how to ensure the survival her children.

My grandma grew up in poverty with a large family. She raised a large family with an abusive alcoholic in a small two-bedroom house, feeding anyone who came through her doors. She was the keystone of the family. She held all the pieces together. I lived with Grandma and Grandpa years after the event with that little girl. I stayed in their extra bedroom working for my uncle's drywall and metal framing company. It was long hours in the Bakersfield heat, working for just $8 an hour. But they let me live there for free and fed me. I loved living with them because every day I would go to work early in the morning, come back exhausted from the day, and as soon as I had had a shower, my grandma would be waiting to give me a hug and ask how the day had gone. These moments with her were the most precious moments of my life. I tried to return the favor by cleaning the kitchen every night. I wanted to return the love they had given me, but didn't have a whole lot of practical skills at this age. This was most noticeable during work.

I worked with a man who had lived a harder life than me and would remind me of it daily. Andy was a 60-year-old Basque-Mexican man who hung sheet rock and metal lath, who had been to prison twice, was missing all of his front teeth, lived in a small trailer, and abused his body with alcohol and other drugs. He was understandably bitter about the way life emerged for him. I would tell my grandparents about his pains or I would tell them about how Andy, from this place of hurt, would act out and try and fight me while we worked together. One day in particular he pulled the scaffold out from under me, because he wanted to tell me I was doing a bad job and it was the fastest way to get me down. When I stood up to him after I hit the ground, he took off his tool belt and said he was ready to fight.

I remembered Grandma telling me about two or three weeks into the job that I needed to be nice to him, he probably needed someone to talk to. So I told him I wasn't going to fight him, walked off around the corner with him following me, cussing me out, and telling me what a lousy person I was. I climbed into the car as fast as I could, locking the door behind me. He banged on the window for me to come out and fight him. He eventually just left the job site and came back the next day—upset, but apologetic.

"Patrick, I am sorry." He said.

"Don't worry about it."

"No, really. I am sorry. I think you might be the only person who listens or puts up with me. I am sorry."

"Don't worry about it."

"Want to come to my trailer for lunch?" This scared me a bit, given that he had just tried to fight me the day before.

Still, I accepted: "Sure."

I went to his trailer for lunch and he told me his life story. He talked about how one day he was working on a high rise and fell, but a friend caught him. They were working on the 30th story. He said had it not been for that man, he would have died.

"You know. I think sometimes people know how to catch us," he said.

"Yeah."

> You have to be aware of your own strength before you just reach out on a high rise and catch someone when they are falling. You have to know who you are and what you are capable of. You also just have to survive the moment.

"No, really. You have to be aware of your own strength before you just reach out on a high rise and catch someone when they are falling. You have to know who you are and what you are capable of. You also just have to survive the moment." We sat in his trailer in silence after this moment, each eating fruit and the small sandwiches he had made, reflecting on the wisdom in this moment.

I developed a close bond with Andy. I don't know if it was because I would not confront him about his anger or engage him during a rant. I think it was more because I was genuinely curious about his life. The summer only got better as he opened up more and more. He told me stories about his marriage and children and how proud he was of them. He told me how his brother stole most of his money after the first time he went to prison. He invited me to his trailer to see the trinkets he had collected while overseas, and told me again how the friend had saved his life while working on the high rise. He asked me to tell him about the books I was reading or about what I wanted to study in school. He didn't think people studied to become priests, but that I would be a good one if I wanted to do that. When he passed away, I didn't remember the anger, I simply remembered his stories. He taught me that we have to know our strength and catch someone who is falling.

My grandma knew these conversations took their toll on me. I would come home and share how I hadn't said a word the entire day or that Andy whacked the living hell out of me with a piece of framing again—his usual form of telling me I had made a bad cut or had messed something up. But she always told me, "Paciencia, mijo." Yet it wasn't just *this* man's pains for which my grandma wanted me to care. While she cooked dinner—her tortillas still fill my stomach just thinking about them—I would head out to the front porch with Grandpa. He would be sitting on the front porch smoking his Pall Mall non-filtered cigarettes. If he wasn't smoking, it meant he was out of cigarettes and he would send me to the corner store to buy more for him. I would sit there and watch traffic and people go by the house. He would yell at people, *"¿Que paso, pendejo?"* I would laugh at their responses to this little, old, decrepit Mexican on a porch. As trust was built through this nightly ritual, our conversations turned, just as had happened with Andy.

The first time they did, he talked about driving home drunk from work one day. There is a large hill on my grandparents' street that swoops down and to the left, ending with my grandparents' house on the right hand side of the road. He was driving his car and he crested the top of the hill to start coming down and to the left. He had passed out at the wheel. The car crashed in the yard across the street from our house and sent him flying into the adjacent yard. He survived without any serious injuries. He had driven home drunk, he said, more times than he could remember, and that was why he didn't drink anymore. As he told the story, he reflected on waking up in the neighbor's yard—mainly, he said, because he couldn't remember anything else. He talked about how he didn't know to whom to apologize or whether anyone would forgive him. He felt he had done so much wrong he didn't know how to make any of it right. Then, he put his cigarette out and we just sat there. Most nights unfolded something like this.

For about two more months, we went out to the porch and he would talk about things he did. Confessions before death, I suppose. He talked about the abuse he had inflicted on his family. He talked about the abuse he had suffered as a kid. He talked about his childhood and what his own father had to do to ensure his family's survival. He said he didn't know how to talk to my father. He knew that my grandma would take the kids out for drives for hours on end when he would be in a drunken fit, and that sometimes they would stay out all night. Or, he told me about the times when he wouldn't even come home. He cried when he told me that he knew my father hid under the bed from him when he came home. "Don't ever be that kind of papi. Keep reading your books," he would tell me as he stared out at the traffic.

I often wonder what interventions my grandpa needed. Who called this man to life? I also thought about my father: Who called him to life? As I pondered this question, I would begin to seethe. These were conditions, addictions, abuses, that were largely out of my family's control. How could anyone survive and imagine a better life while

> These were conditions, addictions, abuses, that were largely out of my family's control. How could anyone survive and imagine a better life while dealing with these struggles?

dealing with these struggles? I remember one night after hearing all these confessions, I was tired and sad for my grandma, my father, my aunts, my uncles. Bear in mind, this is after my grandma had already called me to new life and ensured my survival, and was once again providing a house full of love for me when I was mostly lost.

We were sitting at the table and I had just heard another long story of abuse. I looked at my grandpa, who was sitting there eating his plate of meat, corn, beans, and tortilla. I was angry. I was angry that I knew that by saying out loud what he had done he was feeling some relief from what he had put my family through. "Grandpa," I said, "Don't just smile! Say sorry to Grandma for all that stuff you've been telling me." He looked up, not confused one bit by the demand, and apologized. Upset by how unsatisfying the apology was, I took my food into the backyard and finished my meal so they could talk alone. I am not sure what they talked about, but they never called me back into the house.

God's call is a call to life that transfers from generation to generation. Virgilio Elizondo wrote that the "Mexican-American historical odyssey can be seen as a passage through three phases," the first being survival. The phases also include development efforts including becoming part of U.S. society and *"moviminetos de liberación"* (Elizondo 2010, 19). While all three are currently happening in our communities, I believe that all three are happening simultaneously. This vocational call to life in my own family certainly could be read as a quest for survival, then a struggle to find our place in society, followed ultimately by realizing our own liberation. However, as Delores Williams reminds us, survival *is* an act of liberation. In many ways, for those who are the sons and daughters of the disinherited, our lives are one long act of survival. Our communities are not negotiating these phases singularly, but are actively redefining what it means to survive, thrive, and define our own realities. God's call is active in every part of our personal and communal discernment.

> This vocational call to life in my own family certainly could be read as a quest for survival, then a struggle to find our place in society, followed ultimately by realizing our own liberation.

My father carried much of my grandma's love and care for family with him. When my parents split, he moved a lot. He did his best to make whatever place we were in feel like home. The divorce took most of his money, so we didn't have much. We made do in small places, as I've said before. I didn't know all the stories he had from his home life until I lived with my grandparents. I can't imagine what it would be like to parent with that trauma haunting your own notions of parenting, to be a single father, and have a father of whom you were terrified—and, worse, who knew and admitted that he was a bad father. I could never imagine hiding from my own father under my bed or having to go for all-night car rides just to stay safe. How does one come into such a narrative? How does one "fit in" to the U.S. context when one's day-to-day reality is about sheer survival? How does one parent with memories like these? One becomes like my grandma, I suppose, as my father did—loving, nurturing, making the best of our daily reality.

I can also imagine it is one of the hardest things for parents like my father to endure when they hear stories such as those recorded in this book. The pain they, as grandmothers, as fathers, as caring elders, tried to shield their children from, not only suffered similar pains at the hand of someone who was not their child's parent, but also new pains, new forms of violence they are not equipped to deal with. Where does one turn to find solutions?

My father's own method of survival was to get an education and get away from his home community. My father, like many Latinxs, saw education and work as ways of "getting out of" one's material conditions. The conditions have to be right, though. My father, an incredibly brilliant man, had two recruiters from Harvard come out to visit him and persuade him to attend their institution. I suppose he checked a lot of boxes—poor, brown, Mexican, and smart. Did he attend? No. Why? Because he was to be the first in his family to get an education and no one knew who or what Harvard was. Now, before you roll your eyes, think for a moment that this was before the Internet. This was before mass communication. Bakersfield, the town he grew up in, is one of the poorest communities in California. The Central Valley had migrant farm laborers and some services, but didn't have any emphasis on education. Such farm laborers didn't know the world of Harvard and Princeton. I said earlier that Salinas was rated the second-least-educated city in the U.S. It was followed in the report by Central Valley towns such as Bakersfield. It is not that he wasn't smart enough to choose Harvard. It was that the powers of colonization, oppression, and insidious trauma had clouded his world in a smog of violence and oppression. Harvard had never appeared in Bakersfield to recruit someone until that moment! There is no innate power or authority granted to prestigious institutions in places they have never been, have no respect in, or have never educated individuals from. Instead, he wanted to go to a local school that he had actually heard of—thank God he did, and thank God he wanted to go to school at all! I wouldn't be here had he not had the courage to leave for college in the first place.

You won't hear him or any of my aunts and uncles ever say they were poor growing up, and yet they didn't have money. You may not hear them talk about their household traumas. This is only possible when you have Grandma Reyes, who did everything she could to make life abundant.

My father was not able to be present like my grandma, who was home most of the time. I often ask myself how my Father was able to raise us: more directly, what happens when you as a parent fail to protect your children from the violence you hoped to escape? As a parent, I feel a deep responsibility to echo the sound of God and create the conditions for my son to hear God's voice clearly.

I am sure my father wanted the same for me. Education provides this escape for him and for my family. "If you get an education, you are able to make it out." Whether there is validity to this sentiment or not, it is nevertheless the Latinx dream. He instilled in me from a young age that getting a good education opens up doors. He provided this dream for me. And as the first in his family to do this, he set an example for me. He laid a foundation on which I could build our survival narrative into something liberative. I could escape only because he did. I looked for this liberation in theological education.

I have seen people ground themselves in the practices and stories of their traditions in powerful ways. In a sense, this naming of our experiences that have threatened our existence is a good starting place for many people of color. When we can see our longer histories and narratives of survival and life, we can begin to imagine our own lives anew. However, there are few texts and scholars that reflect our histories and our narratives. This became abundantly clear to me in graduate school.

When I started my studies, a professor asked us, "What prepared you for this experience?" The purpose of this question was to research our collective wisdom and skills that we as a student body had developed over the years so they could be capitalized on during our studies. Many of my classmates responded by offering their educations, showing their academic pedigrees and impressive resumes: "I studied with XYZ scholar; reading these important, classic, and canonical texts; producing this incredible and field-shaping thesis—in undergrad. I traveled to this place, to work with these poor people or urban [black and brown] youth, liberating both them and myself: them from the shackles of global poverty and colonialism, and myself from my own ignorance of how the other half lives." I am being a bit tongue-in-cheek here, but this is basically what was being said. All beautiful work, and in many ways just thinking about some of their answers still intimidates me today. I am sure it did make a difference to someone. At least they broadened their own vision of the world I had inherited.

When the professor got to me and the first thing that came out of my mouth was, "I survived to adulthood." I remember the class laughing. My face turns red even now recalling this event, because this sentiment came from the very heart or gut of my experience. *Why was I here?* That is how I heard the question. I was here not because I had some great experience in communities of color helping the poor (*we* were that community), or because I studied at some great university (because I hadn't), but because I knew how to survive. At their laughing I defaulted to how I would respond back home. I puffed out my chest, pulled down my baseball hat, and hid behind a veil of anger and rage. The professor asked me to give a real answer. Give a real answer?! Apparently survival does not translate. The "struggle" isn't real for everyone. *La lucha* was something the other students and this professor read about in books. But they never knew anyone personally who had survived or struggled. We were all supposed to learn about such suffering together. God forbid that it might actually be among us.

Like a mute, I just sat there and gave the class the best *macho cholo* face I could conjure up. No one in that class understood what I was doing and the laughing continued. By laughing at me, they laughed at my father. They laughed at my grandma. They laughed at my ancestors. They cast us out of their collective histories, the dominant narratives that line our textbooks! We were something else. Of course they could go out into the "world" to experience what I survived, but this was their space, their classroom, their world. To have my world in their space disrupted the norm.

But it was the truth! To learn and tell the story of our ancestors is a privilege that only those who survive long enough get to tell. For those of us who do survive to adulthood, passing on wisdom is a matter of life and death. By grounding ourselves in our tradition, we are able to draw on wisdom from those stories that inspire us to survive. Of course, these stories include the narratives of our own families, as I have recounted here. They are inclusive of survival narratives, but we are inspired to survive from other places as well. I was determined to find what would be inspirational in this space despite the laughter. In this way, I was responding to the call to life I had heard from God.

As Dorothy Day, one of the founders of the Catholic Worker movement as a twentieth-century Catholic activist, says of her experience in the depression of her own life: There was something particular about the tradition that made her carry on. She had been arrested for her activism and for spending time in marginalized communities, which mirrors the experience of so many people of color in both our neighborhoods and our own experiences of going to the poor— not because we are necessarily activists, but merely because we breathe, live, and exist in these spaces. These are the spaces we occupy, not because it is part of a movement, but because this is the accident of our birth. These are those forgotten, lonely spaces that dominant culture has designated for us to inhabit. Day wrote that it was in part her faith in God that carried her through the day-to-day. She said:

> And always there was the New Testament. I could not hear of Sonya's reading the gospel to Raskolnikov in *Crime and Punishment* without turning to it myself with love. I could not read Ippolyte's rejection of his ebbing life and defiance of God in *The Idiot* without being filled with an immense sense of gratitude to God for life and a desire to make some return. (Day 1952, 108)

Here I was turning inward just as Day had. Day, reading Dostoyevsky— who was possessed with exploring where God was amid the suffering and the fundamental questions of human life, such as purpose, love, and faith—was forced through her exploration of theological texts to find meaning in her life and live out of that meaning. She found something powerful in the Christian narrative that suggested we needed to enter into communion with the poor and suffering. I was determined to make something out of this experience and the opportunity to study my tradition and to transfer its message of survival to future generations. I was reading the texts of my tradition to find my immense sense of gratitude to God for life, despite the laughter at my very presence.

The Bible provides a narrative for God's people. I tell people that as a professional theologian my task is to "wrestle with our tradition and texts." I ground myself in our shared holy text because it gives me a way for me to see myself in God's longer narrative of those who have survived and have been liberated. It grounds me in a community of others whom God has called to life.

I feel blessed to be alive. I am lucky that I can find biblical examples in which this message of surviving to adulthood is true.

Surviving is an important concept that appears throughout the biblical narrative, but it is rarely the focus of our theological musings. So often we focus on the courage or strength of leaders such as Abraham, Moses, David, Daniel, or the disciples. From Abraham, God asks for incredible obedience. God asks Moses to challenge Pharaoh and have faith to go into the desert. David stands before Goliath, Daniel before the lions, and the apostles spread the good news in the face of a world that seeks to destroy them. These bold and courageous leaders defy death and challenge their own mortality because of their sense of calling. These narratives are important for understanding that God calls despite dire circumstances. These are examples of those whom God called to a "new life," one in which their fleshed experience may have become secondary. They, however, do not focus on the number of times that God's people have been called to survive. Often survival stories are woven into the very fabric of these courageous leaders' narratives.

When God calls God's chosen into new life, it is with the promise of something—the promise of a kingdom, the promise of land, the promise of progeny, or the promise of a new world. With all of these promises comes incredible sacrifice and work on behalf of those whom God calls. Rarely does God simply call out and say, "Survive." However, when one looks closely at Abraham and that call narrative, one might find threads of survival at the very beginning of our tradition. But it is not Abraham whom God calls to survive, but rather Hagar and Ishmael—those whom Abraham and Sarah viewed as subordinate, as slaves.

After Sarah offers Hagar, her slave, to Abraham because she fears she will not be able to have his children, Hagar becomes pregnant with Abraham's son Ishmael. But then Sarah does become pregnant with Isaac. However, Ishmael is Abraham's first-born son, and so represents a threat to Isaac's inheritance in Sarah's mind. Hagar and her son Ishmael are thus cast out into the wilderness—with just a loaf of bread and some water. As Delores Williams tells us, "[E]conomic realities, specifically inheritance, are the central issues here. Hagar is poor; and apparently Sarah does not want Hagar's situation elevated, as it no doubt would be if Ishmael received the inheritance from his father that the firstborn son was supposed to receive" (Williams 2013, 27). As one can imagine, the bread and water run out quickly. Hagar, not wanting to see her son die, tells him to walk far away from her so that she does not have to witness him perish in the wilderness.

I am often reminded of that young mother standing over her murdered daughter in the park. She was not able to see death approaching. Pained by a world that seeks to destroy her child, Hagar retreats. No parent should have to watch her child die, especially from a death that comes from hate, spite, or power. In both Hagar's case and the case of that young mother in Salinas who watched her daughter die, conditions of violence and material inheritance determined whether or not their children would survive. For that young mother, her daughter was not to inherit the neighborhood, the power to define what was safe. In Mexican culture, drawn deep from practices of our ancestors, it is one's death that determines your fate in the afterlife. These violent deaths are unfit for the innocents.

> When the water in the skin was gone, she put the boy under one of the bushes. Then she went off and sat down about a bowshot away, for she thought, "I cannot watch the boy die." And as she sat there, she began to sob. (Gen. 21:15–16, NIV)

But God does something miraculous with Hagar and Ishmael. While Abraham and Sarah damn them to the wilderness, God calls out to the hurting, the *damné,* to the experience of the disenfranchised:

> God heard the boy crying, and the angel of God called to Hagar from heaven and said to her, "What is the matter, Hagar? Do not be afraid; God has heard the boy crying as he lies there. Lift the boy up and take him by the hand, for I will make him into a great nation. (21:17–18, NIV)

In this story, I find hope that God can call and promise life to those of us who have been cast aside. God can promise great things from those who have been cast out.

We Latinx are not intended to inherit this world. Cast out, people from my community have been deemed unworthy. Society does not recognize that we bring gifts, talents, and charisms to the common table. We are relegated to the margins of our own community. In this story, I find hope that God can call and promise life to those of us who have been cast aside. God can promise great things from those who have been cast out.

When I, ultimately, did indeed return to seminary for my second year, I read Delores Williams's brilliant work *Sisters in the Wilderness*. She looks at Hagar's position, not as of one of simply fulfilling God's promise, but as one of survival. Williams sees this in part as being due to the conditions of Hagar's ethnic identity. As an Egyptian, she is an outsider, one who is not to inherit the land or the promise to God's people. As I recalled the stories of my grandma, the women with whom I worked in the sheds, and all our ancestors, I felt as if I read a text that spoke profoundly to the Mexican, Chicanx, and abused experience, though Williams wrote for her own community.

Williams's attention to Hagar and her experience with the Divine in the wilderness opened up a space in my theological imagination that spoke to my desire to survive and investigate how this call to survival is vocation. This was not simply a story of going to war, as so often was the case in the Hebrew Bible, and as I sometimes wanted to do in my own neighborhood. This was an experience of survival—not cowardice or violence—but survival in life-threatening circumstances. Hagar and Ishmael were being called to survive, to inherit God's hope for God's community, despite society and their own context actively working against them to do so.

Williams claims, following the work of Elsa Tamez and Phyllis Trible, that God does a few things with Hagar. First, when she is pregnant, God invites Hagar to speak, to have voice, to be one of the only persons in the biblical narrative to name God. This is not insignificant, and we will return to this idea of naming God in the suffering as a condition of a theology of the soil; however, for now, let us say that this naming of God comes for Hagar, as read by Williams, as an expression of inheritance.

> The angel of the Lord also said to her: "You are now pregnant, and you will give birth to a son. You shall name him Ishmael, for the Lord has heard of your misery. He will be a wild donkey of a man; his hand will be against everyone and everyone's hand against him, and he will live in hostility toward all his brothers." She gave this name to the Lord who spoke to her: "You are the God who sees me," for she said, "I have now seen the One who sees me." (Gen. 16:11–13, NIV)

To be seen by a God we can name personally, this is being called into new life. Just as the Christian Brother saw me, God sees Hagar. Beyond seeing, they are also naming each other. In naming God, Hagar is drawing on her heritage and practice of naming the Divine, where naming holds power. Williams raises the question: Is naming God, a power not afforded by her masters, an act of defiance of the patriarchal structure and ownership Abraham and Sarah have over her body? This resonates deeply with my experience with my grandma, who was a devout Catholic woman, who performed miracles as far as I and anyone who knew her was concerned, but was at best able to help with Communion at church; and, at worst, was told she was subordinate to all men—not just priests, but all men. I would sit with my grandma in her home where she actively questioned this, and her response was to name God in our own ways and practice. Ways familiar to me. Ways familiar and unfamiliar to the church. She named, challenged, and called to question the events of my life (and I am sure the lives of others) both in private conversation and in her own prayers. She once told me, "I will always be here, even if the rest of God's people are not. You will always have me and God." This was a radical act of defiance, because she knew that healing from the wounds we were experiencing required the presence of God and God's people at the daily level. She felt it was necessary to commit to this daily survival if I was going to live a full life.

> She felt it was necessary to commit to this daily survival if I was going to live a full life.

She put before all things the relationship between her and my own broken body. This imbued her with a power to name God that she found liberative. Whether it be in the small altar at her front door with the icons of Mary and saints, or the crucifixes in every room, or the prayer cards to the patron saints throughout the house, or the God she talked about in the beauty of her roses in the backyard and the Holy in her marigolds, my grandma had multiple ways of invoking God. She had the power to know that, at the end of the day, by bringing people into her home she was providing sanctuary and life. By her owning this right and doing it daily, she empowered herself to call others to life. She, like Hagar, could call to God by name.

The call narrative continues with Ishmael, who was not to inherit the kingdom because of his mother. Today, one does not inherit the kingdom unless both of your parents represent freedom. We are born with certain societal expectations. With God and the help of the elders, we can also be free. But God first calls for us to survive. This message of survival is one that deeply resonates in the Latinx community.

Whether it is surviving on the borderlands or surviving the material conditions of our neighborhood, God and our community challenge us and, even more importantly, the next generation to survive. The next generation faces incredible challenges, just as Ishmael did. This is the vocation of the disinherited, the oppressed, the marginalized—all those who find themselves on the brink of death. We are called to live.

It is not inconsequential to me that Ishmael, whose name means "God hears," will also be "wild," and will live in hostility toward his neighbors, his hand being against his neighbors and their hands against his. Drawing on the experience of our community, this does not read as a character judgment on Ishmael, as if he is some unruly, selfish, violent man, who wants to fight all of his neighbors. Rather, it reads to me simply as recognition of a truth about what it is like to grow up in a context that wants to destroy you, forsake you, and forget you. For those of us who are not named heirs of this world, who are not the privileged, hostility is not necessarily something that we breed from one generation to the next, a natural inclination to fight. For those of us who have been cast out into the wilderness with little food and water, violence is not encoded in our DNA. We are not inherently evil in our bodies, souls, or bones. It is the social conditions we are born into that make us want to turn our hands against neighbors. We inherit this hostile landscape. And we respond by surviving in whatever way we can.

We walk out our doors into a war zone. We are constantly on guard. Surviving to adulthood is a challenge when everyone turns his or her hands against us. Consider for a moment that I have survived multiple shootings – outside of the shooting recorded earlier. That does not count the number of times that drive-bys and shootings occurred in my neighborhood. We are talking about being able to hear the whiz of bullets flying in my direction. This includes being targeted for execution. Think of the terror that happens to a person when this is a reality. Think of the Stranger climbing those steps daily, tossing my almost lifeless body around, casting racially charged slurs as he did it. Or, consider for a moment that I grew up in a community in which these realities were all too common for people. Think of what opening one's door in the morning to head to school must feel like. Wouldn't you be on guard if your home and your neighborhood, places of supposed refuge, were really sites of such extreme violence? What if your people's true history, the history of your ancestors, was never told to you in school—and, indeed, actively kept from you? What if the colonizers' story of conquest and victory replaced your own family's history of surviving in the wilderness? What if your ancestors were part of forgotten generations, their stories, practices, and traditions lost to you because of the deliberate obfuscations of colonial genocide and violence? What if classmates, teachers, and, indeed, the entire educational system told you that you were always less than those who they had chosen—and that they laughed at you in class? What if they told you every day that you were going to inherit the fieldwork but not the fields, so don't worry about being good at math or science, because you won't be needing it?

> Worst of all, what if you believed all of it? What if you had no one like my grandma to tell you differently? Vocational discernment does not start with a spiritual practice: it starts in these contexts with day-to-day survival.

Worst of all, what if you believed all of it? What if you had no one like my grandma to tell you differently? Vocational discernment does not start with a spiritual practice: it starts in these contexts with day-to-day survival. As David Brooks reminds us, "[T]he first big thing suffering does is it drags you deeper into yourself... [S]uffering gives people a more accurate sense of their own limitations, of what they can control and not control" (Brooks 2015, 94).

When I read that Ishmael will turn his hand against his neighbor, a small part of me agrees: "That is necessary!" He is experiencing deep pain and suffering. He is struggling to define his own limits. He is experiencing social conditions over which he has no power, and by asserting himself in his space, he is attempting to claim what little power he may have. He was cast out by his own father, for goodness sake! I would be pissed off too. I am pissed off about the abuse and violence I have had to endure and I can't imagine being thrown out into the wilderness with just a little water and bread. As Howard Thurman reminds us, "Fear is one of the persistent hounds of hell that dog the footsteps of the poor, the dispossessed, the disinherited" (Thurman 1976, 36). This is the world we inherit: one of fear. One of violence. When we respond in violence, it is not a matter of choosing the wrong path, but merely choosing what has been presented to us as our reality. As Franz Fanon famously said:

> The violence which has ruled over the ordering of the colonial world, which has ceaselessly drummed the rhythm

for the destruction of native social forms and broken up without reserve the systems of reference of the economy, the customs of dress and external life, that same violence will be claimed and taken over by the native at the moment when, deciding to embody history in his own person, he surges into the forbidden quarters. To wreck the colonial world is henceforward a mental picture of action. (Fanon 2005, 40-41)

> The violence which has ruled over the ordering of the colonial world, which has ceaselessly drummed the rhythm for the destruction of native social forms and broken up without reserve the systems of reference of the economy, the customs of dress and external life, that same violence will be claimed and taken over by the native at the moment when, deciding to embody history in his own person, he surges into the forbidden quarters. To wreck the colonial world is henceforward a mental picture of action. (Fanon 2005, 40-41)

We Latinx are conditioned by the violence of a colonial world that has rendered us a people without a history, without an identity, without significance. We have been relegated to what theologian Ivan Petrella (2008) named as the zones of social abandonment, those places from which society turns away. We are the barrios that dominant society created and the spaces defined through colonial policies and practices. We are surviving a violent world.

This theme of surviving to adulthood was one of the most resonant for all my following years in seminary. I didn't want to turn my hand against neighbor, because I sincerely believed that we had other options—Jesus's third way, as Walter Wink so aptly put it. But my third way was not a replica of Winks's interpretation, where we seize the moral initiative, find a creative alternative to violence, break the cycle of humiliation, refuse to submit, shame the oppressor into repentance, be willing to suffer rather than retaliate, and so on (Wink 1998). My approach took a bit of Wink with the realism of Miguel De La Torre's explanation of what Jesus could represent for the Latinx community: "Jesús makes a preferential option for the marginalized, for the outcast, for the dispossessed, not because they are smarter, holier, or better, but simply because they are the disenfranchised" (Torre 2015, 59). This third way is one of survival from the most unlikely of places. Nothing good was supposed to come from Nazareth, just like nothing good was/is supposed to come from Salinas. Surviving these conditions is enough. I am good enough because God was good enough in that space. I am called to life in these conditions to both change them and to better the global community of believers, and that is a divine call—a call to which my community and I respond daily. For us, being alive in itself is living into a heavenly call.

In my studies, I looked for the survival narrative everywhere. I was convinced that writing about this survival as best I could through all the various theological concepts would bring me to some sort of revelation about my own conditions back home. I treated every topic, whether it be theology, biblical studies, church history, or spiritual practices, as if it were a matter of life and death—because, for me, it was. If I could not discern how all this knowledge would save bodies, I was wasting valuable time, money (a lot of it), and effort seeking answers in the wrong place.

I needed what I did at seminary to inform my own work back home with building programs to ensure the survival of young men and women into adulthood in an effort to move them away from gangs and provide viable opportunities for people to escape the fields. This seemed to support that this survival motif was one from which I could draw wisdom.

I returned to Jesus as an example of a person surviving through a world that wanted his destruction and eventually did take his life. He also represents someone who heard a very clear call from God. His vocation, as it is recorded in the gospels, is clear: to spread the good news of loving God and loving others. In church and in seminary, I often found myself struggling to fully get behind the teachings of the church, as they so often focused on "Christ the King." I didn't know this "King" version of Jesus. He was not familiar to me. Conquerors had claimed my body multiple times. That is the work of "kings," not the work of saviors and healers.

> I didn't know this "King" version of Jesus. He was not familiar to me. Conquerors had claimed my body multiple times. That is the work of "kings," not the work of saviors and healers.

What happened to the Jesus who accompanied us as we survived in the wilderness? Returning to Thurman: "[M]any and varied are the interpretations dealing with the teachings and life of Jesus of Nazareth. But few of these interpretations deal with what the teachings and the life of Jesus have to say to those who stand, at a moment in human history, with their backs against the wall" (Thurman 1976, 11). Where is the Jesus of my community? Where is the Jesus of the communities that exist on borderlines between death and life? I am not seeking a judge to save us from oppressive rulers. I am not seeking a prophet in the wilderness calling for unflinching faith in the face of adversity. I am not seeking a king to rule a new, more faithful kingdom. I am seeking a Jesus who accompanies me on a journey to survive.

Enter the late Virgilio Elizondo's *Galilean Journey: The Mexican-American Promise*, a book one of my mentors in seminary recommended to me. I read every single word as if it were my last. He wrote about the experience of being between cultures, surviving in a place of rejection. As someone who was always on the outside, always set for death, this text reminded me that God was born on the border, in a community also set aside for rejection. Elizondo writes, "[W]hat the world rejects, God chooses as his very own... In the wisdom of God, it is precisely here in this impure, culturally mixed, freedom-loving, rebellious region [Galilee] that God made the historical beginning of his visible reign on earth" (Elizondo 2010, 53). That text, that idea, breathed life into my studies. Could God choose me as his own in a world that sought my destruction? Elizondo continues:

> It is in the Galilean identity of Jesus that the ultimate meaning of cultural identity of an oppressed people is to be sought... God chooses an oppressed people, not to bring them comfort in their oppression, but to enable them to confront, transcend, and transform whatever in the oppressor society diminishes and destroys the fundamental dignity of human nature. (Elizondo 2010, 103)

Fundamental to this human nature is the right to live, the right to survive despite a culture that wants to destroy you. Where was that Jesus? How does Jesus come to accompany us in our suffering and in our own survival?

I believed Jesus provided a model in Luke-Acts. In Luke 24:13–35, we find two men going to a village called Emmaus, some distance away from Jerusalem. Fresh from witnessing the violence brought against Jesus, they were actively walking away from that sight of violence. Unknown to them, Jesus comes up beside them and walks along with them. For some reason, most likely the deep trauma they had just witnessed, they do not recognize Jesus walking with them. Jesus turns to them and asks them what they are talking about. Cleopas, one of the travelers, asks him if he hasn't heard about the violence that has occurred, and then proceeds to tell him about Jesus of Nazareth:

He was a prophet, powerful in word and deed before God and all the people. The chief priests and our rulers handed him over to be sentenced to death, and they crucified him; but we had hoped that he was the one who was going to redeem Israel. And what is more, it is the third day since all this took place. In addition, some of our women amazed us. They went to the tomb early this morning but didn't find his body. They came and told us that they had seen a vision of angels, who said he was alive. Then some of our companions went to the tomb and found it just as the women had said, but they did not see Jesus. (Lk. 24:19–24, NIV)

Then Jesus calls them fools for not believing what the prophets had said and then teaches them about the prophets. The two invite Jesus to come to stay with them at the end of their journey, and that is when Jesus broke bread, gave thanks, and gave it to them. It was at this point that they recognize Jesus and they say, "Were not our hearts burning within us while he talked with us on the road and opened the Scriptures to us?" (v. 32). They tell the other disciples what they have seen—the risen Jesus, a God who survived death.

In popular culture, Cormac McCarthy's *The Road* tells the story of a man and his son, two nameless characters on the road after the "end of the world." In McCarthy's story the Father, known in the book as "the man," fights off cannibals and starvation while caring for his son and passing on the wisdom of survival and his love to his son, telling the son always to carry the fire. This fire can be read as a hope of a better tomorrow, a better today, a better yesterday—the fire of ethical living, the fire to live into love despite the post-apocalyptic status of the world. However, I choose to read it as the fire of life, as the fire of survival. Like McCarthy, Octavia Butler's Parable of the Sower tells the story of a young person discerning a connection to God in a post-apocalyptic world. Butler's main character, Lauren, is on the road as the world around her deteriorates due to racial violence, ecological devastation, poverty, and addiction. She is searching for a place to form a Christian community. These fictional journeys on the road(s) through the wilderness reflect our own struggles to find God and community in a broken world.

McCarthy's story reminds me of the road to Emmaus and causes me to ask: What is required of us who venture out on the road with no signs of the resurrected Jesus and who are merely trying to survive the violence we experience and witness? We have in the gospels something quite incredible. We have a God that calls for us to live, despite the violent realities of the day. The two disciples see the resurrected Jesus. Like the disciples on the road to Emmaus, I had witnessed too many violent deaths. I was on my own road to Emmaus, on my own road to the Northeast where knowledge supposedly was located, away from Salinas.

Like the two on the road to Emmaus, I say to you, as they did to Jesus, "Are you the only one visiting my community of violence who does not know the things that have happened?" Let me broaden this question: Are you the only one visiting this world who does not know the violence, the struggle, the pain in this world? Survival is the first vocational call. It is first shout, whisper, murmur, and call from God that I hear. Religious and political wars rage on for years. Today, 925 million people do not have enough food to eat. Domestic violence invades our homes and the trust of those dear to us. In this country, shootings happen on a daily basis, taking the lives of innocents. Survival is the first vocational call from God. Will we hear and amplify that call to life? Will you?

After seeing that girl murdered a body length away from me, I set out on the road to Emmaus. And like the two on the road, I have been widening that gap between my community and where I should go to survive. I hope one day that I will be brave enough to return, to set sail from the shore of my lived reality, to that island of salvation, from my despair to the hope of a community liberated from such violence.

What does a call to survival look like in my vocational imagination? Here I am, a student of the scripture and inheriting a tradition, looking for Jesus, ready to tell the story I know, a story of violence in my home and in my community, and a deep desire to hear God's call to life, to call these bones to rise. I am approached by that little girl all those years ago. She walks with me down the road, away from the park where she was murdered. I invite her to sit with me at my table and I try to tell her the story of what I have seen. As we share a meal, I see who she is. She disappears. Was she an apparition? Did my heart not burn when she was with me on the road away from my home?

Imagining these moments draws me into the scripture, draws me in to imagine a resurrected life. Imagination is the only thing that can make this moment real for me. I am not testifying to that little girl's actual resurrection, only imagining it. I saw in that girl's face, that murdered face, which is always before me: the murdered Jesus. For years I have been walking on the road. Like McCarthy's Father and Son in *The Road*, I continue to travel, keeping the fire of her life alive. I want to live, survive, and thrive. This is the call of vocation: simply to breathe.

I don't want to be too hasty and get off the road from wherever we are traveling. Jesus caught up to the two disciples and walked and talked with them, slowly, never announcing his presence, but walking with them. Just before night, the disciples invited the stranger into their home. They shared a meal, as we share meals. One day, I will see the spirit, the spirit of the innocent before me, and she will catch me on the road and walk with me, as I try to make sense of what happened.

Barbara Brown Taylor, in *The Preaching Life,* suggests that the primary purpose of the Church is to foster such imagination. She writes:

> In order to discern the hidden figure [God], it is often necessary to cross your eyes or stand on your head so that all known relationships are called into question and new ones may be imagined. When earth and sky are reversed and it seems entirely plausible that lawns may grow down instead of up, then you are in a good position to glimpse the hidden figure, because you are ready to approach it on its terms instead of your own. (B. B. Taylor 1993, 51)

For so many of us, our lives are turned upside down by our lived realities. We crave God to join us on the road. I want to imagine God with me. I have faith that God is with me. Imagining this walk with God helped me survive my daily realities. As Rubem Alves writes:

> Things become clearer by means of images. Children are playing. One of them points his or her finger at the other and says "bang I killed you!" Adults are playing. One of them points his gun at the other and bang: "I killed you!" Children's play ends with the universal resurrection of the dead. Adult's play ends with universal burial. Whereas the resurrection is the paradigm of the world of children, the world of adults creates the cross. (2009, 91)

And so I imagine a resurrection on the road of life that I travel. Together, we have imagined vocations with the daily struggle. This is where we survive, where Jesus comes to meet us in our deepest pains, where we can imagine resurrection, not the cross.

These pains are varied and wide. We suffer from the pains of heartbreak, from addiction, from blended families, from deception, from lost friendships and loved ones, from cancers and pains, and from deep sadness and depression. Our pains come from losing battles with life. The beauty of our tradition is that it calls for us to live. God calls for life to spring forth. In order for our images of resurrection to be returned to the imagination of a child, we must grasp the imagination that allows for the glorious resurrection of bodies. It's the type of faith that not only claims that Jesus was raised, but imagines actual bodies being raised from the dead. We must venture out onto the road! Jesus must catch us on this walk, not the other way around. To imagine resurrection for me is to say, "She is risen, that innocent of our family, that girl I saw murdered before my eyes." Imagining anything less would be to take that angel out of heaven. Imagining anything else would be to fail to share the good news, the good news of God calling us to live. If we are so hasty to get off the road, we might miss our meeting with Jesus there. We might miss the meal where we see her face to face. We might miss our call when Jesus walks side by side with us, calling us to new life.

For those from communities like Salinas, the road represents a space where we are processing our deepest traumas and cuts through a wilderness we must survive. The wilderness seeks to destroy our very existence. The road can represent a path that is lit through the wilderness where we meet those who will walk alongside us. I can imagine the little girl resurrected on the road. I can imagine my grandma coming alongside me on this road, listening to me talk about the harrowing acts of violence I witnessed. On the road, I can meet those who will walk with me and help me see a resurrected life. The road is holy ground, leading us from the wilderness to the ground in which we feel safe. It is this holy and safe ground to which we now turn.

Chapter 5

Grounded in New Life

People forget that the soil is our sustenance. It is a sacred trust.
It is what has worked for us for centuries. It is what we pass on
to future generations.
—César E. Chávez, excerpt from March 1989 speech at
Pacific Lutheran University in Tacoma, Washington

How often do we pay attention to the ground under our feet? How often do we reflect on the soil that sustains our generations and the generations to come? Coming from an agricultural community, I know that the soil determines our livelihood. The ground beneath our feet sustains us across generations. One of the most common things to say at the start of spiritual practices, healing practices, religious rituals, or when we gather as groups is that we need to "ground" ourselves. Too often the act of grounding is abstract and does not consider the conditions beneath our feet. And this is not to say that we don't pay attention to the connection between our feet and the floor, but rather we don't know the conditions for life in the soil in which we are raised. We can feel in our bodies how disingenuous abstract grounding is when we are in an environment that frightens us or where we experience great fear and abuse. In these cases, we can attempt to ground ourselves, but very rarely do we succeed. This is for two reasons: First, we do not want to be grounded in the reality in which we currently find our bodies; and, second, we don't know what ground we are talking about.

A good example of not wanting to be grounded in a space was when I was very young and had experienced the abuse at the Stranger's hand. Like many of my generation, adults took me to a therapist so I could process my feelings because I was acting out and fighting too often. I was told that this was something that was wrong with *me*—not wrong with the context, but something wrong with my person. Or, so they told me.

Therapy wasn't my choice, but I had to sit here with this person who didn't look like me, who couldn't empathize with my experience, but who had been trained to listen and look for the signs that would cure me of my pain, of my violence, and ultimately, I think, of my own brown Chicano machismo.

We opened this book with a story about what happened at one particular time when I had challenged the Stranger and had started a fight. The idea was that I was a bad kid who was out of control and that is why the Stranger wanted to hurt me. It was my fault. The therapist said that what I needed to do was "ground" myself so I could see other perspectives. We breathed. I looked straight at the concrete slab beneath my feet. "Ground" myself in what? "Ground" myself where? Ground myself surrounded by what group of people? I breathed in deeper. With every breath, my body became smaller. Like that time with the Stranger, my body began to feel as if it was shrinking, shriveling up, curling in on itself. My breath quickened. The ground opened up and began to curl all around—and swallowed me whole. I hyperventilated and nearly passed out. To everyone, this was a sign that something was wrong with me. The therapist apparently never considered that this was a sign of the instability of the very ground on which I was forced to place myself. This was unsafe and unholy ground for me.

This "grounding" never really worked for my own spiritual practices, because I was never taught that it should be tied to the actual ground beneath my feet. The ground underneath our feet matters. We need to know the space, know the people who occupy and live in that space, and, more importantly, we need to know whether the ground on which we stand will provide life. We often neglect the fact that this grounding works well for those who can close their eyes and feel safe. The deep grounding often works for those who do not hear gunshots going off at night, who have never heard the whiz of bullets, who have never had to struggle to breathe as the life is being choked out of them. It works

> The deep grounding often works for those who do not hear gunshots going off at night, who have never heard the whiz of bullets, who have never had to struggle to breathe as the life is being choked out of them. It works for those who trust complete strangers with their bodies.

for those who trust complete strangers with their bodies. It works for those who are okay in the dark. It works for those who don't have to put their backs against the wall to ensure no one comes up behind them to close their eyes for eternity.

With these concerns and questions, it is incredibly difficult for us to think about grounding ourselves before much needed vocational reflection. That doesn't mean the practice of grounding needs to be lost, but its abstract referent needs to be reimagined. We need to ground ourselves in a place, in a time, with a people, with our own bodies, and most importantly *in a place where we feel safe*. We cannot let go of the fact that material existence is what grounds us in our own vocational call to survive, to live, and to thrive in this world.

This grounding takes place on soil that will provide life. It is, as César Chávez said, the soil that we pass on to the next generation. This soil must be cared for and tended to, because it is the ground on which the next generation will stand.

Having grown up in Salinas, a small agricultural town riddled with poverty and gang violence, I find myself always contemplating the quality of the soil beneath my feet. I think about the soil beneath my feet as a native to California who has put his hands in the soil and has literally bled into it. Anyone who has worked the field has bled into this soil because of cuts from machines, cuts from tools, cuts from the produce. We bleed into the soil that provides the food you eat. Yet my community cannot afford to put this same produce on our tables. Blood has been spilled on that soil and what springs forth is inaccessible to our own people. This ground pulses with my blood, the blood of the elders, and the blood of my ancestors.

That call from God to life I believe is grounded in a theology of the soil. To clarify, I tether my notion of God to the very material and raw experiences of our everyday lives. This theology of the soil is a theology of paying attention to (1) our "ground of being," as the German theologian Paul Tillich so rightly named it, though he failed to mention that this occurs in a community; (2) the footprints we leave in the soil; and (3) those footprints that walk alongside our own. The soil identifies the ways that we ground ourselves, or literally plant our feet in communities. The footprints in the soil, as a metaphor for the attentiveness to one's own narrative, can be a powerful tool for discerning one's own vocation. We will find ourselves naming and defining our vocations by the very ground beneath our feet, and find ourselves called to communities and life in particular places. By celebrating God's and our community's footprints, which journey alongside our own, we are able to see how a narrative approach to vocational discernment is part of a larger call from God to God's own community. This theology of the soil will challenge us to think about how planting one's feet commits one to being in relationship with all that is in that space in the particular moment.

I was about to start my Ph.D. program and had returned home to work with a small organization addressing violence in my community. During a visit home to consult on the project—*consult* being the professional word for what we actually called in the community helping—I had just started training to run my first marathon. I left my father's home and drove out to the fields to start before sunrise. I went to a small field near Castroville, the land of artichokes, and under the cover of dawn I laced up my shoes, stretched, and began the 20-mile-long training run.

The run wove through the fields between Castroville and Marina (just North of Monterey). I ran on dirt roads that surround the fields and end along the recreational trail that connects communities such as Monterey and Santa Cruz. The fields in full growing season were beautiful: lettuce row upon lettuce row. I smiled at the greens and reds that meandered over the slightly convex hills. The sun began to rise over the mountains, and I could feel its warmth on my back as I ran toward the Pacific Ocean. It was a surreal experience. Running through the land I love, watching the sunrise over the fields and the Pacific Ocean, I was clearly in God's country. After a few miles and as the daylight officially broke, the fields closer to the ocean revealed that there were people already hard at work in the early dawn. They were stretching with the local supervisor, preparing for a day of backbreaking labor. As I got closer to the group, one of the younger workers stood out to me. I ran by the group that was stretching, when this person began yelling out to me. I realized it was a classmate from my elementary school, Sammy. He was dressed for work in the fields—covered from head to toe, bandana around his neck, big broad hat, and shoes that had been abused by the hard work. He had a big, beautiful, inviting smile on his face. He asked the supervisor if we could talk, and the supervisor told him to make it quick.

Sammy was one of the smartest in my class. I remember competing with him in class over who was better at multiplication. He always beat me in our school work and sports. We were in the same catechism class on the weekends, and even there he was better than me at remembering the prayers and history of the Church. We lived only a few blocks from each other growing up.

Sammy asked how I had been and what I had been up to. I tried not to say much, except that I was about to do more school in Southern California.

"I knew you would make it out, Patricio."

"What have you been up to?" I returned.

"I dropped out of high school. Remember Monica? She lived a couple blocks from my apartment. Well, we had a baby, and we are together. So I went straight to work after school. Our daughter is 10 now. I have been out here all this time. They pay okay... Look, I want to talk but have to get back."

I pulled out my cellphone. "Can you give me your number? Let's talk."

He gave me his number. "Look, be careful. You might hurt yourself running out here in the dark and through that mud." The sun had risen at this point, and he pointed at the long row of footsteps I had left behind me on the dirt road. "You see, you could get hurt," gesturing to the footprints. We hugged and he returned to work.

I ran a few steps and turned back to wave to him. He had already rejoined the line. Bent over in the row of lettuce, he also left footprints in his muddy row. The shoes he wore, not made for the mud, left deep indentations in the wet soil. With each step, there was a loud sucking sound followed by the squish of his shoe being absorbed back into the ground. He bent at almost a complete 90 degree angle. He didn't look up as I yelled good-bye.

> I stared at those footprints for a long time, reflecting on the meaning of where my feet were planted, where Sammy's feet were planted, and where we were going to plant our feet in the future.

We leave our footprints in particular places, and in particular ways. In that moment, I had left footprints on a path that ventured around the soil in which my family, friends, and I had all worked at some point. My footprints, however close in proximity to the fields, were not in the fields any longer. I stared at those footprints for a long time, reflecting on the meaning of where my feet were planted, where Sammy's feet were planted, and where we were going to plant our feet in the future.

Contrast these footprints with my arrival at the Pacific Ocean. This pristine beach, my destination, full of tourists and those who could afford to live near the bay, was beautiful to look at and to enjoy. As I reached the part in my run where I would turn back, I took a moment to walk out to the water. I took off my running shoes and put my feet in the waves. The water was so cold, but soothing for my tired feet. Here was the destination of my run, but my feet didn't leave a mark. The water washed away my footprints.

In my academic journey, I also had a destination in mind—surviving and ensuring the survival of our wisdom and stories in theological education. Yet I could not reconcile that destination and the pursuit of the Ph.D. with the vocation of being called to life. Like the ocean, I wondered whether the game of becoming a scholar would take my experience and erase my footprints in a larger ocean I could neither control nor thrive in. I wondered whether the stories and people that formed me were just going to become another story for the privileged few to point to: "Look at him, the one who made it out; the light-skinned brown person in the room with stories!" (a statement that was made when I first entered my academic life). As I journeyed closer to home, my feet left more permanent indentations on the path and in the soil.

Even here, the recreation trail was surrounded by homes owned by wealthy community members who wanted to be near the ocean. The academy, similarly, was made up of those wealthy community members or their descendants who had the resources and means to enter into disciplines that offered prestige and respect. I had not officially arrived, but when you put your feet in the Pacific or theorize with some of the most brilliant people in your discipline, it sure does feel as if you have. The feeling is only temporary, though, because sooner or later your footprints will be washed away by the ocean. You will be forced to return home to be with the community that raised you. The undertow of oppression reminds scholars of color of our secondary class—our work is "cultural," "less than," too "passionate" to be considered real scholarship. I looked out into this ocean. I stood on the same beach that in high school had taken the life of a childhood friend, also named Patrick. The undertow swept him out to sea and drowned him. This was far more than just a metaphor for what was happening in my life. These were examples of the power that the world has over our community. It has the power to swallow us. I turned away from the beach and started the long journey home.

Running into the heat of the sun, with its light shining directly into my eyes, I tried to make it back to the car as soon as possible because of how draining the run to the ocean had been—a similar feeling to that of my academic journey. I crossed over one sand dune, and then back into the valley of fields. Way off in the distance, I could see Sammy's field crew. I couldn't make out which one was him. He was just a speck in the distance. As I came to the place where we had embraced, I noticed the ground on which we had stood. The path I had chosen to run on, that road that surrounded the fields, was designed to keep us— the Latinx field workers, the poor, the oppressed—inside its perimeter. It was also a clear path for the supervisors and owners to drive on, to ensure that we stayed in the rows that were designed for us to pick their food. My footprints had all but disappeared on that path—some under truck tire marks, others just from not being deep enough in the soil, still others because of the way I had avoided the mud in the dark. In many ways, it was a reminder that I could gain temporary access to this road, but it was not mine. My feet would not leave a permanent indentation in this space. My friend was incredibly insightful: I could get hurt on this road.

In contrast, I looked down the row where my friend had begun his work. I could make out every single one of his footprints. It was as if I could almost hear the sucking sound of his shoe coming out of one footprint, and the squish of it returning to the soil. These footprints seemed permanent—part of the soil—venturing away from my path and deeper into the row of vegetables.

> A theology of the soil does not simply look for our own footprints. It also calls us to look for the footprints of our community. These are the footprints through which God speaks to us.

A theology of the soil does not simply look for our own footprints. It also calls us to look for the footprints of our community. These are the footprints through which God speaks to us. It was God's voice saying to me in that moment by the field not to follow the footsteps I had taken previously. The way of the owners, managers, and field supervisors was not my path or my road. The only footprints left to follow were those into the fields. Those were the only footprints left in the soil, and there were many to follow. Those were the footsteps I had inherited. And it was not just one row in which these prints appeared. The community had left its marks in every single row. It was a reminder that we not only work the soil, but that we feed bodies through our labor, though sometimes our own bodies feel pain and hunger.

I knew that my work would be grounded in this soil, in this reality, and in this community. I was going to follow the footprints of my community. Because, while I had managed through a variety of social factors to find a way to this road designed to keep others in their oppression, I also had the sight to see where God was walking. If I didn't follow God into the fields, then I was no better than those

> A theology of the soil sprouts from the understanding that we are all grounded in some place.

supervisors who drove around in circles on these roads, ensuring that *mi gente* remained oppressed. A theology of the soil sprouts from the understanding that we are all grounded in some place.

For those of you who may not feel physically grounded due to a lack of connection to a particular space or to moving between multiple communities, consider the place in which you are sitting right now as you read this book. There is a particular amount of attention needed to notice where one's feet are located. When we think about our footprints in the soil, we can begin to see our commitments and values being expressed in very tangible ways.

I once had a white, male supervisor who had dreams of being a big part of the movement for justice, especially for communities of color. Yet when he traced his steps, he found himself walking in white neighborhoods, worshiping in white spaces, surrounded by

> If, while planting your feet you trample the footprints of others, you cannot walk for justice, you cannot walk alongside people of color.

white neighbors. When it came to shared work, he once said of my preparation, "You come from a labor background; I come from a professional background. That is why you work more hours." And later, "You can tell the stories, because that is what you do. I can do the theory, because I am an expert in those areas." Though I had done all the work and had a Ph.D. in the matter (both of which he did not), it was jarring for me to be relegated to the "stories of my people," while my intellectual contribution was dismissed or it was implied that the stories of my people were all that I was there for—the representative minority. At those moments when there were people of color in the room, he needed to be upfront, speaking, being the center of the movement, never tracking where his feet were or how they related to others. It was an expression of one's relationship to God. If, while planting your feet you trample the footprints of others, you cannot walk for justice, you cannot walk alongside people of color. If you yell so loud for justice that the cries of suffering are drowned out, you are drowning out the cry of God. It is not just about your *desire* to live into a vocation, it is also about how you actually live and walk. Where are you grounded? Who are your people? Who are you surviving alongside?

This is the challenge of a theology of the soil. While it does matter that psychologically, spirituality, and intellectually we construct our own vocational narratives, the soil under one's feet ultimately grounds that vocation. Where do you spend time? With whom do you associate? What do you do when you are there? How is this the work of the kin-dom in that space? How are you hearing and cultivating the space for God's call to life to be heard clearly? Do you have any control over the ground under your feet? Can you escape your violent reality, if it is indeed violent? Can you move about the ground without being stopped by the police? By rival gangs? By neighbors? Is the ground a war zone or a place of nourishing?

How do we cultivate the space and time necessary to discern where our feet are grounded? It starts with a clear understanding of the now. As people of color, we have an incredible burden to speak and write from places that meet rigorous standards not afforded to other communities. In order for me to "do" theology, I must observe a double standard. I must meet the burden of the white academy; I must know their canon. And if I am going to be liberative, I need to know our own as well. This is an issue of the soil in which we were grown. The soil of the academy was not prepared for scholars of color.

I once had a debate with a white colleague, Tom. Tom insisted that he did not need a Ph.D. in theology to teach theology. He had a full-time job teaching theology with a Master's. I had a Ph.D., as much experience, and a few extra Master's degrees to boot, and yet he still made more money than I did, taught the theology courses he wanted to teach, and was not challenged on his credentials in a single classroom. As a scholar of color, I can't tell you how many students start by challenging my education or background. They asked questions such as: "Mr. Reyes, why are you teaching and not Dr. Tom?" "Mister," for me, "Doctor," for him, when it was the opposite. When I was considered to teach theology, it was to offer a Latinx interpretation of that literature. While he did theology proper, I was relegated to Latinx or contextual theology—as if I didn't know the broader field of theology—when I had to prove competency in order to get the Ph.D. in the first place. Students assumed he had something universal to teach them. I had some brown stuff to teach them, some stories to tell. He was raised in the conditions that were supposed to produce a scholar of theology as a third generation pastor/scholar. I was "lucky" to be teaching them in the first place, as an inheritor of generations who work the land. He had been called to teach. I had been called to labor.

Credentials matter for people of color. In order to build our theologies and our movements in the disciplines of education, theology, and religion, the Ph.D. is a requirement. Even then, institutional racism and societal expectations are such that we are not regarded as being as qualified as our white colleagues. Where the footprints of our ancestors are located define how and where we may travel.

We have to plant our feet in multiple bibliographies, multiple communities. We have to know our feet are grounded in our community and the dominant culture. I needed a Ph.D. and so much more. The soil that sustained me in my youth was also soil that was not designed to produce scholars. Field workers—yes. Scholars—no. Those footprints in the soil that led out to the rows of lettuce were not just the steps of God with my community; they were also the constructed steps of colonialism, oppression, and marginalization by the dominant culture. If society had its way, my boots would have remained firmly planted between rows of lettuce. The difference between Sammy and me was a few lucky breaks and a slight difference in birthplace in society. If we paid attention to a theology of the soil, then we would know that I was now on Tom's ground. The soil had been prepared and tilled for him to grow, not me or Sammy. Society said God had called the Toms of our world to teach, the Toms to drive on the road that surrounded our fields, ensuring that we Sammys and Patricks stayed in our rows, whether of lettuce or of teaching about our God.

Let's root this theology in scripture. Of the many pastoral parables in scripture, I want to focus on that of the sower and the seeds in Matthew 13. Those seeds that fell onto rocky soil would never grow, but "Still other seed fell on good soil, where it produced a crop—a hundred, sixty or thirty times what was sown. Whoever has ears, let them hear.'" (Mt. 13:8–9, NIV). This parable, which appears in Mark, Matthew, and Luke, offers a glimpse into the reality of Jesus's time. This parable would have resonated with the agricultural ways of his community. I think this is all the more relevant for today, especially regarding vocational discernment.

The passage gives us a glimpse into the three broad categories of a theology of the soil that I wish to talk about. Jesus names those "other" conditions in which the seeds are not able to grow. These conditions in a theology of the soil are those that tear us away from that which gives us most life and allows us to thrive. This category we'll call bad soil.

We will talk about what conditions make for bad soil, looking both at the narrative presented and also at other examples of lives in which the conditions just do not allow good seeds to grow.

Next is fallow soil or soil at rest. Wouldn't everyone love a sabbatical? Well, for someone to do good vocational discernment, this time-honored practice is necessary. In order for soil to provide ideal conditions year after year, the Bible notes the importance of giving the soil time to rest, to regain its nutrients, and to build the capacity to hold new life. This is not inconsequential.

I will save "good soil" for the next chapter, but know that this is soil that is rightly tended to, has the right mix of ingredients, and is cared for long after the seed has been planted. We'll evaluate what conditions are needed for a seed to germinate, to sprout, and to form into its most authentic self. Regardless of one's conditions or wrongdoings, one can grow if one is rooted in good soil. Even if a person has perpetrated great violence against people or committed other grave sins, I do believe a seed with great potential for growth still lies within. As Howard Thurman said:

> There is a reaping of precisely what we have sown, with the extra thrown in guaranteed by the laws of growth. Thus the insight from the scriptures: 'Be not deceived, God is not mocked, for whatsoever a man soweth that shall he also reap.' The good and the not-good alike. All of life is a planting and a harvesting. No man gathers merely the crop that he himself has planted. (Thurman 1984, 64)

We reap, even from the bad soil.

Bad soil is everywhere! That doesn't necessarily mean the earth is quintessentially evil or violent, but in many places the conditions don't favor growth. As one can imagine from my opening stories, the soil in my formative years was not full of nutrients, nor was it properly tended to. When I moved away from my community and into the academy, not much changed.

Bad soil happens for a number of reasons, but the most common are neglect and lack of understanding. As any person who has tended a garden knows, neglect can be deadly—not just for the seeds in the earth, but for the earth itself. These conditions are where potential change makers lose their ability to grow and flourish. Neglect unfortunately claims too many seeds early. I remember how in grade school some students in our class would come and go, due to the unstable nature of their parents' work. They would be present in the class for a few months and then would disappear, either going to a different school or leaving the neighborhood altogether. One such student was Carlos. Carlos was the son of undocumented migrant farmworkers. He was in my second grade class for only a few months. He came in one day and the teacher placed him in the back row: the first mistake. She then continued to mispronounce his last name, although he would correct her every time: mistake number two. When he ran away in the middle of class out of frustration that the teacher was refusing to call him by name or take the time to try and translate into Spanish what she was teaching, she didn't even realize he had left until a police officer escorted him back to the classroom: mistake number... Is it really a mistake at this point? He lasted only another week before dropping out of school for the remainder of the year. I knew this because, later in the year, on a day his mother didn't have to work in the fields, she brought him to the park to play with us one last time during recess before they moved back to Mexico. The call to life looked very different for Carlos.

Neglect can be most damaging for vocational discernment. When no one in authority tells young people they are seen, they disappear. Carlos disappeared from our community. In my own family, my youngest brother disappeared for some time. He dropped out of high school, was hooked on drugs, and at one point was considered a "gang lord" by the local police—though it was a title he neither deserved nor fully understood. He did not understand the conversations I had to have to keep him safe, nor did he or the police realize how incredibly stupid the police were for mislabeling him and his clout in the community. After one incident with a group of gang members from a more notorious group, in which one of his friends was stabbed, I rushed home from college to negotiate his safety. I offered to bring him up to where I was living at the time, but he refused.

While my father provided a place of deep hospitality, care, and safety for me and one of my other brothers, this particular "gang-lord" brother elected to stay with my mother. He had friends live with him and was provided a cash stipend for food and other necessities by those around him. He was only sixteen. I don't want to belabor the point, but neglect by all of our family members, myself included, allowed him to be (mis) fed by a community that did not address the call to survival in a way that was liberative. Instead of hearing the call to life, he heard the call to captivity and addiction.

One night in particular, I came home from working a 2–11 p.m. shift at the local Home Depot. I needed to use the home computer to submit paperwork for my college by midnight. I was in the middle of my undergraduate program at this point, and every assignment seemed like the most important one. I went to my mother's house because it was closest to my work, but I found my brother and two of his friends in the basement on the family computer. They had been doing cocaine and were understandably unsympathetic to my need to turn in schoolwork. I asked repeatedly for them to let me on for just five minutes so I could e-mail my paper. I had been called to life by the community and I needed to get on the computer! Didn't they understand this?

Ten minutes later, I yanked my brother off the computer so I could sit down and do my necessary work. Immediately, one of his friends, high on cocaine and also half-naked for some reason, ran up the stairs and out of the house, screaming, "He's going to kill us!!" My brother and his other friend immediately began to fight me. Wrestling and punching ensued, but with both of them in a drug-induced haze, they couldn't land anything. Eventually, I had my brother held in place and his friend had run up to find my mother. As soon as she came down, my brother and his friend took off down the street, following the first friend out the door. My mother told me I was never welcome back in her house.

There is an assumption that birth order means a lot in family dynamics, and to some extent that is true. As the oldest, I wanted to set a good example. In order for young people to set examples, there need to be the conditions for thriving. My brother was neglected, plain and simple. Whether it was his undiagnosed learning disability, his unchecked drug abuse, or his living on his own when he was way too young, he had no good examples to look up to (myself included), no one tapping him on the shoulder calling him to life. Even that Christian Brother, who had been so kind to me, asked him to leave our school because of his bad behavior and his lack of performance in school. I, so intent on my own survival and getting away from home as quickly as possible, left him there. His friends all enjoyed being high school dropouts, but I am sure they were struggling with survival narratives of their own. Communities succeed when a village raises the next generation. His village had not been activated; his elders were not present, and no cloud of witnesses walked him through his traumas. And the consequences played out pretty explicitly that night.

I called my father to tell him to go find his son that night. He refused to go drive around looking for his lost child. My guess is he was taking the prodigal son approach to parenting, a tactic that may still be in place. I was so mad. I was mad because I hadn't turned in my paper and now was dealing with family drama—for what? How was any of this calling any one in our family to new life? This is the experience of those who are raised in bad soil. They're neglected, afraid, and confused. But more importantly, they are negotiating the call to life on a visceral and immediate level. Though I wish I could have focused on finishing my schoolwork, I was called to the very immediacy of life. I needed to pay attention to what was occurring in the moment. I was responsible for my brother.

Like the story of Cain and Abel, I was at a crossroads. Sometimes I wonder whether Abel was asking for it. I imagine Cain felt angry toward his brother, much like the anger I held toward my young brother as I drove around looking for him that night. But, unlike the biblical stories we hear in Sunday school, our story is not set in stone. I had a choice: I could either bury my brother and focus on my most holy of offerings—my education, my work in the community, my love for pursuing an education—or, I could embrace this brokenness of the world and forsake that narrative. Those whose first vocational discernment call is one to survival are also called in a community that is also suffering. Bad soil doesn't just affect one seed; it affects the entire crop. My brother and I, while having inherited slightly different soil, were from the same ground. My call to survival—getting out of Salinas—was going to be put on hold this night.

After committing myself to my brother's safety and well-being, I felt my responsibility acutely. I went out to look for him. I drove around the community. I spoke to neighbors. I called my own network to see if people would join the search. A village had responded. We weren't going to let him and his friends get lost tonight. In Luke 15, the parable of the lost sheep, Jesus says:

> Suppose one of you has a hundred sheep and loses one of them. Doesn't he leave the ninety-nine in the open country and go after the lost sheep until he finds it? And when he finds it, he joyfully puts it on his shoulders and goes home. Then he calls his friends and neighbors together and says, "Rejoice with me; I have found my lost sheep." I tell you that in the same way there will be more rejoicing in heaven over one sinner who repents than over ninety-nine righteous persons who do not need to repent. (vv. 4–7, NIV)

I thought I would find him, our lost sheep, bring him home, and we would all rejoice. But after a few hours of searching, I went back to the house—only to find out he was right there in the backyard. When I learned he was back in the house, I was prepared to embrace my inner

Cain. But my mother, true to her word, did not allow me back inside the house.

Angry and confused, I drove to my grandma's house to stay the night. I got to her house just after 5 a.m. She opened the door, sat me down, cooked me some huevos y papas, made some hot chocolate (the real stuff), heated up some tortillas, and listened to me tell the whole story. She said, very calmly—after I had vented for about an hour—that sometimes I should focus on what gave me life. Confused, I didn't know what that would be in this moment.

She said, "Mijo, I spend hours at home making sure there is always food to cook for people and a place for them to sleep." Lacking the maturity to understand the wisdom she was offering, I asked what that had to do with any of my problems. In her sage-like wisdom, she smiled and asked if I wanted more food. I did. She cooked more and I continued to vent. When I was done, she offered me some blankets and told me to get some sleep on the couch. I woke later that afternoon. She gave me a hug, asked if I wanted more food and told me I was always welcome in "our home." I drove back to school with a full stomach, a few hours of sleep in the safest place I knew, and a renewed sense that I had family. The full wisdom of her words did not occur to me until years later, after she had passed away. Focusing on what gives life—providing the basics for survival, such as food, a roof, and deep, unconditional, and unending love—my grandma showed me that the only response to neglect is to offer care. In order for one to hear the voice of God calling out, these basic needs have to be met.

I was once sharing the story of the sower with a group of youth and when I said that the sower threw seeds on the road, a hand immediately shot up. "Why would the farmer do that? Is he stupid?" Youth often get to the heart of the matter quicker than the adults, who want to focus on the idea of growing these seeds to adulthood. But even the youth knew that if you don't cultivate them in the right conditions they will not grow, and that it is indeed "stupid" to put them in soil that will not allow for the seeds to grow.

When I eventually went to seminary, I felt like a seed on the road waiting to be picked apart by crows. While I had found my new sense of calling and was pursuing it, I was a square peg forced into a round hole. I had chosen this particular seminary because of the pastor who recommended it to me when we were working in the packing sheds, because of its prophetic past, and because I had anticipated there would be support there for me to pursue a prophetic present. I ran intervention and prevention programs in my community, but just hadn't done so formally. Often those closest to the conflict do a lot of the work and organizing, but never benefit from the paycheck, job title, or line on their *curriculum vitae*. We intervene in the violence because it is a neighbor, a family member, a friend that is caught in the insidious web of violence, because the contested borders cross our neighborhoods. We offer food, safety, and activities for our neighbors to prevent them from embracing violence. We do this for survival.

There were a few professors who really got "the need for this work," but didn't understand that imagining, writing, thinking, reading, reflecting, and most importantly doing were a matter of life and death for my community. They were committed in theory, but in body they didn't carry the open wounds I did. I did my best to focus on the classes that were all in practical areas or areas that dealt with my community, with very specific sets of skills and learning that would serve my project and community well. In a particular class covering liberative theologies, my final assignment was on contextual theology: a perfect opportunity for me to connect the theologies I was studying in seminary with my home context of Salinas; a perfect opportunity to talk about confronting "gang-lords," high on cocaine, in the pursuit of an education. This was all ideal, right?

That particular paper came back practically bathed in red ink. The professor's issue with my paper was not so much grammatical or structural, but with how I was applying the texts to Salinas. The professor said I was "using the texts for a question for which they may not have been designed." And more directly, "You run the risk of not 'reading' the text, because you asked questions that were not relevant to the era in which it was written." This implied that in order for this learning to be of value, it was only to be understood within the white academic context in which I found myself, within the framework in which it was designed. These were the rules of the game. Someone should have told me there were rules at all. Contextual theology meant I needed to know the dominant culture's context first—the entire curriculum was designed with this in mind.

I attempted to translate Paul Tillich's "ground of being" for my context. Tillich, a German theologian who is considered one of the great theologians of the modern era, authored classics such as *The Courage to Be*, *Dynamics of Faith*, and his three-volume opus *Systematic Theology*. I used Tillich's notion of ground of being and applied it to Salinas to see what it might yield.

I am in no way a Tillichian scholar, but my mind works pretty well. My community formed me to understand texts and, more importantly,

> My community formed me to understand texts and, more importantly, contexts. My mind and heart work from a particular place, just like my professors were working from a particular place and reference.

contexts. My mind and heart work from a particular place, just like my professors were working from a particular place and reference. Tillich states:

It [being] must be the ground of our being, that which determines our being or not-being, its infinite ground or "being-itself," expresses itself in and through the structure of being. Therefore, we can encounter it, know it, and act toward it. Theology, when dealing with our ultimate concern, presupposes in every sentence the structure of being, its categories, laws, and concepts. Theology, therefore, cannot escape the question of being any more easily than can philosophy. The attempt of Biblicism to avoid nonbiblical, ontological terms is doomed to failure as surely as are the corresponding philosophical attempts. The Bible itself always uses the categories and concepts which describe the structure of experience. On every page of every religious or theological text these concepts appear: time, space, cause, thing, subject, nature, movement, freedom, necessity, life, value, knowledge experience, being, and not-being. (2012, 21)

Reading this, I thought I had finally found a writer in the "canon" and the academy who understood how our existential realities were tied with our notions of the Divine. Here we have Tillich naming that God or being is the ground of all being, that in our theological musings we cannot escape experience. There is an existential dimension to theology. God takes into account all the laws, categories, and structures that govern existence. A God that understood how the road for the managers and owners around the fields were designed to keep us in the field picking. A God that understood the tension between wanting to get out of my community, but ultimately being responsible for transforming it. A God that understood my pain. This God is truly a God of the soil—or so I thought. These categories and structures include the marks of oppression, the rules that the disinherited had to live by, and that there was in fact liberation in that in speaking about God. These categories were not foreign to God. God was in context. God was in my context.

I was naming a reality: the ground of being in which I found myself, in which I operated, and for which I was searching. It wasn't abstract in the slightest. Those searching for God's call to survival know hunger and walk with open wounds, not abstract concepts. We are existentialist in the very fabric of our understanding of the Divine. I thought I had finally grasped and connected with a German thinker in a way that could provide a bridge from my Salinas experience to this credentialing experience.

The paper came back from the professor with a quotation from that same page of Tillich (emphasis mine):

> The theologian must take seriously the meaning of the terms he uses. They must be known to him in the *whole depth and breadth of their meaning*. Therefore, the systematic theologian must be a philosopher in critical understanding even if not in creative power. (Tillich 2012, 21)

This was followed by, "Patrick, you need to spend more time reading German thinkers before you make bold and creative claims about how useful or not Tillich is in Salinas. You write too much about Latinos and Salinas. Please write for a more diverse audience."

More time reading "German thinkers?" Write more about diverse audiences? Are Latinxs not diverse in our own diasporas and homelands because of migration and colonization? More importantly, to write about Latinxs and Salinas was a matter of life and death for me. People were, and still are, dying—literally! People are dying! I shouldn't have been at seminary. That is not a statement about institutional "fit." It is statement about the fortunate conditions and people that helped me survive and get me to this place. My ability to survive was thanks to a few people calling me to life and a few lucky breaks, and the response to my application of the knowledge that was given to me was that I needed to spend more time to learn about German thinkers before I was qualified to speak on the usefulness of the text for my context. We had not read a single brown or Latinx thinker in this class. I was the only person of color in the class. If I didn't read or write about us, who would? I struggled the next morning reconciling my daily prayer of thanking God for the opportunity to get out of Salinas and I could breathe with learning from a professor of theology who thought I needed to read more German thinkers before I was creative with the texts that talked about God.

> I was the only person of color in the class. If I didn't read or write about us, who would?

This professor was tilling bad soil. I was never told I was using Tillich incorrectly or that I had misread him, simply that I needed to demonstrate mastery over this context before I could speak to my own. The underlying prejudice was I needed to demonstrate I belonged before I could claim a space to speak. The academy was not for my people! My theory for that paper was that the ground of being was deeply contextual and addressed the struggles of my community on a day-to-day level. There was an actual ground to my ground of being. This was inaccessible to this privileged educator because such a notion of being grounded in *la lucha* was again something such educators read about but did not feel in their bones. Their hunger did not pull on their stomachs, their scars did not burst open from having to bury young people, friends, cousins, and community members. Therefore, my contribution could not—must not—be good.

More importantly, what educator writes "you write too much about Latinos?" At least I had the courage to call my papers and theories what they were and identify where I was writing from and for. Never in Tillich's work did he write about his "white, German theology." Never did our professor give us her own papers with a title "white theology." I never said she should stop writing and teaching about "white stuff." They claimed to write universally. It was as if they took Tillich's notions—that theology cannot escape the question of being and that being is the ground of being—to mean that if they write "Theology" (capital T) proper, they are writing the ground of being itself. For them, whiteness is the unquestionable ground of being. It is the assumed center of discourse.

Because they are naming God universally and I named God too particularly, they had the power to claim that their contextual understanding of the ground of being did not have an actual ground to reference. We were back in my grandma's house with her telling me that when God's people did not see me, hear me, or help me survive, she would be there. She would be there not only to see me, but to help me name God in a way that was authentic to our experience. This was our ground of being and this ground was inferior in their eyes. It was limiting to the academy, because God's preferential option for me and my community left them out—or so they thought. God's preferential option historically had always been the other way around; God served the inheritors of the Kingdom, right? They just didn't name that from their privileged position. Yet it takes great courage for people like us to write from a place that has been rendered to death, where there are bodies scattered in our physical location and in our collective memory, where one is searching desperately for God's call to life. As Chela Sandoval put it in her book, *Methodology of the Oppressed,* such privileged thinkers as my professor could deny the ontological reality in which they stood because they had always claimed it at the center, but for those of us from the margins, our being needed to be claimed for survival.

When one has been relegated to death, it takes incredible courage to boldly claim that this is also *my* space, *my* text, *my* God. On the flip side, it takes very *little* courage to write disparaging comments in the margins of a graduate school paper of a person surviving and trying to wrestle away wisdom of the academy to take back to his community. This to me epitomizes bad soil and a perversion of the ground of being.

When one has been relegated to death, it takes incredible courage to boldly claim that this is also *my* space, *my* text, *my* God.

While my classmates were assumed to have come with certain knowledge banks that allowed them to provide commentary on the canon, the assumption was that my community brought only a remedial understanding of the texts. Such an assumption is a remnant of colonial thinking, a type of thinking that considers us to be inferior. More importantly, *my* questions, which were life and death matters to my community and me, did not matter to the academy. My life didn't matter. Or better, the life of my community didn't matter. The academy stood on different, safer, sterile, lifeless soil. The soil I found in the Northeast supported the ivory tower of the academy, not the *campesinos* who sustained it.

What does one need to transform this bad soil into life-bearing soil? Soil needs time to be fallow or rest, just as we often need time and space apart to hear God's voice clearly. In my undergraduate years, I worked at Home Depot and did construction work on the side. A lack of funds prompted me to transfer to a less expensive state school in Sacramento, where I lived with a group of people from my hometown, sharing a room with my best friend and my younger brother. I worked full-time, went to mass almost daily, partied, and went to school full-time, often in that order. Toward the end of this experience, I began discerning next steps.

During these years in Sacramento, the father of one of my friends from high school had purchased some land in Wyoming. He wanted to build log cabins on them. My friend and I made the case to go out there and help build. After all that experience working in Bakersfield and at Home Depot, I had a variety of skills that would be useful. He agreed.

At the time I had a motorcycle, so we put that on the back of their pickup truck and headed east. We rode up through the Sierras, passed through Tahoe, and hit Highway 80 through Salt Lake before we headed North toward the Grand Tetons. The landscape was beautiful: long valleys, open wilderness, forests, and mountains that mingled with the heavens. We stayed in a little village with maybe a few hundred people. While I grew up in an area that I thought was beautiful, in which the soil under my feet was near perfect, Wyoming was a close second. At the base of the Tetons, I was able to look out over beautiful valleys in relative peace. During the day, my friend and I worked as much as possible to earn money, and at night I would read a bit before sleeping, waking up, and starting over.

One long weekend, my friend returned home to celebrate a birthday. I was working with the contractor on one of the cabins and I was finishing up the trim on this beautiful archway that looked over the Snake River. After only an hour of working that Friday, the contractor cut me loose early and told me to go and experience the area. I was so close to Yellowstone, I felt like this weekend was a once-in-a-lifetime opportunity. I went home, took a shower, packed up my saddle bags with food, rope, plastic bags, an extra pair of underwear, and strapped to the rear seat a small canister of gasoline. I hit Highway 89 North through Jackson Hole. I rode my motorcycle through several valleys, keeping the Tetons on my left. I remember thinking how incredible the mountains looked with their tops lightly dusted with snow. I rode right out of Grand Teton National Park on 191 into Yellowstone Park. I remember getting to Yellowstone Lake and thinking I should stop and try and get a room, but something told me to keep going. I stayed on that highway, past Beaver Lake until I hit a valley near the Wyoming-Montana border. There was a clearing and I decided to pull off the road and camp for the night. I pulled my motorcycle behind some trees, because I didn't know whether or not it was legal to sleep under the stars just off the highway. I walked a bit deeper into the woods, tied my saddle bags to a rope, slung the rope over a tree, and pulled them well off the ground.

I have never seen so many stars. In comparison, the sky seemed completely empty back in Sacramento. The entire night went by and not a single car passed me. I have never experienced anything like it. I was so far away from all of the trauma and violence I had experienced. I was still scared because I was sure a bear or wolf was going to come and attack me, though neither did. This was a night of complete stillness, wonder, and majesty. This was the closest that, outside of those times with my grandma, I have ever felt to the Divine. The stillness suited me. It was in that moment that I began to think clearly about my vocation.

This was a night of complete stillness, wonder, and majesty. This was the closest that, outside of those times with my grandma, I have ever felt to the Divine. The stillness suited me. It was in that moment that I began to think clearly about my vocation.

There were no expectations, no violence, no trauma immediately affecting my body. I had the space to ask the question: Who is God calling me to be? I had survived! I was alive! I was *profoundly* alive in God's creation! So now what? Surrounded by wonder and beauty, with money in my pocket and my tank full of gasoline, God could call me to a life worthy of living. For most of the night, I just took in the beauty. I didn't seek answers to my questions about the future; I only offered them up to the universe.

God, how did I make it to adulthood? God, what do I do with all the suffering in the world? God, how do I ensure that others don't suffer? God, I want to go home, but don't know how to thrive in that environment. I am scared to go home. God, do I forgive the Stranger? God, do I reach out to the monsters that shoot children in the park? God, how do I do the work you have called me to, and still put food on the table? God, will I find love? God, will I find a community that holds me and carries me when the ghosts of a past life emerge? God, will I ever see you face to face? God, why me? Why am I still alive? God—I shouldn't be here. God, please, that little girl, resurrect her body. Take me instead. I will replace her. God, do you hear me? Do you hear us?

The void of the night's sky responded with silence. The late Brazilian educator, philosopher, and theologian Rubem Alves, in *The Poet, the Warrior, the Prophet* (2002), writes about this void. He says that we must unlearn in order to learn again. When we peer deep into the void, we can ask it questions, waiting for it to respond. We can be strung about on the safety of our web of understanding over the void, waiting for a response, but only in leaping into the void do we find the stillness and chaos of its deep, dark, and never-ending contours. That is what was happening in this moment. I was, for the first time, peering into God's beauty, unshackled from the threat of violence. This is not a new space for God. In the beginning, God also stood over the void, over the surface of the deep, hovering over troubled waters, and called life to our earth (Genesis 1). In many ways, God was there, hovering over my troubled body, not calling it to a particular type of life. God

> I was given time and space to ask the questions I needed to, without having to attend to my immediate survival needs.

was separating the light from the darkness in me. This moment of stillness was part of God cultivating the space for me to grow, providing soil that held the nutrients for me to discern what I was to do next. This was a time of rest for my body and soul. I was given time and space to ask the questions I needed to, without having to attend to my immediate survival needs.

On the ride back the next morning, I was reminded of reality. I ran out of gas and was happy to have that extra canteen with me. While I was filling up, I saw a coyote off in the distance just staring at me: two scavengers on the brink of survival, looking for a place to be in the world. I saw what I thought were two black bears, perhaps a mom and a cub. They were most likely making a life in this forest. I saw a group of deer and a whole bunch of tiny mammals. I was surrounded constantly by life, I just needed this quiet space to realize it was all around me.

Through my motorcycle helmet, dressed in my black and yellow leathers, I was experiencing God's beauty in a completely new way. This ride back made me think I could do anything I wanted, and what I wanted to do was become an educator. I wanted to write, think, and educate people about the beauty of God's call to life. Not just the beauty I was lucky to experience on this trip, but the beauty I could find in the mundane life of my community. Howard Thurman reminds us:

> There is the rest of detachment and withdrawal when the spirit moves into the depths of the region of the Great Silence, where world weariness is washed away and blurred vision is once again prepared for the focus of the long view where seeking and finding are so united that failure and frustration, real though they are, are no longer felt to be ultimately real. Here the Presence of God is sensed as an all pervasive aliveness which materializes into the concreteness of communion. The reality of prayer. Here God speaks without words and the self listens without ears. Here at last, glimpses of the meaning of all things and the meaning of one's own life are seen with all their strivings. To accept this is one meaning of the good line, 'Rest in the Lord—O, rest in the Lord.' (Thurman 1984, 62)

I entered into this state of pervasive aliveness, where God was speaking without words. I was finally at rest in God.

When I returned to Sacramento for my final year of college, I decided to take the standardized test to get into graduate school and began to follow the suggestion made by that pastor to go to Boston. Coincidentally, that same friend who hooked me up with the job in Wyoming asked if I was still considering Boston just after graduation. At the time, I was planning on attending graduate school in New York—my bags were packed, ticket was purchased, etc. But his question and remembering my co-workers' encouragement to go to the "school of the prophets" and head to Boston convinced me to reconsider. God was calling me to that place to train for the next part of my journey.

Sabbath soil provides stillness. While I found this elsewhere, whether in books or on retreats with others, this moment when I was alone with the world opened up my eyes to the vast beauty and life that God is calling us to tend to. It looks like friends collaborating to see that each other's vocation is realized. I was thankful for this leap of faith, or, as Kierkegaard would call it, a leap into the absurd. I would not have had the courage to do it on my own.

Where do we go to survive that gives us the time and clarity to faithfully discern our next step? Who walks alongside us during these times? Vocational discernment is never a completely solitary process. In the soil, there are always footsteps alongside our own. Whether it is seeing them in the fields in which I grew up, in the family and friends that guided me along the way, or God's own footsteps in the quietness of the world, we always walk with others.

> Where do we go to survive that gives us the time and clarity to faithfully discern our next step? Who walks alongside us during these times? Vocational discernment is never a completely solitary process. In the soil, there are always footsteps alongside our own.

There may be times when we need to go to a quiet, gentle space, to care for our innermost thoughts. There are also those social places and people that are the lifeblood of our inner workings. Holding this need for personal reflection and contemplation alongside a need to be in community is difficult for many people to understand. Today, especially in North America, we pride ourselves on our individuality and moral aptitude to wade through our own personal mishaps. I hope it is clear by now through my story and my understanding of God that even in the quiet, or the most violent, of moments, we are not alone. Others, including God, are always present. The ancestors are always watching. However, we are not adept at inviting others into this process of deep reflection and contemplation, or, perhaps more accurately, we are not skilled at seeing when these vocational moments are happening in our very midst. As Parker Palmer reminds us:

> We must come together in ways that respect the solitude of the soul, that avoid the unconscious violence we do when we try to save each other, that evoke our capacity to hold another life without dishonoring its mystery, never trying to coerce the other into meeting our own needs. (2000, 92)

Part of this gathering to respect the solitude of the soul happens at home. As you can imagine, growing up in a crowded home or going to Bakersfield to be with my large and loud Latinx family, there were not often those moments of quiet solitude. Bakersfield is literally and figuratively a long way from the stillness of Wyoming. In the hustle of the day family members would play out their problems and tough life decisions over dinner, often yelling, laughing, and sometimes crying about the hardships or tough moments we were facing; an aunt would correct an uncle with a joke, and the uncle would shoot back with some smart ass comment; someone else would be getting food for one of my cousins but offer a question or clarification to the person who raised an issue, the person would respond, cut off by another joke, and so on. Every day this pattern of interruption, questions, jokes, and commentary displayed communal discernment in a distinctly Latinx way.

It was loud, noisy, filled with family and community members, and food was always involved. Everyone was in your business. Everyone had a thought or question for you, and someone else always had an answer to try out. This was a space of communal discernment, though I admit that to an outsider it might not look like that.

While Palmer writes about his practices of communal discernment, namely the "clearness committees," which come from a distinctively white, liberal, quiet, Quaker space—and a good one, by the way, if you have never tried the practice—my context for vocational discernment had this other more familial dimension to it. It was loud, noisy, filled with family and community members, and food was always involved. Everyone was in your business. Everyone had a thought or question for you, and someone else always had an answer to try out. This was a space of communal discernment, though I admit that to an outsider it might not look like that. When I examined those places and spaces where others' feet traveled alongside my own, ensuring my survival, my vocational calling, this is where it happened.

Grandma's house was one of those places where the footsteps of others came into the home to discern alongside others. For those not familiar with Latinx guest politics: Our doors are always open. Come anytime. Come as you are. This was our soil. While it was never named explicitly, people would come to visit, old and young alike, because they wanted to fellowship, visit, and seek the wisdom of the elders. For example, I recall one of my cousins coming to see my grandparents in the middle of the day. This particular cousin had not really been involved in the family for some time. He was estranged from his parents, estranged from his own kids and wife, and was in trouble with the law. Upon his arrival, he named the day when he was heading back to prison. Though we were all profoundly sad this was why he had come, we were also happy to see him.

We began cooking, calling people to come over, and telling the rest of the family he had come home, even if it was for just a short while. A true prodigal son moment, because that was who my grandma was. I followed him around the house as he visited with my grandma and my grandpa. He talked with my grandpa about the details of his arrest, what was going to happen to him once he got into prison, and, sadly, how he was excited to be going to see some of his friends there. My grandpa stared straight ahead at the TV and asked what channels he was going to get on the TV. They talked for a bit about this, but it was clear my grandpa was talking about more than the channels. He wanted my cousin to know that the TV in the prison was not the TV in our family room.

With my grandma, my cousin just sat quietly at the bar while she cooked. Grandma asked about his children, his wife, what he was going to do when he got out, what his wife was going to do without him. He continued to go deeper and deeper into himself, until, finally, he said he had to go home. He hugged Grandma for a long time. She packed up some food for him to take home. He said good-bye to Grandma, Grandpa, and me, and headed home to be with his family.

Vocational discernment in these moments of trouble takes wise and discerning hearts. My grandma and grandpa had welcomed him into the house. They asked the deep, self-awakening questions that allowed him to wade through his own heart. He was challenged and heard the call of life, specifically to be in the presence of those who gave him life. My grandma's house and my grandma in particular was the elder who

> Grandma's house was a place of rest and discernment. It was a place where the troubles of the outside world were put on hold while we figured out how best to experience life.

walked alongside us all through the valleys of our pain and suffering.

Grandma's house was a place of rest and discernment. It was a place where the troubles of the outside world were put on hold while we figured out how best to experience life. It was different than that space in Wyoming under the stars, but it served a similar purpose. When you walked through my grandparents' front door, the violence of the world outside stopped, you were safe, and you had a community to hold you and your deepest questions. My grandparents created a space, a ground, for your soul and body to rest, necessary conditions to open one's heart to the fullness of God's call. These are the conditions for what we will call good soil. These are the conditions for one's thriving, and it is to those conditions that we now turn.

Chapter 6

Sources of Inspiration and New Life

Tell your heart that the fear of suffering is worse than the suffering itself. And that no heart has ever suffered when it goes in search of its dreams, because every second of the search is a second's encounter with God and with eternity.
— Paulo Coelho, *The Alchemist*

Paulo Coelho, in his masterpiece *The Alchemist,* tells the story of an Andalusian boy who goes out into the world in search of his personal legend. The boy encounters a number of people who help or impede him along the way. Coelho conveys through the story that when someone knows his or her calling, the "universe conspires in helping you to achieve it." At the end of the journey, after he truly believed in his own personal legend, he told bandits that he was searching for treasure and they laughed at him. They said that they too were looking for a treasure, but that it was in Spain, leading Coelho's main character to realize that his personal legend was waiting under a tree back home.

The first time I read this work, I realized that home is where my own personal legend and wisdom journey began. Despite all of the knowledge I was searching for in grad school and during my other studies, in my travels and my projects, the wisdom I really sought was back home. But like in *The Alchemist,* I never would have learned that had I not gone on my journey, had I not experienced leaving my homeland, had I not spent time in classrooms or in the lands in which

I didn't fit in. It was after a long narrative of survival and learning that I was opened to God's call to life.

Vocational discernment is connected to one's home community, one's survival, and being resilient through realities that seek one's destruction. This is not a prescriptive dictum, outlining that one must endure suffering or move through it in order to experience this call to life, but it is to say that the universe will help one live if one can hear God's call to life in these moments.

I want to celebrate those narratives that give us life, focusing on the relationships that call us to be our better selves. I open with those conditions that allow one to thrive, and in many ways allowed me to form into the educator I am today. These conditions include those people in my life who called me to life out of the conditions that threatened it. They shared my love of life. And we supported each other as we lived into our own Christian narratives. As I explained to you in the previous chapter, this for me is grounded in the space in which we live and among those who surround us.

Good soil is hard to find. It takes a lot of naturally occurring ingredients, care, time, attention, water, and just the right amount of fertilizer. A little shit is okay. In fact, shit in the form of fertilizer is necessary for good growth. Thinking about the parable of the sower, finding the good soil sounds as easy as making a choice. But we don't always get to choose our ground. Good soil needs to be cultivated. As religious people, we don't spend a lot of time thinking about what makes good soil, or what would make our "soil" good. The scientists and agronomists reading this book know that the right balance of nitrogen, phosphorus, potassium, and other elements are needed for "healthy" soil. As Diana Butler Bass put it, "Soil is sacred, holy, and good. When we care for it, we are doing God's work. Soil is life. And it is time for us to reclaim the dirt" (2015, 58).

When I worked in quality control and in the fields, you could anticipate the type of soil you would find in fields that produced "good" quality vegetables. That doesn't mean there is an "ideal" mix of soil, like what you would buy at garden or home store. But there are important components that make up good soil, like a significant amount of the local soil in every mix. Good soil requires attention to the way the mix is being cared for. When one should fertilize, dig it, let the land lie fallow, plant certain crops, weed, etc., all become important factors both for the garden and the fields that feed you. This mix mimics our call to life from God, because both are about having the right conditions for life. In my case, it was being loved by the right people and finding places to discern my call to life. Discerning one's vocation necessitates being surrounded by people who want you to flourish as a whole being. Cultivating the conditions for such flourishing takes time and a recognition that we control very little about how these conditions are cultivated in the first place—a paradox.

> Discerning one's vocation necessitates being surrounded by people who want you to flourish as a whole being. Cultivating the conditions for such flourishing takes time and a recognition that we control very little about how these conditions are cultivated in the first place—a paradox.

As I stated at the beginning of this book, several people stepped in and provided these conditions for me from a young age: the Christian Brothers, my grandma, my father, friends, etc. I had no control over how and when they did step in, but it wasn't until I became responsible for cultivating relationships on my own behalf—nurturing and tilling my own soil—that I realized how important this process was to learning to hear God's call to life.

Tending to our relationships is an important part of discerning vocational commitments. Most of our emotional, intellectual, and spiritual energy is spent on our loved ones, our closest friends, and community. The companions we choose for our journey are significant. They support our call to life.

Finding an intellectual and spiritual community that would sustain me took time. When I moved away for college, I made sure I was within driving distance of both my father and my grandma. But I needed more than just them to sustain me in this new environment. I didn't have a lot of resources to go and do what I wanted during my first years in college for two reasons: First, because I didn't stay at my first undergraduate institution long enough to build lasting community and, second, because I couldn't get by without working full-time jobs. I wasn't able to spend much time and attention on my studies or on my spiritual friendships.

Yet despite having little money and lacking time, there were always a few friends who supported me. My first college roommate, Lemec, was one of these people. We took many of the same classes, played all the same sports and games, and genuinely enjoyed each other's company. He also understood me in a way a lot of other people didn't. I liked to study and be around friends, but I preferred intense and sustained conversations with a few people rather than being in crowds. I liked playing sports. I liked being with people, but financial realities ensured I needed to work.

Lemec and I met because all of the students of color were put in one wing of the dorms, both a sad reality and a life-giving situation: sad that we were segregated, blessed that we were in immediate proximity of people we could talk to about this. One night Lemec and I were driving back from getting food at a Wendy's. It must have been past midnight, because we would often play ball until the gym closed at 11 p.m. A cop pulled us over. He yanked Lemec out of the car and put him on the sidewalk. The police officer's partner stood by the window, flashlight in my eyes, pressuring me to give him our food. Through organizing in my hometown, I had seen enough of this sort of behavior that I knew not to confront these police officers. It was the best course of action, as we sat on a non-lit back road. Anytime I confronted police, I was reminded of that "gang task force" and their intimidation tactics. I was reminded that if they had the opportunity, they would drag me out to be killed thinking they were upholding the law.

Lemec understood we needed to survive these experiences. He remained quiet and we hoped to make it back to campus. After about an hour, the cops let us go. On the way back, before I could say anything, Lemec looked at me and asked if I was okay. I wasn't. Neither was he. But we were thankful to be able to drive back. This is not to say that all police are bad or malicious. Having to navigate at best an implicit bias and at worst direct prejudice at the hand of law enforcement made us nervous.

Living with Lemec reminded me of what Thomas Merton said about his decision to join a religious order:

> By this time God had given me enough sense to realize at least obscurely that this is one of the most important aspects of any religious vocation: the first and most elementary test of one's call to the religious life...is the willingness to accept life in a community in which everybody is more or less imperfect. (1976, 419)

We did pretty much everything together, and our community was imperfect. Imperfect does not mean there are perfect communities or perfect people out there. It simply means that we recognized the brokenness in each other. Embracing this imperfection meant we knew that each one of our members needed mending and tending to that brokenness.

Lemec hooked me up in my sophomore year with a job working at a local elementary school in Helm. Helm was a small community in the middle of the Central Valley. There were no homes near the school, just miles of fields and orchards. The school served mainly migrant farm laborers, many whose parents lacked documentation. In the parking lot of the school was a post office in a trailer. These kids would come to school hungry and tired, and we were assigned with helping them with their homework and providing fun afternoon activities. Lemec was in charge of seventh and eighth graders, and I was in charge of kindergarten through third grade.

One day one of the young boys started to act up. He had had enough of the *"putos"* who came to the school. I sent a runner next door to get one of the teachers from the older grade levels and Lemec came in to watch the other kids. I asked the boy about what was going on that he felt he needed to throw things, swear, and threaten to harm himself and others. He kept throwing punches, kicks, and would not stop screaming. This was not like him. He was usually kind and had the biggest laughs in the class. He was the kid who wanted to hug the teachers as much as possible because of the joy he experienced in the classroom. After inviting him to do some deep breathing and sprinting in the fields to get our anger out, we sat down.

"My dad left. He hasn't come back for a couple of years."

"How old were you when he left."

"Kindergarten."

"Is that why you are mad?"

"No, I am mad because a stranger moved in. He steals our food. He hits my sister and makes her scream." His sister was in junior high school. "My mom just yells at him, but we can't stop him. He eats all of our food and doesn't work. I am hungry."

"When do you eat?"

"At school."

"Is he home with you now? When does he do this?"

"Every day."

Given my own story, this was particularly hard for me to hear. I had only just escaped my own community. I had no training to respond to others' stories, other than my own my life experience. Rather than go back into the class, I swapped out with my supervisor, to whom I reported the abuse and lack of food. Then I went to the bathroom to vent my own frustration. I was broken all over again. My body started to feel small again. This little boy, who didn't even remain in the school through the year, didn't have anyone to intervene on his behalf. He was plagued by a stranger. I knew exactly how this felt. He had no food. There were times when all I had had to eat in a day was bread—I knew the pain of hunger as well. And what could I do? What power did I have? I had been provided good soil to thrive in similar circumstances, but what could I do for him? How could I call this young boy—and others like him—to life?

On the drive home, I was noticeably quiet. Lemec didn't ask what was going on, but he treated me to In-N-Out on the way home. No words, just a shared meal. He understood that something deep was moving and stirring in me. God was at work. God was at work on my soul.

> God was at work. God was at work on my soul. God was calling me to life again, but this time it was different. *God was calling me to call others to life.*

God was calling me to life again, but this time it was different. *God was calling me to call others to life.*

When we got back to our college campus, Lemec said he knew it must be hard for me to hear what the boy said. I thought about how God had surrounded me with people who supported me and cared for me deeply. How would I respond?

Here is the thing about good soil: It's not mine alone. It doesn't belong to me. I don't try and take it home and put in a pot to grow only the seeds I like. It benefits everyone growing in it. I wasn't alone in hearing this call or being called in college. All those in my social group in college became educators. They are currently calling students like that little boy from Helm to life. They are living into this call in a way that inspires me. It calls me back to that moment with that boy when I was in my early twenties. God calls on a community to respond. Good soil—being nurtured—requires a village of people who respond to God's call, not just one person. I pray that little boy found community. I am thankful for Lemec and our group of friends who stood by me through good and bad times. I truly felt loved and cared for by this community.

Finding love is part of the good soil as well. We spend an incredible amount of energy and time trying to hear God call through people who do not understand or cannot cultivate that sense of call in us. Even Augustine of Hippo, in his famous theological and spiritual autobiography *Confessions,* written around 400 c.e., wrote the now-famous line in Book VIII: "Give me chastity and continence, only not yet." Please don't think I'm inferring that love is only sexual. I'm just making the point that our quest for a romantic (and sexual) partner is not something new in our tradition. We have been writing about it shamelessly and beautifully for a long time. It has always been a part of the narrative. For me, love was connected to the body. Unfortunately, this part of the journey is not easy. Often, we are attracted to people in whom we cannot or do not have the maturity to nurture that call to life. When I read *The Long Loneliness* and learned about Dorothy Day, co-founder of the Catholic Worker movement, and her long and complex love life, I knew that matters of the heart could not be separated from one's vocational call.

During the same time that friends such as Lemec were supporting me, I found community with people who loved God and wanted to answer a call to teach. These relationships, both in the romantic and communal sense, provided a love and validation of life that was necessary for survival. My vocation was gaining clarity, beyond my call to survival. I was quickly discerning what it might take to live into God's call for me, specifically as an educator. I was clear that I wanted to be an educator like that Christian Brother who saved me all those years ago. I also wanted to return home to my community with a partner by my side. I thought this was enough clarity. The plan was set. Perhaps in another coming of age or vocation book, you would think that life then would have conspired to help me find love once and for all? God's plans don't always match our own.

Relationships are never that clear and clean. When I fell in love in college, I was so excited to be in a relationship. We had a shared Latinx culture; a shared love of God; shared community; shared values; a shared call to teach; and shared passion. When so much is shared or common, the differences become sharp. That Latinx background you share is not the same Latinx context. That love of God is expressed differently in different communities. In this case, I loved being part of dual worship communities: one was a bit more charismatic and biblically based, while my own worship community was tradition-and-scripture-based and more contemplative in practice. I was being spiritually fed in both, but these communities do not always intertwine in ways they probably should. I found out my community of friends was not uniform. The value systems and life experiences these friends brought challenged my way of being in the world. I learned that what, how, and where you want to teach becomes a clear difference. This particular relationship ended as they usually do—with confusion, sadness, and a broken heart. I deeply loved this person, but not at the same time nor in the same way. And in that moment, at the ripe age of 20, everything seemed so final and dire: apparently I was to be love-less.

It took many years for me to develop a profound sense of respect and love for that person that did not include romantic hopes. We may not have called each other to life, but it was clear that God calls incredible people to do incredible work. As God calls one to life, one begins to see the deep beauty and magic in others without needing to be in a romantic relationship with them. I was blessed to see God at work, God calling others to live, and to see a response to that call embodied in such a beautiful person.

I did date again after this relationship ended, but never really anything that was beyond shallow, surface-level relationships. All of them were with beautiful, wonderful, intelligent people, but they were not truly life-giving relationships for myself or them. I definitely was not my best self. Years later, after I began seminary, I wanted to pursue a call to ordination. I told my roommate in seminary, now my son's godfather, that I wanted to "fall in love with a community." Having given up on finding a romantic partner who understood my deep need for sustained partnership and support to do God's work, I started to discern a call to teach and offer education through and with various religious communities: The Society of Jesus (Jesuits) and the Christian Brothers in particular. As the men in these fraternities know, the process of becoming a member is long and invites one into a deep personal discernment process about the call of the community. I would go on retreats and have regular calls to ask questions and discern whether this was the life for me. I chose these groups because both had a commitment to social justice and education. I had all but decided to join an order when I met my life partner.

I had signed up for most of the intramural sports at the university. Softball/baseball is a Reyes family pastime, so in the spring I joined the team. When I got to the first game, there was my future partner, Carrie, waiting for someone to play catch with her. As we played catch, I rambled on about nothing in particular, just talking nervously, until one of my best friends at the time came up and said she wanted to play catch with this magnificent and interesting human instead. I gave her my spot and played with a more earnest teammate, who took warming up a little too seriously. I came to find out later that for half of that season Carrie didn't even know I went to school with her and was convinced by my backwards Giants hat (a staple of my attire in those days), baseball pants, and decent athletic skill that I was some ringer that the school had brought in just to play softball.

When we finally did go on a date, I found that Carrie and I had next to nothing in common. She was Jewish. She was studying the relationship between religion and science. She didn't normally play sports, but was playing because she had a few friends on the team. She loved classical music, so much so that she was a trained and a degreed classical vocalist. She sang in a high church setting—with bells, banners, and professional singers. She was quiet and shy. She came from a small family. She grew up moving around in a military family and didn't have a sense of home or connection to a particular location. She only read white, European philosophers and theologians.

QUE?! This was the exact opposite of everything I knew and believed in!

I can't tell you how different she and I were and are. But this was exciting! What we shared was a commitment to learning more about the other person and supporting each other in their own call to life. I wanted desperately to know how she had been formed, and she wanted to know how I had survived. I told her about my revolutionary ways, and the deep pains and scars I held on my body. She told me about her formative experiences in sacred music. We fell into that beautiful, early stage, starry-eyed love, giggling at the mundane, playfully pushing each other as we walked to and from school, smiling and winking at each other when we would see each other across a crowd.

We had known each other for only a short time before I had to head off for the summer. She was going to rent a room from my roommate, and I was heading off to England to work in a logistics firm office. That summer we sent a 300-page-book's-worth of e-mails. I e-mailed her every morning and night. We came to know each other fully and more deeply. I knew I loved her, because she wanted to know who I was and what had formed me. She wanted to know how she could participate in that call to life. I wanted to do the same for her. I just didn't know if she wanted that in return. What I did know is that she didn't believe in providence, and thus that to her there was nothing pre-ordained in our meeting, while to me it felt predestined. She wrote in an e-mail on August 30, 2010:

> Fate is lame, and boring. If fate existed, then what would be the point of even trying? If we are fated to end up a certain way, or in a certain place, then why even bother anymore? What's the POINT?!? Fate sucks. Good thing it's not for real. Yes, let's go to Salinas and meet some of your people, that sounds great. I'm glad you believe in me, I think that's just lovely, and I believe in you.

While we may never reconcile our theological differences, this was a clear call to life. These were the very questions I had been asking. I hadn't been called to life for some pre-ordained purpose. I was simply called to live. I couldn't reconcile that I had survived to adulthood to tell the stories of my community, especially for those who didn't. I struggled with this question of fate just like her. I was called simply to live, to survive. Is that still fate? Carrie just let it go all together, but affirmed that "belief" in each other was an expression of love and care. This was what I needed in order to hear God's call to life.

I came back from that summer away ready to find out whether Carrie and I were going to commit to being together. Luckily for me, the feeling was mutual. When we went to the local bar to have the "Will We Get Married?" conversation, we were joined by our landlord, Erik, and his housemate, Peter. They lived above me during my time in seminary, and Carrie during the summer, but had little idea that their two tenants from different times were having a conversation about spending the rest of their lives together. It somehow seemed fitting. Erik bought us beers, provided some wisdom and thoughts on theology from the Jewish perspective, and told us "good luck" as he walked out of the bar. Carrie and I laughed, because the conversation took less time than either of us had anticipated. We said "salud," smiled like giddy, young people in love, and said we were going to do this! We were married a year later.

I said above that having Erik and Peter there during the conversion was fitting, because Carrie and I have committed to believe in each other *and* to do our best to make time for others. An artist wrote on our Ketubah, a traditional Jewish marriage contract that sometimes serves as a piece of artwork and reflects marriage vows and values, these words that capture our love:

> The walls of our home are trust and commitment, and its spirit is filled with our love. Our doors will be open to family and friends, and our windows to the view of the land and to the reverberation of our community. Our garden will be fenced with justice and compassion, peace and forgiveness, growing deeply rooted trees with ever-fresh foliage, connecting past and future through solid trunks. This house will provide secure space for the uniqueness of each of us as well as for our common strivings and mutual endeavors. May our marriage be our fortress and safe base for a long and satisfying life together.

I have never been happier. It takes work to delve into someone's life, to commit to being present, to call one to life. She does it, though.

She does it with beauty and with grace. Every day I fall more deeply in love.

God calls us to life in miraculous ways. Everything seemed to get better. My friendships deepened with others, as my perspective on the world had changed. I had far more compassion for the world around me. I could hear God more clearly calling me to life on a daily basis. I could share my deepest pains and hurts with a person who would be present, and whom I wanted to reciprocate that space as well. I could share those depressed spaces, when the sadness and violence of traumatic memories reemerge unannounced and uninvited—those times when I ventured into deep depression and sadness about the loss of homies and community members—and she would wait patiently for me to emerge from my time lost in the wilderness, and, when necessary, know when and how to enter into that wilderness with me and help me get out. Our relationship became a place where we could store our collective hopes and fears.

Because my mind and heart had been opened, my scholarship and writing improved, as Carrie asked provocative and challenging questions from her context. I didn't have to justify to her why I thought what I thought, or why I was committed to the liberation of my home community. She understood and wanted to further this call. Carrie had invited me into her narrative, where she was also making incredible life and faith choices. We had entered into a process of discernment together, and it focused on what would provide us life. Love is an incredibly powerful call to life. This is good soil—the soil that continues to offer the conditions for life to thrive.

While the game is rigged, I believe sometimes you can laugh at it. The first was when I wanted to ask Carrie's family for their blessing on our relationship. At the time, Carrie's father was an Admiral in the Navy. My grandpa was the only one I had ever talked to about the military, and none of my friends who joined ever even became low-ranking officers. We went down to Southern Georgia to visit the family. Her father, one of the fittest men I know, asked if I wanted to go for a bike ride. We went out for a ride, pushing as hard as we could go. At one point I tried to draft behind him. There was no wind, and it was also Georgia, in summer, so I might as well have been riding my bike through a lake, the humidity was so thick.

About halfway into a ride on which I clearly couldn't keep up, nor breathe, he asks me what I think the state of the country is? What do you say to an Admiral about the state of the country? After stumbling through an answer that would make any politician proud, he followed up with, "So you like my daughter?" How do you respond to that? I said, "Yes, very much." And did everything in my power not to pass out while riding the bike.

I found out years later that the gears on the bike were broken, perhaps deliberately, and the bike was permanently stuck to prevent me from keeping up. The game is rigged. Not in the same way that it had been, but rigged nonetheless.

The second time was about a year and a half later. Carrie and I had just become engaged and we were spending our first Christmas holiday with her family. My future father-in-law had received his second star and was working at the Pentagon. After giving me a tour of his large office there, which was intimidating in and of itself, along with going through security and walking the Pentagon's internal corridors, we went to their home just down the road from George Washington's home in Mt. Vernon. Keep in mind, Salinas tracks a different history. We have history on the West Coast, but it is a history of indigenous people of California, and Spanish and other colonial powers occupying our space. To be in the Pentagon and down the road from the first President's home... this little boy from Salinas did not know how to function in this space. My future father-in-law, known to me as Admiral Dad at this time, escorted me down to the basement, where I would be sleeping. He pointed to a door that clearly led to the area below the backyard, and said, "Don't open this door." He left me nervously wondering what was behind that door. Later that night, Carrie came down to check on me. Frightened by the entire day's events, and now a door that clearly was designated for some secret ops and intelligence stuff, I freaked out. *"GET OUT OF MY ROOM,"* I shout-whispered. *"GET OUT!"* The game is rigged, I am telling you. Carrie may have called me to life, but I was not sure of it then. She was going to get me killed.

This is all supposed to be humorous. Truth be told, my in-laws are some of the most down-to-earth and lovely people I know. They are truly living the American Dream, coming up from humble beginnings in Arizona, community colleges, and state schools for education. It is an incredible story, which I am sure they will write about in a book at some point. It was never just Carrie that called me to life. It was her entire family. It was her family's embrace of me as an individual and my own sacred worth. While there may have been humorous moments like those described, there were countless times early on in our marriage during which her family showed their support for us—whether by coming to celebrate the birth of our son, or my Ph.D. graduation. They have always been present. Love extends far beyond just the one you love, but also to the ones they love. This love supported me in some dire times.

Yet the call to life does not just come from our peers, friends, and lovers. In Christian literature, we very rarely focus on our elders. In vocational or biographical "coming of age" literature, elders tend to perform a particular function. They appear in the person's life at a critical moment, and then disappear as if they existed solely for that purpose. This is in part because so many of the vocational discernment

> A narrative approach to Christian vocation shows how narratives are intergenerational and are a connection between the living and the dead. We need to celebrate the narratives of parents, grandparents, and all those departed who clear the path for new life.

texts and practices have turned us inward, to look at ourselves or "whole selves," without understanding that our whole selves include our elders, ancestors, and our communities. A narrative approach to Christian vocation shows how narratives are intergenerational and are a connection between the living and the dead. We need to celebrate the narratives of parents, grandparents, and all those departed who clear the path for new life. I celebrate the inspiring lives of those who surround me currently in theological education, and the mutual call to new life and new scholarship.

As many people are aware, in Mexican culture we pause on *Día de Muertos,* not to contemplate death, but to celebrate life in the midst of death. The three days of festivals and remembrance coincide with the Catholic calendar days of All Saints' Eve, All Saints' Day, and All Souls' Day. Originally the celebration commemorated and celebrated the goddess Mictecacihuatl, a deity who watched over the departed. We still remember the dead on these days, building *ofrendas* to honor our ancestors, or those who have departed, with the classic sugar skull, flowers (usually marigolds, but my grandma loved her roses so I bring those or both), food, and drink. These three days hit hard for me every year. On the first day, *día de los inocentes,* we mark the passing of children. Children from events of my own childhood, named and unnamed in this book, are invited to return and be with us. I don't know why I have survived certain death and the innocent remain resting in what Édouard Glissant calls the submarine, that place where the colonized are rendered to death (2010). I suppose they, in their own way, call me to life. They call me to tell our story and to call others to life. As Immaculée Ilibagiza named in her heartbreaking memoir

Left to Tell: Discovering God Amidst the Rwandan Holocaust, God not only calls us to life in the most murderous and violent of situations, but those who survive can and should tell their stories. It is not to equate our suffering with others, but, as she puts it, it is a matter of being left to tell the story.

Later in the celebration, we remember the elders we have lost. Being so far away from family, my own *ofrenda* is an unsightly piece of artwork. I have no artistic sensibility. When I do find time to pay attention to what is displayed, I make sure to have pictures of the innocents, my grandparents, and items that remind me of all those faithfully and violently departed. These days of remembrance for me are the closest I get to the Divine each year. I remember all of the lessons my family has taught me and the many times they intervened in my life. I remember those who were not able to be with me today. I remember those who did not make it to adulthood.

> This act of remembering is an important one to my own sense of vocation. In remembering, we recall those people who called us to life.

This act of remembering is an important one to my own sense of vocation. In remembering, we recall those people who called us to life. I've said it before: In many ways, I should not be here. Yet I am. I am because of them. By honoring them each year, I remember that I have survived thanks to them. I remember that they held me in their arms when I thought I wasn't going to live, and they watch over me now. They called me into new realities, guiding me as I sought to find how I could call others to life.

I have written a lot about my grandparents. They were instrumental in my own vocational call. They empowered me to be a better person and to seek ways in which I could better my community and family. But like all living things, their health started to decline. This was devastating for our family.

As my grandpa was passing, we each took turns caring for him in the hospital. One night, the doctor told us he was doing particularly bad. It was my father's and my turn to watch Grandpa that night. I left the hospital to get some food, mainly for my dad because he had not eaten anything since getting to the hospital. When I went out to the car, I was mugged at gunpoint.

Having stared death in the face several times in my life by this point, I had started to see moments like these as opportunities to meet with people who were on the edge of death themselves. I assumed some sort of immunity from death, but, then again, what young man in his twenties doesn't? I began to see those moments right before violence erupts as opportunities for God to break in and build peace. God had called me to life too many times for this to be the end of my life.

"Give me your wallet and keys," he said loudly.

"What the f— do you want?" I asked seriously.

"I need your wallet to buy food and your car to get me there."

"How about I buy you some food?" I offered.

"How about you give me your wallet or I will take you out!"

Having little patience for the tough guy routine, I pushed the conversation toward what I thought this man really wanted.

"Look, mother f—, I am asking if you want to have a meal with me when you pulled a gun on me. Who does that? Step up either way. Pull the f—g trigger or go to dinner with me, but that is all we got. My grandpa is dying inside, and I don't got time for this f—g shit."

Steve, as I found out later was his name, put the gun down by his side and engaged the safety. "Fine," he said, disappointed.

"Really?" I asked in disbelief.

"Fine."

I led him to my father's jeep and we drove to the Sonic down the street. Not the most wholesome of food joints, but I was in college and only had the cash my father had given me. Over the course of that dinner, God was speaking. This poor man had hit hard times.

"Steve, why are you pulling on people in a parking lot?" I asked.

"Look. I need money, plain and simple. I need to get my hit. I have no job, because I need to get high. I have no family, because I like to get high. My wife, ex-wife I guess, kicked me out of the house because she said I was a danger to our family."

"Really??"

"Well, I am." He pulls up his sleeve. "See this needle mark here? Or, was it here...?" He stared at his arm for a moment. "One of these put me out. She had to call the ambulance. I was out, man. I think I died, really. She told me right at this hospital that she didn't want me to come home. So I won't. I am f—d up, I know. Probably wondering why you even are sitting here with me. I get it..." He continued to speed up his rambling.

"Nah. Addiction is real. There is no 'off' switch. I get that," I said to keep the conversation going.

"You don't think I am a pile of crap?"

"Well, sure I do. You pulled a gun on me, right? Who the hell does that, man?" We both laughed. "But nah, I don't think you are a pile of crap. In fact, I doubt you just ended up in that hospital parking lot. I bet there is more to the story. There always is."

> We split a large order of fried cheese sticks.

Drug addiction had taken over his life. He had lost his job. He had lost his family. He had lost his livelihood. This was the only way he knew how to live. We split a large order of fried cheese sticks. With this new invitation to tell his story, he talked about his childhood, which was just as rough as the more recent turn of events. He had an abusive father, who worked out in Delano, which was far enough away that he didn't come home all that often, but when he did he made sure he beat Steve up a bit. His mother was a prostitute. He went to East Bakersfield High School, the same high school at least three generations of the Reyes family went to, and he knew one of my uncles.

"What do you want out of life, Steve?" I asked.

"I want to live. I just want to be able to live a life free from this shit."

"What do you need for that to happen?"

"I thought I needed money. What I guess I need is help. I need someone to help me."

"Who might that be?"

"I really don't know. I mean, I know there are clinics and stuff. I had a teacher my freshman year in high school who was always nice to me. I wonder if he is still around." We both laughed before he continued, "I'm being serious, though. He was the only one who took the time to get to know me."

We continued to talk about his high school teacher and it was clear that this teacher had been the only positive influence in his life in his formative years. He needed mentors and guides to have interceded for him at a young age. But the

> One mentor is not enough. We need a community of support.

system is rigged. It failed him. One mentor is not enough. We need a community of support.

We finished our meal and I drove us back to the parking lot of the hospital.

"I am glad that we had a chance to meet, Steve. Can I get that gun from you though?" I asked.

"I wish I could give it to you, but I need it. I don't feel safe at night. I need it to sleep."

"Where are you going?"

"Down by the rail yard. Thanks for the food." This was the same rail yard at which my great-grandpa worked to get out of the fields. I hoped that Steve wouldn't pull the gun on anyone in the future. He gave me a hug and walked down the road. I don't know if he pulled the gun on anyone else. I did my best to call him to life, by simply offering a meal during a time when I was suffering another death. It was a lesson I had learned from my grandma and grandpa, from my own elders and mentors.

The next week my grandpa moved from this world to the next.

Often, when I remember my grandpa and all those conversations we had on the porch, I am drawn back to my time with Steve. I am drawn back to that gun he pointed at me. I am moved that through my experience, my elders, and my narrative, I had developed a capacity to see these moments as opportunities for God to call others to life, as God had called me to life.

Grandma began suffering from dementia soon after Grandpa passed away. While I was studying at seminary, her language skills left her altogether, to the point that she was not able to speak to me in English *or* Spanish. She remembered things and people from her childhood, but could not for the life of her remember or even speak the names of her grandchildren when they came in to visit. She began to see things on the walls, like water and fire. And when she finally had lost her ability to speak, she would have violent outbursts. Dementia is a horrible disease.

People who used to flock to her house to be at her side now would show up confused about how to be around my grandma. We were all so used to being cared for by her, we had not made time to learn how to care for her, save my aunts—who to this day, embody that deep love for others.

When the disease had really taken over, I was discerning my next steps toward becoming a Christian educator, now looking at options that involved being with my wife Carrie. This was both exciting and disappointing for my grandma. She told me one day over the phone that she thought I was studying to be a priest. When I corrected her and said I was getting married and I wanted her to be at the wedding, she said, "Oh, that is okay too. Is she pregnant? Grandma always knows."

I had applied to the only program that was close enough for me to be home with my grandma and would support me in my liberative Christian education and formation work. I wanted to be close enough that I could help take care of her on a daily basis, as she had taken care of me. I wanted a program that would equip me to be a theological educator that embraced the multiplicity of religious practices and cultural inheritances.

When the seminaries and universities first started sending out their letters of acceptance and rejection, many of my brilliant colleagues received rejection letters. My letter came a week or two after my classmates. Not wanting to be embarrassed in front of them by what I felt would be certain rejection, I kept the letter secret when it came to my apartment. I brought it to my little room in Boston. With Carrie there, together we opened the letter—which proclaimed my acceptance into the program that matched my desire to change my local conditions and to study with the scholar I most revered.

Carrie and I decided at that moment to go to Southern California. She knew how important it was for me to be present with my grandma and to fulfill my call to become an educator who calls other to life. Grandma, more than anyone else in my journey, had raised me spiritually and religiously. She, with a handful of others—such as the Christian Brothers, friends, my father, and community members—had kept the pulse of life beating in my veins.

We moved to Southern California, and spent as much time as possible in Bakersfield, while I waited for my program to start. My commitments in theological education were solidified the day orientation for my doctorate started. Those commitments included, above all things, honoring the elders and mentors who had supported me by becoming a theological educator with the sole purpose of calling people to life. It was not a stretch, given my story. So I committed to God that day that my life would be turned over to God's work of calling people to new life.

I prayed something like this:

> God, you called me through her; you called me time and time again to life. You called me those times when people sought to kill me. You called me when that man lifted me off the ground to squeeze

the life out of me and tried to smash me out of existence. You called
me to live when people were being gunned down all around me. You
called me to live when negotiating peace in my neighborhood meant
standing between drawn guns. You called me to live when I was
isolated, depressed, and wanting to end it all. You called me to live
when I felt I didn't have anyone left. You called me to live through
her and others, who stepped in and told me I was valuable. Told me I
was worth your love. Told me I was worth their love. I want to honor
them. I turn my life over to you.

On that first day, the day I said this prayer, I didn't even appear on
campus. The academy would have to wait. While I had found my
calling and my vocation was clear, it was also the same day that my
grandma passed away.

My grandma and grandpa had formed me. They taught me the loving
power of Christian hospitality. They provided a roof over my head and
wisdom for me to learn from. More than anyone else, they encouraged
me to pursue my educational dreams. When I talked to Grandma about
what I was studying in seminary, she would say, "You are learning to
heal the soul." She told me at my college graduation she had never
imagined she would have two college graduates in the family—my
father being the other one. When I got my first Master's, she was so
moved to have a family member with an advanced degree that she
told me, "You can perform miracles now!" And she meant it. We
Reyeses weren't supposed to get advanced degrees. We were expected
to die early deaths. And when I said I was going to pursue a Ph.D. to
serve the church and my community, it was as if Jesus had personally
blessed and visited my grandma—or, at least that is the way she talked
about it to her friends. She was the first and only one in my family to
understand how important faith can be in the vocational call to life.
She knew what the stakes were for me to pursue this line of work. She
knew it was a matter of life and death.

Rather than recount the way I responded to her death, I have provided
here what I said at her funeral. Honoring my grandma is the least
I could do for her in this text, and these words in many ways still
guide my work. These words reflect as accurately now as they did then
that, by taking time to honor our elders and mentors, we are not only
obeying the commandments of our sacred text, but are recognizing
that God calls us to live through others.

Hello. My name is Patrick Reyes and I am Carmen Reyes's grandson.
Let me start by saying it is good to be here.

It is good to be here.

It is good to be here to participate in the life and death of Carmen Reyes. It is good to be here with our loving family and community. It is good to be here to see old friends, lost family members, and to remember Carmen Reyes. It is good to be here and we thank you for coming.

When my grandfather, Julio Reyes, passed, I was asked to say a few words at his funeral. As I reflected on what I wanted to say when asked to say a few words at Grandma's funeral, I thought to myself, "What better way to honor Grandma than to offer her a personal letter, as I did for Grandpa, highlighting the images, the influence and inspiration that was my Grandma, Carmen Reyes?" Grandma, we all have words, prayers, and thoughts we want to lift up to you, and I am proud and honored to do so publicly.

Dear Grandma,

Grace, embrace, *and* faith *are the three words that come to mind when I think of you. But before I tell you why, let me start by saying, the best lessons I have ever learned—and I have and will continue to spend my time being a lifelong learner—have been with you. Grace, embrace, and faith are traits I learned from you and mimic every day of my life.*

Grace. *Grandma, you had this way of inviting everyone into your home. Whether they are family, friends, or those people who are not friends and family but we somehow can't get rid of them. Grandma, you offered grace to everyone and anyone. Your grace was the complete definition of the word—it was elegance and beauty; it was dignified; it was the generosity of spirit; it was the liberating power of your refusal to let one's past/present/future dictate your love for them. It was a grace freely given.*

A quick side note, Grandma. I must say, though, I am glad you had Grandpa, at least when I lived with you, and Aunts Mona and Carrie in those last few years, because your grace needed just a "little" bit of discretion. You can't let all the crazies in.

But that was just it...wasn't it? You let all the crazies in. You let me in. You let me in when I was prepared to die. You let me in when I was no good to anyone.

One of the lasting lessons you gave me is that when you offer a roof, a meal—when you offer sanctuary to another—you offer more than just the physical needs of the body. You offer God's love, you offer God's grace. For nearly 2,000 years the Catholic Church has been venerating lesser men and women; popular stories like Victor Hugo's Les Miserables *focus on this liberating power of grace—the type of grace you offered on a regular basis. Lessons taught to me in all my theological training were repetition, as I had learned them already through the invitation to your table—to break bread, to share a meal, to hold hands, and say grace. I am alive because of your grace.*

Embrace. *Grandma, you held love for all people in your heart. Grandma, you never spoke ill of anyone, at least not around me, and you thought of your babies until the very last of days. Like the grace you extended to all people, you embraced all people with love.*

Grandma, your embrace... Grandma, your hugs, your kisses, your smile and offering of prayers will always be in my heart. One of my final memories of you will be when, toward, the end of your life, [when you were] possessed by that horrible disease that took your mind, my Dad and I were in the room with you and you grabbed my hands and said, "It's my baby. It's my baby. I'm sorry. I'm so sorry." I don't know why you are apologizing. You saved my life. You saved my life when I was in Salinas. You saved my life by allowing me to live in your house. You saved my life by being another example of living a life of compassion and courage.

What I want to say to you in this letter is that it was never you who should have been sorry, Grandma. I am sorry. I am so very truly sorry.

I should have been there at that end to hold your hands and tell you, "You are my baby." Grandma, you are my baby and I'm sorry for not being there these past few years. Everyone in Boston knew about you. In fact, I wrote my final paper for seminary about you. I knew you were proud of me for being there, and I wanted to the world to know that I was proud that you were my grandma. The final words in that paper were: "To both my Holy Mother and my Grandma, you are both Holy and I thank you. I offer these words of meditation in reverence. In reverence for your love, for your beauty, for your grace and compassion for all people, a love without borders. Because of your Motherhood, I spread Grandma's good news. Amen."

Grandma, you are an inspiration. As I begin this new step in my academic journey, I hope to write only works that reflect my love and reverence for you, and works that embody your spirit so that my words might inspire people to offer grace, to embrace others, and to have faith.

Which brings me to my final thought, Grandma, and that is on faith. You were a believer. Grandma, you had the faith that could move mountains. Your faith was of being sure of what we hope for and certain we do not see—Hebrews 11:1—or, you lived by faith but not by sight—2 Corinthians 5:7. Or, perhaps all this is better put, Grandma,[by saying] you placed your faith in me, your living grandson. You put your faith in your children. You put your faith in your grandchildren. There was no reason to. You could have let me die. I wanted to die. You could have let me fall like I probably deserved.

Grandma, you believed in me without me doing anything to prove myself! Grandma, you moved me to be a better person, simply because you would tell me you were proud of who I was—without knowing exactly what I was doing or how damaged my soul was. Grandma, you may not literally have moved mountains or been able to perform miracles, but you moved me, a mountain of pain, hurt, and suffering, and you were certain of my life though you did not know my future.

My future is bright because you had faith in me, as I am sure you had faith in others. This is not to undermine or demean the faith you had in God, but merely to show the combined power of your heavenly grace with your warm embrace.

It is to say that anything and everything I do—that we do—will be changed for the better because of your lasting smile, because of your love, because of you.

Before I finish writing this letter, I want to say something to you, wherever you are: If your new landlord didn't give you your own room and a place to get a break from grandpa, write me back or send me a sign and I will raise a complaint, protest, or pray excessively to make things right! A lifetime with that man was too much...God should give you some grace, like you gave me. I will join you soon and look forward to the time when we will see each other face to face once more.

I honor you. I miss you. And I love you.

Signed—one of your children.

These words reflected my deep love for Grandma. And I wish you could have been at this funeral. It was a packed house in that church. People from all over Bakersfield came to see my grandma. Love filled the church. She had cultivated good soil and everything she grew came to that room.

She guides my work. When I talk about vocation, I talk about being called to life—but, not just by God, but by people such as Grandma. I want to call others to life, because I was called to life by her.

All that was left was to live into that call.

> And I wish you could have been at this funeral. It was a packed house in that church. People from all over Bakersfield came to see my grandma. Love filled the church. She had cultivated good soil and everything she grew came to that room.

Chapter 7

Calling Others to New Life

There is always something left to love.
— Gabriel García Márquez, *One Hundred Years of Solitude*

There, in the soft language, life centered and ground itself in me and I was flowing with the grain of the universe. Language placed my life experiences in a new context, freeing me for the moment to become with air as air, with clouds as clouds, from which new associations arose to engage me in present life in a more purposeful way.
— Jimmy Santiago Baca, *A Place to Stand*

My two favorite writers and poets, Gabriel García Márquez and Jimmy Santiago Baca, remind us that language, storytelling, and naming our experiences can thrust us into more fulfilled lives. As I read these two authors over and over again, I came to the understanding that they wrestled with the suffering of their characters (Márquez) or their own lives (Baca). I related to how they both pointed to life through these very hard and real times with how it was through my own putting into language of this experience in my research, in my work, and in my communities that I began to feel completely alive. However, I don't want you to think for a moment that it was because of these writers, books, or the university that my mind and body were liberated. In fact, when it comes to the body, the experiences and traumas I experienced remind my mind and soul that the damage afflicted to it informs how I often act and react, before the logical or artistic side of me has a chance to intervene or create alternatives. It is often in deep reflection on the body that I am helped to make meaning and words out of the experiences of my life. It is this reflection on my body, in relation to other bodies, that demonstrates for me that I am not in this alone, that God calls us to life with and through others.

In 2013, I ran the San Francisco Marathon with one of my mentors. The day before I spent visiting a friend in the hospital who was battling cancer. I ate little food, drank little water, but was filled with the spirit of good company and necessary love.

The race was off to a terrific start. We started down by the wharf, running along the beautiful bay, and then followed the water to the Golden Gate Bridge. We ran over its beautiful red-beamed and concrete-slabbed back. Did you know it is uphill both ways if you run out of the city and then back? We followed the course down and around the Presidio and then through Franklin Park. For the first 19 miles, I was running the marathon of my life! I was making incredible time. I whispered to myself at mile 20, though I was slowing down by this point, "Patrick, you have the body of a god!" Then, at mile 20.5, my entire body began to freeze up. I was cramping up in every single part of my body. I had run several marathons before and knew that I would be stiff and sore, but this was something new.

At mile 21, my mentor, Dr. Frank Rogers, ran by me and he looked at me and I whimpered, "You passed me."

He very calmly turned as he graciously passed me, "We are all running our own race, together. Just keep moving!"

> We are all running our own race, together.

By mile 21.5, I had completely stopped moving. A woman passed me, and, trying to encourage me, said, "Don't look back." As I turned to meet her eyes, she followed with, "Oh, my God, I hope you finish. I am so sorry." By this time, tears had begun to flow down over my face and my sweat tasted of pure salt. The 3:15 pacer had just finished her shift and ran to my aid, taught me how to stretch, and ran to the electrolyte station and came back with something for me to drink. I managed to move my body again, and finished the race. It wasn't a "god-like" time, but I finished.

We are all running our own race, together. This phrase has stuck with me. The Reyeses aren't exactly built for running. We are short-legged and rotund in stature. We are accustomed to monotonous work and being on our feet, but running marathons has never been part of our narrative. This notion, however, that we are all running our own race together made sense. In the running community, everyone wants to see others finish the race. You won't see people at a marathon hoping people fall on their faces before the finish line—partly because so many exhausted folks do. Everyone who has finished the race already, or who has come to support the runners, stands somewhere in that last mile to cheer on the runners as they finish the race they came to run. In my first marathon, I ran with a pack of strangers, five of us total, who organically gathered at mile 23 because a person who was struggling asked that we encourage him. The group of us all finished around the same time, cheering each other on all the way to the finish. We are all running our own race, together.

God calls us through people and experiences simply to breathe, to continue to run our own races. But we are never alone. While you may never know the depths of my suffering, depression, or pain, I feel that when I recall stories like those recorded in this book, you can run alongside me as you make your way through your own race of life. I, likewise, have been called to and will continue to run my race alongside others.

In my role in higher education, I have a responsibility to use my education as an opportunity to seek out others who need to be taught at mile 21 how to stretch, who need that extra boost of electrolytes. We need someone to show us how to stretch out those muscles that have been overused. We, ourselves, may need to be encouraging to ensure that others make it to the finish line. I live this life for others through my scholarship, administration, and teaching. I want to share with you the stories of being a Latinx in religious higher education and the plight to provide opportunities for students of color, first-generation students, and other historically marginalized groups. I am working to expand God's call for higher education to be life-sustaining and liberating for students to find a little bit of sanctity and liberation in and through education. As the Brazilian educator Paulo Freire put it, "[E]ducation as the practice of freedom—as opposed to education as the practice of domination—denies that [one] is abstract, isolated, independent, and unattached to the world" (2011, 80). This work desperately needs to be done, as the privileged and those with power continue to widen the gap between themselves and those without opportunities.

During my doctoral studies, I was able to find work to support my studies. I always held a full-time job during my studies. One job during this time was a Director of Communications job for a performance-based logistics firm, which had offices across the globe. This job provided me the opportunity to stretch how I saw myself in the world: friends from unlikely walks of life, resources to do my work in community, and an entry into professional work. It was my first time in a nonlabor/trade job. It was, in many ways, like that playground all those years before, dangerous and unfamiliar. In other ways, it was different. I was able to travel and see the world. I was able to have enough money to know where and what I was going to have for dinner. It was a good job.

The friends from unlikely walks of life included my supervisor, who made an incredible impact on me and, in many ways, inspires me still. Coming up from next to nothing and living on his own during his teenage years, he had served in the Navy and was a Director at this small firm. He was humble and hard-working, and dedicated to his family. He was an inspiration to learn with and under as I entered into professional life.

Performance-based logistics is a white male–dominated field. I went to England to serve in one of our offices there and I had the privilege of becoming friends with people such as our Chief Scientist, who lived with me in a small village of around 200 people called Thompson, England. The village has a small pub and church—that's it. Every Friday night, we would go down to the pub, because this was where everyone would gather to talk and fellowship. I could meet and talk to people whose experiences of life—namely, those of village life in England—were drastically different than my own. I was able to meet and talk with our global partners in South Korea, Japan, Brazil, France, Germany, and all across the globe.

This job was perfect for my doctoral studies, not because of who it served or the work itself. Rather, it stretched my skill set, both in terms of developing my professional skills in a field in which I had very little knowledge and through learning the value of working together across different cultural contexts and age groups to accomplish goals. I was the youngest there—by 30 or so years. More importantly, it provided me the income and the time to both complete my studies and work in my community developing programs to address the epidemic of violence. Time, space, people, and resources: God had provided the foundation of what would be a life-changing community project.

Developed during my first two years of course work at Claremont School of Theology, and prompted and supported by Dr. Frank Rogers—the "everyone is running their own race, together" mentor— the project was to build community programs that provided healing and transformation. I started *Nueva Comunidad*. This small group of

> This small group of ex-gang-affiliated young adults met regularly to employ spiritual and religious practices to heal our deep wounds.

ex-gang–affiliated young adults met regularly to employ spiritual and religious practices to heal our deep wounds. As a budding researcher, my imagination was ignited. As Rev. Dr. Gregory Ellison likes to put it, this was when I found my "academic freedom." I entered into a deep dialogue with my community to find out what was already happening on the ground. What were we doing to heal our own wounds? While the community was great at coming up with prevention and intervention programs, we were each trying to be "Atlas," carrying the weight of the world and of our traumas on our shoulders with no one to help us carry our burdens. This needed to change.

The first thing we did was ask questions: *What did we survive? What were unique experiences that we had not been freed to talk about yet? What did we find holy and sacred—family, God, life? Where did we go when things got really bad? Where did we send others when things were bad? What scars do we bring into the space? What open wounds? What techniques, or religious or spiritual practices, do we have to heal our wounds? Who were we before we were broken? Who are we now? What did we want for that time? What do we want for now? What do we want from our time together?*

These questions were not answered directly. We simply posed them. Our group was about 20 strong at the time it started, and almost all men. We didn't know what or how to answer the questions in the first place: a perfect starting point for those suffering from incredible traumas and machismo complexes. We started with just holding the questions, posing them like a litany of prayers to God. We were committed to going as deep as we could just to come to terms with what we had each survived or were currently working toward surviving.

When I started organizing as a teen, we had a group of individuals come from a local organizing/theater group in the Bay Area. They put all of us through a variety of theater games from Augusto Boal's *Theater of the Oppressed* (2000) to get us to express what we had buried deep within our own psyches and souls and allow them to emerge in embodied ways. We did many of those same activities with this group of men, spending time reestablishing the relationship between our bodies and minds.

After building the group's trust and meeting regularly to practice healing together, I was still on my own journey to learn how to facilitate group gatherings and hold a space for disagreement and dissention.

When you are working with ex-gang members and witnesses to heinous acts of violence, the stakes are high and holding the space with compassion is sacred and holy work. As a former organizer, gathering people and creating action plans came easy to me. Holding the wounds of the broken was difficult

> When you are working with ex-gang members and witnesses to heinous acts of violence, the stakes are high and holding the space with compassion is sacred and holy work.

and very different work. I needed help to address this growing edge for me, to help me convene this group of broken bodies. But God conspires to help us when we do the work of healing and calling others to life.

At the time, I was in a class led by Dr. Frank Rogers called the "Practicing Compassion" for social healing. We played with techniques of convening and holding the space in that class. We learned about the power of meditation and various techniques for turning inward, using techniques from the Christian tradition. We also played with techniques for listening to the group to allow the needs of the collective to emerge. We built our knowledge and competency with a variety of facilitation practices, so that we might enter into our communities with not just one method or style of facilitation, but with many. I wanted to work with Frank, because I knew he was doing and had done this type of work in communities, and now here I was, not just being allowed or tolerated for my story and passions, but actively supported in my work in and through my community.

At the time I was also studying decolonial theory with Dr. Santiago Slabodsky and liberationist and decolonial education with Dr. Sheryl Kujawa-Holbrook. Essentially, these theories contend that religious communities played a role in the violent colonization of the globe. This colonization by European powers played a role in destroying cultures and traditions. It played a role in mapping the landscapes between the rich and the poor. It aided the State in occupying and taking over lands. For my community of Latinxs—and even more specifically in my case, Chicanxs in California and the Southwest—we are living into a historical reality in which people had colonized our lands, our families, and our minds. It was not that we wanted to work the fields or live in poverty, but that the historic circumstances that created classes of people—some to work the land and others to manage and reap the benefit of wealth and power—were passing power from one generation to the next. The wounds we were healing in *Nueva Comunidad* were several generations deep.

I would enter into *Nueva Comunidad* standing at the intersection between this historic reality of violence and the healing and liberating power of spiritual and religious practices. I was challenged to live into the tension that the church and religious practices that saved me also had colonized and destroyed my family, my mind, and others. Holding the space where not just our wounds, but the wounds of our ancestors were emerging in the lost memories and stories of extreme violence acted upon our bodies stretched *Nueva Comunidad's* ability to hold each other. I remember sharing my own experience of abuse and playing with gang banging and was reminded by the community of the historic conditions in which the violence of our communities and homes were bred. I was not just carrying the traumas of my childhood, I was carrying the traumas of generations. I was carrying the traumas of a violent migration, and I was carrying the violence of Spanish colonization. I was bringing into every meeting, just as everyone else was, the hauntings of a violent history.

There was another balance for this group I was learning to navigate. While I had been called to life and been fortunate enough to work for my education, this was not the case for the entire group. Being the only one with a college degree in the room, holding the space authentically—not authoritatively, not teaching, not fixing, but holding the space for the spirit to emerge—was exhausting work. The tension took me back to that baseball game, took me back to that Christian Brother's office, took me back to that playground. I knew that my education was informing and forming how I operated in my community, but that tension named on the baseball field all those years ago existed here as well. To get an education is to live into a value of the community. To have an education is to betray your neighborhood homies who didn't get out or have the opportunity to get an education. Building a space where we hold each other authentically, from heart to heart, means that we come to the community as whole persons, not a series of credentials. However, that didn't mean it wasn't still helpful to have an education. It [education] provided a space for me to research our history, our lost religious and cultural practices, our shared religious practices for healing. But what I was sure it would not do for me is place me above the community I served. We did this work together. When you are healing hearts, souls, and minds, it must be the work of the collective. It is the only way the spirit works.

> It [education] provided a space for me to research our history, our lost religious and cultural practices, our shared religious practices for healing.

And this responsibility came with a golden rule. If you have a narrative in which the reason why you are alive is that people "showed up" and intervened in your life, then the number one rule I had for myself and others was "that we show up for each other." If God was going to work through us, we had to be present for that to take place. If I was going to use my knowledge for my community, I needed to show up for *Nueva Comunidad* and bring the spirit of God and of my grandma into the space. I needed to bring my whole self—my gifts, talents, hopes, pains, and sorrows—both prior to and after my education. The stakes were so high—healing mortal wounds inflicted on the soul—that we needed people to show up completely and, as they were able to build trust, to hold each other's stories in love, and to demonstrate we all had a commitment to healing.

While I was translating what I was learning in the classroom for this group, I wasn't the only one bringing to the group his or her research, spiritual practices, or hopes. For *Nueva Comunidad,* we took our lead from each other. We learned from the practices we each brought and researched together. What I learned clearly from this experience was that all my education did not provide me the knowledge, the training, or the

> What my education gave me was a set of skills, an ability to navigate multiple worlds so I could hold the space for new knowledge to emerge, and the responsibility to make an impact with what I was learning in the classroom in my own community. This was my vocational call being played out in front of me.

right to gather and heal this group. I couldn't do that work alone. What my education gave me was a set of skills, an ability to navigate multiple worlds so I could hold the space for new knowledge to emerge, and the responsibility to make an impact with what I was learning in the classroom in my own community. This was my vocational call being played out in front of me. It was not to produce new knowledge only to be found in books. It was not to educate people about what they did or did not know. I was called to lead people to life. It was not a call to be the educator that liberated minds, but it was a call to be a life-giving presence to those who had never been called to life, who had never shared their stories. I was called to create space in which the spirit could emerge, where knowledge of self and our history could emerge, where healing could emerge, where a community of practice could

> This was what God had called me to life for—to hold the space where life could emerge.

emerge. This was what God had called me to life for—to hold the space where life could emerge.

Nueva Comunidad ran for about two years. We met once or twice a month, mostly in Southern California, and usually outdoors. We would open with prayer, follow with a practice or ritual of some sort, a story, and then close with another practice. At one of our final meetings, we had about 45 people present. We opened with a poem from New Mexican poet Jimmy Santiago Baca, whose memoir *A Place to Stand* documenting his time in prison was part of our shared reading. The poem was "From Violence to Peace." We listened as a group member recited the poem aloud. There were words about surviving childhood, words about death, words about taking bullets, words about the strength of blood, and words about how healing may or may not come. We followed the poem with a practice my grandma taught me, a mix of our Roman Catholic ancestry and something deep, ancient, and old. The practice included building an *ofrenda* to all our fallen friends and family members. After we constructed it, we lit candles, turned off the lights, and our musicians and dancers took over, bringing to life through song and prayer those who we had lost. It was as if we were living out the Psalms, crying out to God for healing and health.

> It was as if we were living out the Psalms, crying out to God for healing and health.

When the dancing and singing subsided, we took turns blowing out the candles, until there was only a large candle left in the center. An elder in our community then walked over, took the candle, and looked out at all of our faces. One by one, he stopped and said our names. He called out to each person in the space.

Then he spoke to us: "In our [Mexican] culture, it is not the life that determines where you go in the afterlife, but it is your death. How we release these memories, how we release those we care so much about, impacts how they are received in the afterlife. If you still care for them, if you want to see them at the end of times, we must cleanse our thoughts, prayers, and memories of them. We must make them pure. When I release this candle light and we see the smoke rise, it will represent those lives we have lost. The smoke will rise and we must allow all of our hate and anger to go with it."

He paused. He looked each one of us in the eyes. He continued speaking: "Cleanse your hearts. You will feel the Spirit in this space. Can you feel the heartbeat of life—beating fast, beating slow? It is leaving us. But it is a life we have to let go. It is a heart that is not pumping the life blood of life in this space. It is pumping violence to our body. Let's stop that beat and let's pick up a new one. When I let go of this flame, let that beat go. Let that life go. You will be something new after this moment. You have to believe. Now let it go." And then he blew out the candle.

I saw the smoke drift up into the darkness. With it, I gave up all of my pain and anger about that little girl, about my own childhood of abuse, my own troubles in education, my own anxieties about whether I was worthy enough to live this life God had given me. I saw my own life go up with that smoke. The part of me that was dying over and over again, the part that carried the deep guilt and pain from my childhood and young adulthood, went up with the spirit. My life of sin and violence went up with the smoke. And it wasn't just my life that went with the smoke. Everyone in the room had given over what they were carrying to the ritual.

After Jesus died, his disciples huddled together in the upper room—scared, concerned, guilty, angry, full of pain, and confused. Then a fire descended upon them—the Spirit. In *this* room, I was being baptized anew, baptized through fire, just as those in the upper room had been. I had come to this process broken. It wasn't until this moment that I felt God had put me back together. God had called me to lead others to life through building, creating, and maintaining spaces in which their wounds could be healed and their stories told. Here I was living into that call authentically, holding a space for our broken bodies to be broken over again so that the Spirit, God, might receive our pain and brokenness and repair us.

> Here I was living into that call authentically, holding a space for our broken bodies to be broken over again so that the Spirit, God, might receive our pain and brokenness and repair us.

Nueva Comunidad only met a few more times after this. For the original conveners, we had done some incredible healing and learning over those two years. It was also clear that in order to sustain this level of gathering, we would need to formalize our ministry. It was a unanimous decision that this was not part of our work. After prayer and deliberation, the group decided it had served its purpose for that time—and, perhaps, it will emerge again, but it was time for all of us to try to formalize in new spaces the practices we had learned in *Nueva Comunidad*. Just as the disciples went out, speaking their own languages, the members of *Nueva Comunidad* disbanded to heal our own communities.

For me, the next space I would try to do this work in was the university. This was not an easy move, as I am reminded by Sandra Cisneros's description of joining the university:

> I was too afraid to apply for a teaching job at an institution of higher learning even though I had an MFA from the Iowa's Writers' Workshop. Applying for a job at a college or university might confirm my worst fears—that I didn't belong in the world of letters, that I wasn't smart enough, good enough. In graduate school, I often felt like an intruder, intimidated by the wealth and sophistication of my classmates. So how could I possibly feel I had anything to offer as an instructor? I took a job teaching high school dropouts in the barrio, and, on weekends, when I wasn't too exhausted, I tried to write. (Cisneros 2015, 134)

Like Cisneros, I was scared to start my academic job search, because it meant that I could receive further rejection from the academy. What good comes from Salinas? The academy was a place that was supposed to be inaccessible to me and my community, and here I was attempting to take what I had learned and scale its ivory walls, to be a role model for those in my community, and, ultimately, survive by making a paycheck with what I had been trained to do—create space for God to call people to life.

I applied for what felt like hundreds of jobs. I eventually landed my first job at Northeastern University in Boston. I was enamored by the social justice work they were doing on campus. It was the perfect mix of faith engagement and social justice, which I embodied in my home life and work experience organizing for Interfaith Worker Justice in Boston during my Master's program. Carrie and I moved to Salem, Massachusetts, in a small, two-bedroom apartment downtown. It seemed like a mansion compared to the first apartment Carrie and I had in Southern California, which was a room and a half with just about 450 square feet. Our son, just a few months old at the time, loved the winter and snow when it came. It was a charming New England life. I was still completing my dissertation at the time, writing most mornings between 4-6 a.m., and this job seemed like it would fuel my fire to make a difference in young people's lives.

As one can imagine, getting a job in higher education when you have few connections and little industry know-how is not easy. It is, in many ways, still an old boys' club. If you know the right people and how to make your way into the industry, it doesn't matter if you have any degrees or how much work you have done in the community; you will be granted entrance. This was difficult for me to come to terms with, because I had worked hard to bring my education, experience, and talents to those who were preparing to return to communities like Salinas. I wanted to prepare students, faculty, administrators, and staff to have the cultural competency to intervene in young people's lives in meaningful ways, just as had been done for me.

Higher education is a machine, though. This machine was built for particular people. While my aims were to build programs centered on peace, community capacity building, and cultural competency, what happened was more attuned to what Trinh Min Ha describes for the educated minority educator. I would do cultural competency or peace-building workshops I had developed using all the skills and practices I had gained in my home community, *Nueva Comunidad,* or learned from my grandma, and apply them in this context. However, the response was always the same—clapping, people coming to tell me how they didn't know how or where I learned my practices and knowledge (and if they could pay for it), or that they were inspired but didn't know how to respond. I had one affluent white student come up after a workshop and bow. Bowing is not a practice in her culture or my own, so clearly a message had been lost in my cultural competency workshop. In short, I was like a caged animal on display. While those I worked with regularly in the office, including the 15 chaplains from a variety of traditions and the student workers, saw me for more than just a token minority, it never really evolved to much more than that.

When I would talk about my life or scholarship, those who ran programs imagined visits to similar places to talk with people with similar experiences as an opportunity for them to build their life experience and professional personas. They would travel to these places where black and brown bodies lay exposed and would claim: "I have been there!" From Selma to Ferguson, to the Southwest, to the global South, I was witnessing the very definition of trauma tourism: *Let's go witness suffering so we can say we were there.* These well-meaning, pious neocolonialists wanted to make a difference, but had no local or embodied commitments to *la lucha.* Such trips and site visits became part of the organization's public narrative: *We have traveled to this site or that site, with these poor brown and black bodies. We took incredible pictures. We are incredible for visiting, saving, witnessing, etc. We need to share our experience with the world, because we have been enlightened by suffering.* As one who suffered, this was insufferable.

These visits and narratives slowly ate at my soul. I embodied these very communities. Despite having talents, education, and professional experience unmatched in the community, I was relegated to being a tour guide to pious colonizers. In my community, we have a word/name/person for this role—*Malinche*. Malinche Tenepal is being recovered as a historic figure of survival by brilliant scholars, but her role as the translator to Hernán Cortés, the 16th-century Spanish conquistador who laid waste to the Aztec civilization, associates her name with traitor. I did not want to betray my community or other communities of color. I was walking alongside others while they came to the realization that black and brown bodies were suffering "out there," but not in here, in our very office. Out there in the "real" world, but not in our space, not in our work, not in the tasks we did day-to-day. I felt like a traitor. I felt like I had betrayed the suffering of my people, of my community, of what I had imagined working for the kindom of God was. I was serving as translator to wealthy, white supervisors and students, while they added lines to their resumes for having witnessed the traumas done to our bodies.

> I felt like a traitor. I felt like I had betrayed the suffering of my people, of my community, of what I had imagined working for the kin-dom of God was.

This came to a head after the Charleston Church Massacre. In Charleston, South Carolina, Dylann Roof sat in a group meeting of Emanuel African Methodist Church before he opened fire and killed nine people, all black. My e-mail box began to fill and colleagues began to call and ask where they could go to feel safe. We organized a small vigil, building an *ofrenda,* holding space for people of color to mourn our loss. Having to bury a number of homies and young people throughout my life, holding space for others to mourn, to heal, to be together in safety was part of my calling. As they called me in *Nueva Comunidad,* "Father Reyes" was known for this. Afterward, I was approached by (all white) senior leaders of the university asking why we had not advertised, taken photos, or asked them to speak at the gathering. I told them it wasn't for grandstanding, for talking about peace, or a photo opportunity. It wasn't their moment or space. We were holding a space for people of color to mourn the loss of our own in safety and away from the gaze of others. It was a space created to have a moment together to grieve and to feel safe doing it.

These white leaders wanted to capitalize on our loss, but especially the loss of the African American community. We had lost, even as far north as Boston, a sense of safety. Church was supposed to be a place of sanctuary. It was for me. There was a reason why *Nueva Comunidad* often changed locations. We were frightened, because where two or three or gathered we could all be murdered. And now, after this massacre, this feeling returned in this community, and it was a feeling with which I was all too familiar growing up, having been targeted for murder multiple times. They (these white leaders) didn't get why it was important to create a space for people to survive, or, at the very least, a space hidden from the gaze of sympathetic voyeurism. For those who had written to me and to whom I had extended an invitation, this was a time and space to mourn. The wounds located on my body and in my soul, and those wounds held by our communities continued to be opened, prodded, poked, and peeled back so that outsiders could see deeper into our pain and then, ultimately, return to their safe havens, leaving us open, exposed, and bleeding. I needed to find safety. After this, I needed to return to the comfort of my home. I immediately organized a trip to go home.

> The wounds located on my body and in my soul, and those wounds held by our communities continued to be opened, prodded, poked, and peeled back so that outsiders could see deeper into our pain and then, ultimately, return to their safe havens, leaving us open, exposed, and bleeding.

I took this opportunity to complete my research and writing for my doctorate. Every vacation or time I took off, I would spend at home talking to those from my home community, who were working the fields or suffering from gang violence. They were suffering in the flesh. They felt the pain of hunger daily. They heard the sounds of bullets recurrently. One night I stayed with a family in Salinas to talk about their daily lives. I knew them well. The dad had worked the fields since he was a boy. He would wake up at 4–4:30 a.m., get his kids' school stuff ready, and then head to the fields. The mother cleaned homes. They had a one-bedroom apartment: the parents in the back room and the two boys in the family room. We stayed up most of the night talking. They invited me to stay the night with them so that their kids could hear stories about "being on the other side of the world." They wanted me to share what it was like working at a university. I tried telling them how wonderful it was, because I knew how important it was for me to say to the impressionable young people that they could get out and get an education. I knew how important it was for me to tell them that there is something beautiful on the other side.

What I couldn't tell them was how our bodies and stories were used even there. The system is rigged. God may call us to life, but the world in which we are called is not life-giving. In fact, it is constructed to abuse, use, and colonize us. Maybe one of these children could thrive as the token minority or live with the guilt of translating suffering for those who do not know it. Maybe these boys would find it liberating to have a little extra money in their pockets, though, let's be honest: My first academic job paid less than what I made working full-time in the packing sheds. The system has always taken advantage of black and brown bodies, not only historically when we were absent from those institutions, but also now, when we are present. We are underpaid, undervalued, and underrepresented.

When I proposed this notion in my academic contexts, that black and brown bodies have always been taken advantage of by the system, a challenge from the center was that I had no facts for this statement. I grew angry at this suggestion. One only need to look at the data tables from the Association of Theological Schools, the Pew Research Report on job pay gap based on race, professional guilds reports on representation in the field, or, a novel idea, history. Colonialism has numbers attached to it. Number of lives lost due to the Atlantic slave trade – 60 million plus. Number of indigenous lives lost because of North American colonization – millions. The cultural and physical resources of the countless communities of Mexicans, Mexican Americans, Chicanxs, Latinxs, and Latin Americans who came to the United States or were present when the Treaty of Guadalupe Hidalgo was signed, who all continue to be denied our rights, our culture, our ways of being in the world. And the number of our primos and primas who crossed the Pacific and continue to be exploited for their physical and intellectual labor. The burden of proof, the center would say, is on the oppressed to count our losses. The burden of investigation is for the marginalized, the subaltern, and the forgotten to quantify the damage done to our communities. It was as if it was suggested that we don't know that we make less or know where to look for this data or that at each institution they would prefer this data remain hidden. I didn't know how to translate this for these young boys. I couldn't explain to them why the work of researching our material lives was to illuminate the conditions of colonialism to the colonizers. It was even more difficult to try to explain to them when we are busy burying the dead and building a better world for the next generation, so they are not burdened with interjections of white amnesia.

For my friends, my family, and my community, these boys wanted me to tell them how wonderful it was once you get out of our community. As I was doing so, we heard the all-too-familiar sound that reminded me why saying that we can change the world we inherit is so important. That night with the Salinas family made it clear the stakes were exceptionally high to get out. I was reminded of life that you cannot smile through.

That night with the Salinas family made it clear the stakes were exceptionally high to get out. I was reminded of life that you cannot smile through.

Around midnight, a car came screeching around the corner on the block. We heard the tires against the street. We completed stopped our conversation, and waited for the long delayed snaps of a handgun. *"Dat!...Dat!...Dat!...Dat!...Dat!"* We could hear the bullets hitting a wall. The car's tires, spinning out and gripping the pavement, sped off down the street. The boys ran back to their parents' room as if it was a routine they had prepared for. I joined them. The dad gathered everyone together in the back room. He asked me to pray over the family. I did. Then the dad said a prayer for the two little boys. After half an hour in the darkness, the dad and I went out to check on the neighbors. The townhome next door had a few bullet holes in the stucco. The neighbor was outside, not surprised by the shooting at all. The dad turned and looked at me, asking, "Why would God allow this? This is what you are asking, right? What you went to school for?"

"I don't know what I was asking. But that is the question."

"Do you think God spared us?" He asked earnestly.

The image of that little girl returned to my mind. It paralyzed my answer. I just stared at a hole in the wall where a bullet had struck. I thought about my buddy Jesse, not named in this story here, who was gunned down next to me near the mall in Salinas. I thought about all the funerals of young people I had gone to, the bodies I had helped bury. My mind flooded with remorse and deep sadness. "I don't have answers." I said solemnly. We went back inside. I held one of the little boys for the remainder of the night.

The family moved away not long after that to somewhere in Arizona. The question: "Why would God allow this type of violence?" remains open and stands against what leading others to life might mean. It is a question that still haunts my soul.

The question: "Why would God allow this type of violence?" remains open and stands against what leading others to life might mean. It is a question that still haunts my soul.

I returned from this experience to the cold, frozen air of New England. This was an important lesson for me. If I were to make a difference in my own community, if I was to feel like I was able to make an impact on my home community, even from afar, I would need to serve students and an institution that represented my community, that actively sought out my community to better their material existence. I needed to be in rooms like the one I had just come from, or at least be able to learn from and learn with those who would return to those communities—not because they thought this would be a good resume builder, but because these are our communities. I needed to be able to hold a space for the marginalized...simply to be alive.

During this time in New England, I began to professionalize my experience. While researching and holding down a full-time job, I received an invitation from a friend, Callid Keefe-Perry, who served as a theologian in residence with the Forum for Theological Exploration. I was invited to offer cultural competency workshops for young people discerning a call to ministry. When I went to my first retreat, I told stories and held a workshop focusing on cultural competency, but highlighting our own and collective narrative. I convened and facilitated a process of activities that allowed people's stories to emerge together. I also told stories about my grandma and Salinas. Here, the response was not applause, but a deep engagement with how they were going to take the work back home, sharing stories and contexts that were similar to my own. One student came up to me and said that it was the first time he felt he could "do anything!" This "do *anything*" was not in reference to what many college and university students think about, when one's career and life are truly open for them to do what they choose. Rather, this student's *anything* was simply that he was not powerless or caught in some paralysis. That he could "do *anything*" was a reference to the realization that we might actually have the power to change our material realities despite where we come from.

For me, the call from God sharpened yet again. There were places where my education, experience, and life mattered, where black and brown bodies were not just broken bodies to be gawked at by well-meaning, voyeuristic "do-gooders." People of color had the power and the critical mass to make change. This was a wonderful revelation to gain just before I defended my dissertation. As theologian Carmen Nanko-Fernandez says, "We are not your diversity. We are the church" (2010). We could do anything we needed to better our local communities. We no longer had to ask permission or wait for someone to tell us it was okay to do our work.

After one of these workshops in Los Angeles, I went to stay with my brother (the brother I got in a fight with while he was high on cocaine, all those years ago). He had recently moved to Southern California. I stayed with him for a few days, before defending my dissertation. It was also his son's—my nephew's—birthday. It was great to see my brother, his partner, and my nephew, as my brother appeared to be taking care of himself. Then, on my nephew's birthday, one of my brother's friends from Salinas (which is six hours away from where he currently lives) came into his living room. While I had managed to cull those who wanted to destroy my soul from my life, my brother had not been so lucky. He was still playing the loyalty game. I was, of course, loyal to my friends, to my neighborhood—*mi gente y mi familia*—but only in so far as they were seeking to create life or the space for life to emerge. That does not mean I had given up on this young man. What calling our friends and family to life looks like when we are surrounded by those who continue to take life from us is that we have to get away from those "roots" that hold us in place. In this case, my brother and this young man recycled bad habits, destructive habits, on a day on which we were supposed to celebrate life.

I was hanging out with my nephew for several hours after my brother's friends arrival, because while my brother and his friends went to the backyard to get high, I was the one left holding my nephew. I was in a very different place at this point than I had been in years past. I was not going to fight my brother, or his friends. They were all much bigger and stronger than I am, now anyway, and would have whooped me. However, I have never been so disappointed. Once his friends left, I just told him that I'd put my nephew down to sleep, and that I was going to go stay in a motel closer to my school. He said okay, and asked if I had a problem.

"No, but I do need to focus," and I walked out of his house.

I drove two hours that night to my school and I rented a room at the Motel 6. I was sad and disappointed that my brother was still following this group. I was sad for my nephew, because this was the world he was going to have to navigate growing up. I was tired, because I was scheduled to defend my dissertation the next day. I desperately needed sleep, and it was already very late. Only six of the units were occupied, the front desk attendant told me, "So it should be quiet." I got to my room—and found the door already open. Inside, a few young men and one young woman were shooting up something. A young man in a chair was just sticking the needle in his arm.

I went back to the front desk to tell the attendant he had made a mistake. "Wrong room. Sorry. You are in the room next door." I went back to my room, only to listen for a few hours to these young people do drugs and party. In many ways, it was fitting that on the eve of me completing my Ph.D., I would spend the late hours of the night going over to these young people's room, attempting to "call them to life." I believe God had called me to minister to someone that night—even if it wasn't my brother.

At around 2 a.m. I sat with them for an hour, asking questions that I thought my grandma would ask: "How did you get here? Where is your family? Who loves you?" Of course, since they were high, those who had not passed out engaged me in ongoing conversation. The man who had the needle in his arm when I first entered the room asked a simple question in return.

"What are you doing here?" A good question, because he meant, what was I doing in his room? Well, I wanted two things. The first was to let them know I could see them and that I was genuinely curious about who they were. The second was I wanted them to be quiet, so I could go to sleep. I chose to answer the question with only my first reason.

"I came to talk to you."

"What for? You want to take a hit? How much money do you have?"

"I don't know. You all were up, so I thought I would talk to you." Ignoring his question about taking a hit.

"What are you doing staying in a motel and checking in so late? You sure you don't want some?" He wasn't going to let it go.

"I have to defend my doctoral dissertation tomorrow."

"What does that mean?"

"It means that tomorrow I stand in front of a bunch of people and defend 200+ pages of work I turned into them so I can get my doctorate."

"Like a doctor? In what?"

"In spiritual and religious practices for healing." I figured he wouldn't recognize what my discipline was actually called.

"Oh, yeah. So like a priest or something."

"Sure," I said, "...or something."

"I am sorry." The young man was looking down at his hands, which were scaled and callused. He started to pick at one of his scales nervously.

"For what?" I asked.

"This was probably the last thing you needed before that. And you're probably thinking what's wrong with us. Here you are, trying to talk us all out of getting high and trying to get us to shut up so you can go to bed. Hanging out with junkies isn't what you had in mind, I am sure." He could see right through my subtle talk.

"I came to talk."

"Don't f— with me. I can see right through you, Jedi." We both laughed. "So I'll get these people to shut up so you can do your thing." It was nearly 3 a.m. at this point. "Hey, shut up. The padre is going to sleep now."

"Well thanks, but I wasn't really trying to do anything."

"Whatever, man. But hey can you help *me*?" He was clearly not buying that I was there to talk.

"I don't know. Do you want to be helped?"

"You are good, padre! Yes. Whatever that thing is you do tomorrow, when you talk about being a doctor or whatever, can you help people? Don't be a prick. Hanging out with us is...Well, you could have just called the cops. I don't know anyone who would come over to talk, especially someone that wouldn't want to get high or that wasn't already high. Are you high?"

"No, I am not. I'll try not to be a prick." I said as I turned to walk out the room.

"I am being serious. Not a lot of people would come into this room. Keep doing that. And we will keep it down."

"Okay." I shut the door behind me.

The rest of the night the room was quiet. I don't know how he did it, but he managed it. Looking back now on that night before I went to defend my dissertation, it seemed providential that I would spend it in a motel room with young people with severe addictions, after leaving my brother, and after attempting to lead a good workshop for young people trying to discern their next most faithful step. God calls and presents us opportunities to find life in the diversity of God's world. Some of these places are like the cultural competency workshop, with people with shared commitments. At other times, it is with people who are living in some of the most depressed and neglected places of their souls.

The next morning, I woke up, put on my shirt and tie, and prepared to head to campus. I opened up my motel door and on the welcome mat was a napkin with the words, "Sorry. Thanks. Good luck." Along with the note, there was a cup of the motel's coffee and a doughnut from who knows where. *Sorry. Thanks. Good luck.* I looked for the group of young people, but they had checked out before I did. I drove up to campus, ate my doughnut, and drank my coffee. The origin of the doughnut did concern me, especially since it was left outside on a napkin on a motel welcome mat, but we didn't have much money at the time so I ate the unknown-origin pastry anyway. I was grateful for the gift.

I entered the room where my dissertation committee sat. At the table were sponsors, mentors, friends, and colleagues. One committee member had helped me navigate the ethics board, as my project seemed to the ethics committee at the school as though it might lend itself to some "communal harm in the form of deportation," if people were identified in the study. As the Latinx on faculty, Dr. Santiago Slabodsky helped me through the institutional politics to get my research approved. I had said in my research that deportation was a threat my community was facing, because they were every day. But not because of my study!

White institutions sometimes need assurance that we know how to navigate our own communities. Dr. Santiago Slabodsky helped me navigate the perils of being a Latinx in higher education, knowing that he and I had completely different experiences of being Latinx. Dr. Frank Rogers, the one who had liberated and supported me in my work with *Nueva Comunidad*—and the one who said during the marathon, "We are all running our own race, together"—sat down next to Dr. Slabodsky. Dr. Sheryl Kujawa-Holbrook, my advisor and mentor, walked in with a big smile and said, "You passed with high honors, so let's have a discussion about your work." I have never felt so relieved. Relieved that all that work was accepted. Relieved that my community and the stories located in the text were accepted. I was excited that there were parts in the dissertation and my research, because the work I was doing in the community was *for* the community, not for the academy. I had an entire committee that understood why that protection of my community was necessary.

I was also blessed to have a community of supporters there to participate in the discussion and celebrate the defense. I did my best to focus on the room, but my mind kept coming back to the napkin: *Sorry. Thanks. Good luck.* God was at work. God had already moved me beyond this room and this conversation about my dissertation. God was calling me to something else. In the words of that young man that something else was to "not be a prick" and enter rooms in which I was more familiar and could navigate more authentically—at least more so than this dissertation defense. Though I loved the discussion about my research—because, who doesn't love talking about their work that was years in the making?—I needed to be in different rooms.

I had a conversation at a discernment retreat some time later with a campus pastor, who told me about a small, Christian college, in a small city in the Pacific Northwest. The college had a student body that was majority students of color. When I accepted the job offer as an Assistant Dean there, I remembered the words on that napkin: *Sorry. Thanks. Good luck.* I said "sorry" to those that I grew up with, who I was leaving yet again: I apologized to my past and my community for leaving to search for the "golden ticket" of the academy in New England. I called Michael, the young man from the introduction with whom I had worked in *Nueva Comunidad*, and thanked him for all that he had done to help organize that group. I apologized to those in Salinas, who I labored alongside in my youth and during my dissertation, for leaving yet again. I said good luck and thanks to those who had supported me while in New England. I ventured out with what little luck I had—luck in the form of God and all the angels calling me to life—to take a job as an Assistant Dean for Academic Affairs and the Director of the Center for Community Engagement at a small, Christian liberal arts college in the Pacific Northwest.

I was drawn to this community because the college had a majority of students of color, who had "low opportunities, but high potential." This was a not-so-subtle code for "they are black and brown students." Though problematic, this community was perfect for how I felt called to call others to life through education. In addition, the college provided me an opportunity to direct the Center for Community Engagement. The foundation of the Center was solid. The service-learning program had been designed and refined by a few of the faculty members who did this work with the larger Lutheran church. The prayerful thought put into every detail and the care of the relationships with community partners modeled the ethos and spirit of the college: love, care, and concern for the marginalized. The logical disconnect, though, with which I could help, was that the college had for nearly 70 years educated almost solely white students, and employed exclusively white faculty who could meet this aim. The college was now engaging black and brown communities.

What made this opportunity great was that those who ran the college understood that this disconnect was happening. They understood that white students going to black and brown neighborhoods or black and brown students coming to the college was causing a tension, not just in institutional identity but in the student body itself. If this tension were not addressed with care and attention to how black and brown students would feel about their college, which didn't have a faculty or board member who represented their communities, the community would implode. On the one hand, the college was providing access to education for marginalized minorities, while on the other hand, the college was playing pious colonizer to support their dying institution with the labor and money coming from poor black and brown students. Either way one looked at the student body, the administration was ready to begin to think about what it meant that most of their students now were students of color who came from the communities that the school and faculty were used to visiting and serving through community service.

As an Assistant Dean for the college, I served in administration supporting an incredibly gifted Dean and Vice President of Academic Affairs to try and keep the small, struggling college from collapsing financially. We worked on coordinating our academic offerings, made pedagogical and curriculum innovations, addressed the challenges presented by the accreditation agency before either of us had joined the community, and chaired a number of committees that are needed to keep a college running. Alongside all of these responsibilities, I began to look at diversity and inclusion across the college—curriculum, faculty hiring practices, mentoring, training faculty and staff, student affairs, leadership, and applying a level of critical inquiry to every practice of the college with attention to diversity. This was not simply because I thought these initiatives were a good idea, but because it was a matter of life and death for many of the students and myself. As the only voting faculty member of color, my office was often the first place students of color would visit to talk about their struggles, their classes, and their hopes for their education. Given my background and my story, which some of them had heard before, many came to me with their own stories of growing up in rough neighborhoods or families. Alongside the administrative and educational duties, I again was holding a space for people to engage their deepest hurts, stories, and vocational aspirations. They were looking for someone and somewhere to call them to life. At a faith-based institution, I could claim the way in which I saw God working in and through them and help map their *familia* of support.

For the first time, I had institutional clout and power to make a difference. I, with a core of concerned faculty and administrators, began to ask, "What does education look like in this context? How do we hold a space where healing can happen?" My belief was and continues to be that if education has any purpose, it should be to heal. It should heal the pains of colonialism by using its resources to investigate the lost and subjugated histories and bodies of people of color. It should heal by researching cures to the day's illnesses, cancers, and traumas. It should heal by creating safe spaces, where students can come completely and wholly into the classroom, and educators are able to mine for the knowledge and wisdom of generations that rests in their narratives and cultivate an inner peace and genuine curiosity about life. Education served as a vessel for me to be saved, and God had now provided me a context in which I could extend this saving grace to the students I served. I reflected this in every practice. How I handled student disciplinary proceedings, the committees I served on, how I taught my own classes, how I engaged my colleagues was all predicated on this simple principle: Was what we were doing calling our students to life?

One moment of pushback to this ethos came when a fellow administrator entered my office to confront me about how I had helped a student navigate institutional politics that was destroying her life, essentially evicting her from housing for being an "administrative and academic handful." For context, this "handful" translated to this young woman of color being in a school where no one who taught this young woman looked like her, or spoke from or with her context, in classes she took with particularly hierarchical and underqualified professors; meanwhile, working full-time and dealing with a home life that was tumultuous to say the least. This young student of color was being pulverized by the wheels of a system in which few had power and she had even fewer advocates, sponsors, mentors, or family to help navigate said system. When I was pushed by this fellow administrator for allegedly not working in the best interest of the student by allowing her grace, I asked a simple question: "How were any of the actions taken by you against the student beneficial for her call to life?"

"Well, it is teaching her that you have to work for what you want. That you have to have resilience through adversity and that nothing comes easy. That there are rules to follow and there are consequences if you don't."

"You think she doesn't have resilience or doesn't know that life is hard? Is that the purpose of your class...to teach these lessons? What if she has this wisdom already? Or has learned these lessons through life?" I asked suspiciously.

"No, she is entitled. She shouldn't be speaking up like that in class."

"Did she have something to say?" I asked shaking my head.

"Yes, but she was correcting me."

"Was she right?" I knew the answer to that question.

"That's not the point. And, I don't know. It doesn't matter."

"Well, let me ask you, as a faculty member and administrator of color who has a Ph.D., who has published in the field we are talking about, who has done extensive research on the matter, what if the student in this case is in fact right? What would you do then?" This was the first time I had spoken out loud my credentials, my education, and my experience in a world that had also sought to destroy me. I felt empowered. For the first time in my life, there were no longer any boxes I had to check that someone like this could cite as a reason for me not being able to say or do what I do!

"That wouldn't matter. I don't care about your degrees or research. It is a matter of integrity. I am the instructor. You and she are not."

"So it is about power?" I said, eyebrows raised.

"What? No? It is not about power." She said, backing toward the door.

"You want power over black and brown bodies. You think you deserve that?" I asked from behind my desk.

"You are not listening," she yelled at me.

"You are not hearing or seeing," I said, as calmly as possible.

"What does that even mean? Is that a story or some 'wisdom' from your culture?" she asked mockingly, putting wisdom in air quotes.

"See my qualifications: They mean I know what I am talking about. It means I have played by all the rules of this game and have learned its insidious practices from the inside out. It means that, unlike you, I am qualified to speak on the matter of administration set by the standards you are claiming to uphold. It means a classroom in which white educators dominate brown students or attempt to seem higher because of color of birth over their colleagues has no place in this college." I paused to let that sink in. "Do you see this student we are talking about? Do you hear her, really? She has more grit than you will ever have. She has been homeless. She has worked a full-time job since she was a kid. She has survived conditions you only read about in books. And you come in here and try and tell me that you taking action against her is to teach her life isn't fair and you have to work for what you want? That what she needs to learn about is integrity? Resilience? That life is not fair? I don't know who you are trying to convince. That young woman has integrity. She has resilience. She has courage despite life not being fair. But the one thing students like her have never been given is power, which you think was given to you at birth. But you have assumed your having power is a birthright, so much so that it was a given, something we didn't even have to talk about, and power is not what this conversation is about. Well, you assumed wrong. This is about power. And when you use your power over any student, particularly my students of color, you take our lives. You slay us in the classroom as quickly as we would have been slain on our streets. You enact a psychological violence on us that says we are not welcome, that we don't belong, that we are not to be breathing the same air as you!"

> This is about power. And when you use your power over any student, particularly my students of color, you take our lives. You slay us in the classroom as quickly as we would have been slain on our streets. You enact a psychological violence on us that says we are not welcome, that we don't belong, that we are not to be breathing the same air as you!

"That's not what I am..."

"*¡Basta!* Do you know what that means? *¡Basta!* Let me say it one more time, *¡Basta!*" By this time, I am sure I was yelling. "*¡BASTA!* You don't have power here. You don't have power over that young woman anymore. You don't have power over me. Get out of my office." I pointed at the door.

"You can't talk to me this way." She yelled back.

"You think you haven't been talking to us this way your entire life? You just aren't used to seeing someone like me speak at all. Get out. You have no power here. You have no power over us anymore." I felt as though I were casting out a demon. I was making way for the Spirit to enter. I had moved from that place of survival of my youth to a place of bravery and liberation. I now had the power to cast out demons! Demons of the -isms of today's world. I also had the power, whether I really had it according to the handbook or not, to defend those most marginalized by the system. This was me calling that young woman to life. I was using education as a liberating and healing space for the most marginalized in the society. The difference between the other educator and myself was I understood in my bones that this struggle was about life. It wasn't just about "integrity," or "power," it was about the right to breathe, the right to live, the right to be a member of this human race. We had a right not just to be here, but to have knowledge and experience that was unmatched by our colleagues. We were bringing

> We were bringing something new—the formerly colonized were saying *¡basta!* to the violence and taking our lives back.

something new—the formerly colonized were saying *¡basta!* to the violence and taking our lives back. This was my younger self, all those years ago with the Stranger, standing up and saying, "You will not choke the life out of me or throw books at me that you never read." This was me saying God had called us to life. God had called us to make space through education for people to survive. I never told the young woman about my conversation in my office. The young woman graduated the following Spring.

During this same time, I was actively engaged in several interdisciplinary and national projects that addressed learning in higher education and theological education. These projects all looked at the experience of students and professionals of color. In each of these projects, I was reminded and in many cases talked about being called into new life, called to serve in the ways the elders and the marginalized of our communities call us. I was drawn back to this small college and the people who worked there. I reflected on the bleakness and our own marginal status as people of color. And every time I was told I was too young or naïve or dreaming too big about the impact of young people and scholars of color, I was reminded of two things.

One, my grandma walked right up to that murderer's door and told him to turn himself in. The way we call our community to life is by calling it on its flaws, on itself, on its own violent tendencies, without fear or apprehension. Every time in these conversations something came up that did not call us to life I said: "*¡Basta!* We are not standing for it anymore." If my grandma could face the person who wanted me dead, I could face those in the academy who thought we *were* dead, or didn't belong, or didn't have something to offer to society. My grandma didn't stand for this. She held me up. She said I was capable of anything. She called me to life.

The second thing was being suspended above the ground, powerless over my own life, looking for someone to intervene, with the life being choked out of my very body. After I passed out all those years ago, I made a commitment in *Nueva Comunidad* that I would never be silent again if I had the chance to speak, to be powerless if my feet could touch the floor, to allow another to have power over my body if I could breathe. God didn't call me, any child, or any person to be silent on life and death matters. I had a responsibility to call others to life, to hold a space in which life could exist and grow, and where wounds could heal. It didn't matter whether I was working at a university, at a small college, in a community, or at home, I was going to hold the space just as I did with *Nueva Comunidad,* or as Grandma, the Christian Brothers, and my father had for me. There were other lives at stake, not just my own.

I had finally come to peace with who God called me to be and how he called me to be in the world. Again, I turn to Howard Thurman, who wrote: "But the need of my heart is for room for Peace: Peace of mind that inspires singleness of purpose; Peace of heart that quiets all fears and uproots all panic; Peace of spirit that filters through all confusions and robs them of their power. These I seek *now*. I know that here in this quietness my life can be infused with Peace" (Thurman 1984, 95). I was at peace with myself. The only thing left to do was to stand up and do the work. I had found a vocation. I no longer had to fear not breathing. I was breathing with the help of God, my ancestors, and my community.

Chapter 8

Living into the Christian Narrative

You will always harvest what you plant.
— Galatians 6:7b, NLT

"You need to work faster," the field supervisor said to me as I looked up at him from my knees.

"I am working as fast as I can."

"Do you see the rest of your family? They are working faster than you. They are all the way down there on your row. And you are stuck here. What is wrong with you? If you ever want to be a good worker, you need to pick faster."

I had fallen behind. As the field supervisor walked away from me, that sense of vertigo came over me. The row seemed to go on forever. I saw my family, friends, and co-workers moving farther and farther away from me. We had driven by Soledad Mission to get to this field, yet God had never seemed so far off.

The sun beat down on our backs as we moved through the field. I worked as hard as I could to catch up. Picking the pea pods and throwing them into my bucket, I worked from my knees as fast as possible. When you pick peas in the field, you have three ways of picking them. Bending over to the short vine and pulling them. This process can destroy one's back. Some of the older generation brought a skateboard-like contraption, with two wheels below a short plank of wood that they would sit on as they rolled down the field. This way only worked if the ground was dry and hard. This always slowed one down on mornings like this. If you worked like me, and the majority of

166

us did so, you typically could pick more peas with less strain on your back if you were on your knees. But this meant your legs drove down deep into the dirt. In Soledad, the fog would cover the valley. Mixed with the occasional morning watering, the dirt would be wet, soaking one's clothing.

As I went faster on my knees, standing occasionally to see over my row and find out how far behind I was, I felt as if I were getting closer. When you are on your knees, though, you can't see into another's row; you are alone and isolated. I think the vines are designed this way: to keep us from realizing our collective power; to keep us focused on our work; to keep us from reaching out to our neighbors to help them in their times of need.

> I think the vines are designed this way: to keep us from realizing our collective power; to keep us focused on our work; to keep us from reaching out to our neighbors to help them in their times of need.

Lunch came and I thought I should keep working to finish catching up. The field supervisor had left, so it seemed like this would be fine, when a neighbor came into my row. It was my uncle—in reality, it was my friend's dad, but I always called him Uncle Che. Uncle Che held himself with such power and poise. We all respected him. He walked up to me, still on my knees. He brought an empty bucket, flipped it upside down, and sat down in front of me.

"Patricio, what are you doing?"

"Trying to catch up."

"Catch up to what?"

"Catch up to you."

"Why do you want to catch up to me?"

"I want to be a good worker. I want to be like you."

Uncle Che sat and looked at me, quiet, and just stared down at me with sympathetic eyes. "Give me your hands," he said as he placed his hands palm up on his lap. I put my hands in his. He traced my small hands. He traced my lifelines, the soft callouses, the deeper scars, the open wounds. He followed each and every finger to the end. "Your hands are soft. These wounds are fresh. Your scars are not deep. Don't ever think that is a bad thing. Don't listen to that supervisor. These are not our fields and never will be. They belong to him. As long as he keeps us in our rows, quiet, working hard to earn our shitty paycheck, he will

always own these fields. You need to get out of here. Look at my hands."
He placed his hands in mine. They were old, dry, and calloused, and
dry blood stained his cracked skin. "Trace my hands as I did yours."

I followed every contour of his hand with my small pointer finger.
His hands were swollen in parts. Swollen to the point they looked like
they hurt. At other parts, his hands went down into deep crevices that
seemed rise and fall like the valleys of California. I traced one lifeline
from the bottom of his palm all the way up to the base of his pointer
finger. This line was deep. It was hard on each ridge. It seemed to
represent his hard life, a life spent in these fields.

"That line right there—it is the pain I carry. It is the pain of my
ancestors. It is the pain of my mother and father who worked here.
They worked hard every day to make it to the end of this row. But there
was always another row to go to. So we were tired and hungry. And
when there wasn't a row to go to, we were still tired and hungry. This
was the only option they had. It was the only thing they could do to
survive. This was not the life they chose, but the life that was given to
them. You have been given something else." I stood there holding his
hands. "What do you think that is?"

Tired from the work that day and the heat beating down on my back, I
did not answer the question. I looked down the field row searching for
the answer. On the road that led to the fields, I could see the supervisor's
truck approaching, which meant lunch would soon be over.

"Look here, mijo! That truck will always be driving up here. What do
you think you have?"

"I don't know."

"A chance to redefine how you live in this world. No one is destined for
this f—g hell of a place. And you have an education. You don't have to
be here. This is not your field. This is not my field. I want my kids to see
you. I want my kids to get out of this shit." His eyes started welling up
with tears. "Stand up, mijo." My knees creaked as I stood up. My body
had grown accustomed to being on my knees. He was still sitting on
his bucket looking up at me. "Don't you ever trudge through this on
your knees again. Stand up. Stand up. You understand me?" I nodded.
"I pray to God every day that we won't have to do this forever, and I
believe in a God that will deliver us out of this hell."

The supervisor drove up. "Looks like you caught up. You won't
be too bad at this after all." I stood there and smiled at him. I had
heard Uncle Che. I was going to survive differently. I was going to

live differently. Not just for me, but for our children, for the next generation, for our grandchildren, and great-grandchildren. I, like Uncle Che, believed in a God who would deliver me from this hell, and, in many ways, already had. But I didn't just want to survive. I wanted to call others to life, to call them out of this hell.

> I stood there and smiled at him. I had heard Uncle Che. I was going to survive differently. I was going to live differently. Not just for me, but for our children, for the next generation, for our grandchildren, and great-grandchildren.

Howard Thurman writes, "Sometimes a deep racial memory throws into focus an ancient wisdom that steadies the hand and stabilizes the heart. Always moving in upon a man's life is the friend whose existence he did not know, whose coming and going is not his to determine. At last, a man's life is his very own and a life is never his, alone" (1984, 61). I may have been called to stand. I may have been called to life, but my life is not mine alone. This call to life extends to any persons who have been throttled against a wall, who have been shot at, who have spent time on their knees trying to make ends meet. These are collective memories that go back generations. My vocation is not limited to just me—not now, not ever. Survival is a communal act. When we hear the call to life, we must answer it. When we know that call is muted for others, we must find new ways to communicate it to them.

> Survival is a communal act. When we hear the call to life, we must answer it. When we know that call is muted for others, we must find new ways to communicate it to them.

Throughout my life I have had people such as Uncle Che telling me to stand up. I have also had plenty of people who wanted me to kneel before them, to place my body on the line, so that they might inherit the kingdom: modern colonizers.

But the kin-dom is here. It is now. God calls us to life in the midst of violence and pain. But God does not do this work alone. We must join the call to life. I am reminded of when the prophet Isaiah was called by God in chapter 6.

> Then I heard the voice of the Lord saying, "Whom shall I send? And who will go for us?" And I said, "Here am I. Send me! (6:8, NIV)

As I once heard the Rev. Dr. Roger Nishioka preach, "It would be great if we could end here and this great call—here I am. Send me." And we often do. Here I am, send me. I am ready God. I am ready for this work of calling people to life. I have tried, and tried, and I am ready to continue living into this call. But the call doesn't end there. God continues:

> He said, "Go and tell this people:
>
> "'Be ever hearing, but never understanding;
>
> be ever seeing, but never perceiving.'
>
> Make the heart of this people calloused;
>
> make their ears dull
>
> and close their eyes.
>
> Otherwise they might see with their eyes,
>
> hear with their ears,
>
> understand with their hearts,
>
> and turn and be healed."
>
> Then I said, "For how long, Lord?"
>
> And he answered:
>
> "Until the cities lie ruined
>
> and without inhabitant,
>
> until the houses are left deserted
>
> and the fields ruined and ravaged,
>
> until the LORD has sent everyone far away
>
> and the land is utterly forsaken.
>
> And though a tenth remains in the land,
>
> it will again be laid waste.
>
> But as the terebinth and oak
>
> leave stumps when they are cut down,
>
> so the holy seed will be the stump in the land." (6:9–13, NIV)

We are called to this work forever! "Until the cities lie ruined and without inhabitant." This is a prophetic call, but not unfamiliar for my context. We have been destroyed. We have been driven from the land. We have been marginalized to the point of extinction. This call in Isaiah to venture in the land that is utterly forsaken is a call to marginalized communities such as the one I come from. We have endured so much. Our hearts are already calloused. Our eyes and ears are closed and we are ready to be called to life. The disenfranchised, the marginalized, the poor, the heartbroken, the afflicted, the addicted— all those who have not inherited today's kingdom—are ready for God to call on our communities. Now the question is: What will I say to my community? I have been spared, saved, and resurrected by God's people, so what is my responsibility now? How will I call us together, in community, and to life?

As Christians discerning our vocation through the narrative and life of a savior, it is incredibly important that the discernment look critically at the characters, settings, and biblical narrative. For a Christian educator and religious scholar, these stories have been so influential in calling people to new life. I turn to the biblical narrative and examine those places where the call to life is central. As a Christian theologian, educator, and leader, I feel moved and called to examine the biblical texts for themes, characters, and narratives that provide guideposts for how one might think theologically about this concept of vocation. When read vocationally, we are doing this work of reading God's word for the call, listening for where God calls those into new life. When read this way, much of the Hebrew Bible and Christian Scriptures becomes pertinent to our everyday lives. The following three examples in particular are prescient for how one might hear God's voice for oneself. What holds these stories in common are that God calls over the troubled waters, calls people during and in the aftermath of suffering, and always calls people and the community into new life. This is not the only time that God calls us into our vocation, but it is in keeping with following the mission and teaching of Jesus, spreading good news, and fulfilling the prophetic, evangelical mission of the church. The three biblical examples I draw on for my own narrative follow three themes:

> What holds these stories in common are that God calls over the troubled waters, calls people during and in the aftermath of suffering, and always calls people and the community into new life.

1) Hearing the voice of God to liberate self and others

2) Discerning the call to prophetically announce God's voice to the suffering

3) Wading in God's call for us to be present with suffering in its fullness—to look deeply into our wounds for God's healing presence

These three themes center on the idea that vocation is a call out of oppression and into new life. This is not the only way to think about Christian vocation, but it does reflect what vocation through biblical narrative practice and reading looks like, especially through my work with field workers in California, gang-affiliated youth, first-generation students, and students of color in college settings—or, more radically, offering self-compassion when, where, and how I come to hear God's voice as hearing the cries of the oppressed. Our neighbors, in the stresses of their everyday lives—whether in working shift work, having a desk job with a long commute, troubled marriages, broken homes, spousal abuse, depression, addictions, hard labor, violence (and the list goes on)—cry out for God to call them to life. We each individually cry out from our own pains of addiction, hunger, and desire to be seen and heard—to be accepted—for someone to notice our longing for community and companionship, for health, for respite from the many cancers that plague our bodies and minds, and to be called into new life. I believe that God does this, and provides examples through the Bible of this calling of people and communities into new life.

Hearing the voice of God to call others to life is a recurrent theme in the biblical text. Consider Exodus 3, in which God meets Moses. Moses is out tending to the flock of his father-in-law when an angel of God appears to him in the burning bush on the mountain of God. Moses, curious about a burning bush, approaches it and God calls to him from the bush, "Moses, Moses." Moses replies with, "Here I am." God tells him to come closer, remove his sandals because he is on holy ground, and then tells Moses that the one calling him is the one true God and the God of Abraham, Isaac, and Jacob. Moses, in response, hides his face, because he is afraid of God. Then the Torah records:

> The LORD said, "I have indeed seen the misery of my people in Egypt. I have heard them crying out because of their slave drivers, and I am concerned about their suffering. So I have come down to rescue them from the hand of the Egyptians and to bring them up out of that land into a good and spacious land, a land flowing with milk and honey—the home of the Canaanites, Hittites, Amorites, Perizzites, Hivites and Jebusites. And now the cry of the Israelites has reached me, and I have seen the way the Egyptians are oppressing them. So now, go.

I am sending you to Pharaoh to bring my people the Israelites out of Egypt." (Ex. 3:7–10, NIV)

Moses responds to God, asking, "Who am I?" A question so many of us ask ourselves—*Why me?* God assures Moses, "I will be with you." After protesting again, suggesting that the Israelites might not know whom Moses is talking about, God responds:

"I AM WHO I AM. This is what you are to say to the Israelites: 'I AM has sent me to you.'" God also said to Moses, "Say to the Israelites, 'The LORD, the God of your fathers—the God of Abraham, the God of Isaac and the God of Jacob—has sent me to you.'

"This is my name forever,

the name you shall call me,

from generation to generation." (Ex. 3:14–15, NIV)

God hears the suffering of God's people and calls to Moses. Moses, standing on holy ground, states first that he is there, and then follows with, "Who am I?" Moses hears the call to tend to the suffering of his people.

As with Moses, I believe other people have heard God's call to liberate others. They were people such as my Grandma, such as that Christian Brother, such as my father, who heard God calling to them who liberated me. In each of their own hearing God call to them and responding, "I will serve God's people," they were able to see and hear me crying for life. In answering my own call, it is not simply about mimicking that Brother, my grandma, my father, or the countless others who supported my life. It is also about hearing God's call directly to me to return to those communities that suffer. It was not the suffering in which I found my call, and it is not to the suffering that I call others. Instead, I bring an invitation to new life and a call to survival. Living into this reality is not easy, as one knows from Exodus. Moses did not just go to Pharaoh and say, "Let my people go," and the chains of slavery and the weight of oppression simply disappeared from this earth. It was a long struggle in Egypt, an even longer one in the wilderness, and Moses ultimately did not even enter the promised land. Instead, Moses's vocation took a lifetime, a continuous call for the community to live together. Similarly, the work I do does not have an end. My vocation is to

> It was not the suffering in which I found my call, and it is not to the suffering that I call others. Instead, I bring an invitation to new life and a call to survival.

> Vocational discernment through narrative is about living into God's call to life, not about arriving in the promised land.

call people to life on the margins, specifically to life on the particular margins in which I reside. Many of the experiences that you read about in my narrative are those experiences during which I am still in the wilderness, still wandering. And that is okay! Vocational discernment through narrative is about living into God's call to life, not about arriving in the promised land.

The second theme, announcing God's voice to the suffering, is exemplified in Ezekiel. Deriving from the Hebrew, Ezekiel means "God will strengthen." Ezekiel was a prophet during the Babylonian exile. Born into the priestly caste, Ezekiel had a vision in which he saw the images of four creatures, and then that of the figure of a man. He looked upon these creatures, and described them in detail, when he saw the figure of the man:

> This was the appearance of the likeness of the glory of the Lord. When I saw it, I fell facedown, and I heard the voice of the one speaking.
>
> He said to me. "Son of man, stand up on your feet and I will speak to you." As he spoke, the Spirit came into me and raised me to my feet, and I heard him speaking to me. He said, "Son of man, I am sending you to the Israelites, to a rebellious nation that has rebelled against me..." (Ezek. 1:28b—2:3a, NIV)

Ezekiel is then sent to this rebellious community. What does this rebellious community actually look like? We get a better sense of those to whom he is sent in chapter 37:

> The hand of the Lord was on me, and he brought me out by the Spirit of the Lord and set me in the middle of a valley; it was full of bones. He led me back and forth among them, and I saw a great many bones on the floor of the valley, bones that were very dry. He asked me, "Son of man, can these bones live?" I said, "Sovereign Lord, you alone know." Then he said to me, "Prophesy to these bones and say to them, 'Dry bones, hear the word of the Lord! This what the Sovereign Lord says to these bones: I will make breath enter you, and you will come to life. I will attach tendons to you and make flesh come upon you and cover you with skin; I will put breath in you, and you will come to life. Then you will know that I am the Lord.'" (37:1–6, NIV)

These bones are those of God's people, those who suffered under the oppression of their day. Ezekiel is called to announce prophetically to the deceased, the broken, the long-suffering—in my tradition, they would be our ancestors, the little girl, all those suffering under the weight of colonization and violence—that they will be returning to their land; they will rise; they will be resurrected. Here we see not just God calling out as in the story of Moses, but the voice of the prophet calling on the bones to rise. I often imagine my story, my limp body hanging there in my room and the next day feeling numb, my bones dry from the violence of the night before, then the Brother calling out to me to make "these bones" rise! That is the call. Not just to see the bones of the living, but to see them in the community. The Brother saw my bones and called them to life. However, we also know that so many others in that land are exiled and suffering in the land I call home—longing to return.

For Latinxs, this passage contains so much more. It reflects our connection to our past, to our *familia,* and, for me, to all the lost ones: *los inocentes,* Grandma, my fallen homies. To those who grow and live on the border, or whose families have crossed, this valley of the dry bones is much too real. It exists in our subconscious, our lost and subjugated histories. It exists in our present, with the Sonoran desert that separates the U.S. and Mexico, filled with the tears, the failed journeys, the bones that dried out on their journey to answer God's call to new life. Throughout my narrative, I have talked not just about my plight, but the plight of the community, the struggle of my family, and the journey of people for whom the weight of suffering is so great that the sound of God's voice is muted. This is where we are called.

As Christians, we are all called to the borderlands—the borderlands where people are on the brink of physical, intellectual, spiritual, psychological, and social death. And we are called for these bones to rise. This is answering the call to life and, in turn, calling others to life.

> As Christians, we are all called to the borderlands—the borderlands where people are on the brink of physical, intellectual, spiritual, psychological, and social death.

The final theme is a call to be present with suffering and know God. An often quoted vocational story comes from the Gospel of John. In the Gospel of John, the apostles are gathered and they are speaking about how 10 of them had seen the resurrected Jesus. As the gospel writer tells us:

> Now Thomas (also known as Didymus), one of the Twelve, was not with the disciples when Jesus came. So the other disciples told him, "We have seen the Lord!" But he said to them, "Unless I see the nail marks in his hands and put my finger where the nails were, and put my hand into his side, I will not believe."
>
> A week later his disciples were in the house again, and Thomas was with them. Though the doors were locked, Jesus came and stood among them and said, "Peace be with you!" Then he said to Thomas, "Put your finger here; see my hands. Reach out your hand and put it into my side. Stop doubting and believe."
>
> Thomas said to him, "My Lord and my God!" Then Jesus told him, "Because you have seen me, you have believed; blessed are those who have not seen and yet have believed." (Jn. 20:24–29, NIV)

This is the story in which we come to know "Doubting Thomas," because theologians and biblical scholars have come to see Jesus's words, "[B]lessed are those who have not seen and yet have believed," as referring to people who have privileged faith. I, rather, come to read this story of Thomas not only for his ability to see the wounds of Jesus, but also for his ability to hear the voice of God. Thomas, after witnessing his teacher being crucified, goes to mourn as was the custom of his tradition; he leaves the community to heal from what he has witnessed. He has been psychologically and vicariously traumatized through witnessing a most horrifying and violent act against someone he loves most dearly. While he is gone, Jesus visits the community. When Thomas returns and hears about the visit he says he won't believe Jesus is alive until he can see the wounds for himself. A week later Thomas sees Jesus, who tells him to touch his wounds. These wounds are fresh in his mind. He saw the flesh of God be torn. He saw his friend, mentor, teacher, placed up on an instrument of torture. He saw Jesus left there to die. However, when Jesus first speaks, Thomas sees the wounds and believes. For those suffering or struggling with witnessing or experiencing their flesh being broken—for example, as the apostles all did after watching Jesus being crucified—I see Thomas as an example for people discerning their vocation based on the suffering they experience in their communities and their bodies. Thomas, after such a traumatic event, calls into doubt that Jesus could have been raised—the suffering of this world is too much for him to comprehend. But upon hearing the voice of God, he is called to believe in God's power of life beyond death.

Imagine for a moment that adolescent version of myself—abused, alone, trying to be strong, trying to care for others—and someone comes to me in the midst of that suffering, at that final moment before I blackout, or the moment before the bullet enters that little girl, and states that I just need to believe that Jesus suffered, died, and was resurrected on my behalf. The bruise around my neck would still be deep purple. The bullet would still strike the body of an innocent. The weight of not being able to protect my family and most vulnerable in my community on my shoulders demands not simply that I believe because someone aside from Jesus tells me to, but that my own and God's suffering be seen and heard, and my experience validated. For the suffering, God needs to be fully present.

Like Thomas, before I can hear God calling out to me, I need to see the wounds—or, more accurately—I need the opportunity for the wounds to be seen and felt, and my suffering to be validated. By authentically witnessing suffering and acknowledging the pain, violence, and deep wounds that have occurred, we might be able to hear the voice of God.

> By authentically witnessing suffering and acknowledging the pain, violence, and deep wounds that have occurred, we might be able to hear the voice of God.

Christian vocation, then, is not just hearing the voice of God and then responding, but it is tied deeply to the suffering of this world. In these three biblical themes, we see as part of the call narrative God hearing the voices of the suffering, the deceased, and the psychologically wounded, all calling or being called into new life. Christian vocation is about hearing the voice of God in, through, and beyond the suffering of this world. This is not because all people hear the voice of God this way, or because this is the only way to discern one's Christian vocation, but it is my firm suspicion that God calls prophets and ministers of the kin-dom to respond to suffering. Those who are deeply entwined with marginalized communities know that when individuals or communities experience suffering and pain, we need others who are called to bring us to life, or we need to build the capacities to see the wounds and believe that resurrection is possible.

One of my favorite extracanonical stories about this sort of vocational call comes from the author Toni Morrison and her book *Beloved*. Morrison writes in her epigraph, "Sixty Million and More": "I will call them my people, which were not my people; and her beloved which was not beloved." This relates to the number of slaves murdered in slavery. The novel itself, titled for the central character, a ghost named "Beloved," serves as a reminder of the destructive power of trauma induced by slavery. By quoting Romans 9:25, "I will call them my people, which were not my people; and her beloved, which was not beloved" (KJV), Morrison is gesturing toward the saving power of grace and belief in God that brings one into life with God and community. Never more accurately does she describe the role of those who are called to alleviate the suffering of others, or live into Christian vocation, as when she describes a central figure, Baby Suggs, creating a community called the Clearing. It is here that she gathers the community to share in crying, laughing, dancing, and preaching—all generated toward self-love. In the Clearing, we see healing, but we also see those who are struggling with suffering finding a place and a community. When the main character, Sethe, feels the chokehold of Beloved, what she comes to know as the "circle of iron," Baby Suggs creates a place that is safe from the outside, oppressive world, and allows the community to come to her home and generate a capacity for self-love, and calls Sethe to life. Ultimately, it is the groundwork of community building in the Clearing that removes the "circle of iron" from Sethe's neck.

It is communities such as the Clearing that clear the way for God's voice to reverberate through our bodies and dispel those hauntings of our past traumas. Like the Clearing, hearing this call, the voice that calms our inner storms, is communal, messy, and does not happen overnight. Thinking about my narrative call, the Brother's office was the first place where the bruise around my neck was visible and allowed to heal. Grandma welcomed me when society had rejected me and la raza wanted me dead. I went to her home when manual labor was too much and the open wounds from a life of labor and toil exposed itself on my hands. Friends and my own family called me to live in love and peace. Ultimately, I have now tried to recreate those spaces. *Nueva Comunidad* was my attempt to create the Clearing. Entering into that motel room the night before my dissertation defense was me actively looking for the Clearing. Bringing the spirit of *Nueva Comunidad* and the lessons learned from a hard life, I have tried to carry into education that spirit of holding a space for healing. Calling people to the Clearing is not just *a* vocational call, it is *the* Christian vocational call.

But *this* is a call. This book is a call. There were times when I thought I didn't have it in me to live. I didn't want this world to take my life, so I would venture to God on my own. There were times when my body curled in on itself and I thought I was surely going to die, yet God called me to life. I pray that you are called to life.

I want to finish with a prayer, but not the standard prayer—something different. Like my life, it is messy, disjointed, sometimes out of time and not linear. But it *is* a call for life. It is a reflection on the vocation of survival. It reflects my hopes for you and your vocational discernment, and the hope for us as a community. It is my attempt to call you to life.

In the name of the God that sustains life

Where are you God?

…[Silence]…[Sirens]…[Cries]…

Where are you God?

Why are you not here? Am I not suspended up on this instrument of torture? Feet dangling, life being choked…out…of…me. [Fade to black]

Where are you Father? Mother? Brother? Sister?

Why are you not here to see the pain in this world? Can you not see the little girl that lies before us? Can we imagine her body resurrecting? [Vision runs red]

Where are you educators, philosophers, theologians, liberators of minds?

Will you stop the internal and external violence? When will you join in the work of healing?

[Chalk board covered in ashes]

Where are you friends and companions?

Are you bringing out the life in your partners? Are you calling them to life? Are you tilling good soil or enacting violence on the land?

Where are you?

Now that you have survived, where are you planting your feet? Whom are you calling to life?

I pray that the pain goes away. This is a cry to you God that you call us to life…that you liberate us to live.

I pray for all those in my community who walk in war zones, who fear going into their bedrooms, who are afraid to come out, who walk across the wilderness under the cover of night—for those who are not accepted, loved, or called to life.

I pray for the poor who prepare the table for the world, but can't afford to put the food on their own tables.

I pray for us struggling with addiction, depression, mental illness, and abuse—all things beyond our control. I pray we find communities that hold us, carry us through that which afflicts our bodies and minds. It is not our fault. It is not your fault.

I pray to a God that calls people to life.

I pray that you are called to life.

I give you my breath—because, at times, that is all I have to give.

I give you my listening heart—because, sometimes, that is all we need.

I give you my hands, because showing you my wounded hands is an act you first afforded me. Continue to show me your wounds in your hands and I will believe.

This is a call to life. Don't let it be choked out by the suffering of the world.

I am here. Send me.

I am here, God. Send me.

I am here, and I love you. I love you like my grandma loved me.

I am here like my family loved me.

I am here because I love life.

I am here because I am to till the soil so new life may emerge.

I am here because I survive.

I am here because I survived and no longer fear death…but sometimes am haunted by it.

I am here because of my vocation.

My call. My call from God to breathe life into the world with you.

I am here, send me.

We are here, together, in life.

Amen.

Acknowledgments

When I write, I never write for myself. I do not write to glorify my name, only God's and our community. Writing this book has been a process of pain and healing. It has sent me down into the valley of my own pain. Like Dante's *Inferno,* I was not alone. I had guides and angels walking alongside me, caring for me when a memory was too much for me to write about for that moment, to love me when I felt I could not love myself, and to hold me accountable for the words I put on these pages. I want to thank my partner, Carrie, for walking alongside me in life. Your wisdom, courage, love, joy, and brilliance make every life you touch better. You inspire me to be a better person and call me to life when the rest of the world is silent. Thank you. To my son, Asher, know this book was not easy to write given that one day you will pick it up. The lessons and life I lived in its pages and the stories that exist in the margins, between words, and off the page, helped shape me, but they could have also destroyed me. I want to care for you and your sibling, Carmelita, who has yet to come but will be born soon. I want to help you find your own story. I want survival to look different for you. I want the call to life to be heard differently by you. When you came into our lives and we held your small body just moments after you were born, the fragility and preciousness of your body put into perspective that we do not live for just ourselves, but the innocent children. I love you. To Carmelita, you carry a name full of love and the spirit of a blessed ancestor. May you love and live as passionately as Grandma Carmelita Reyes did. I love you and am thankful that you have come into our lives.

I have to thank my father. When the world demonizes, casts out, shames, litigates against, and abandons fathers, casting them as not having the capacity to be the caring, loving, and teaching parents that they are, you continue to show up. I would not be here today without you. You set a course for me that allows for me to breathe. There were hard times. You survived so much, endured so much. You were the first at so many things. You cleared a path for me to live fully into who I am today. I am because of you.

To my grandparents, Carmen and Julio Reyes—*presente*. There are whole generations of the Reyes family who are alive and thriving because of you. To my grandpa, sitting and listening to your stories demonstrated the power and importance of storytelling. Grandma, you provided the foundation for all that I know. Your wisdom, traditions, ethics—but, more important, your love—will be passed down from generation to generation because you created a space for us to live and to love. You opened up the door for all of us. I cannot give thanks enough for the entire Reyes clan. We are a family, because we show up. I want to thank my Aunts Mona and Carrie, especially, because you were always there, always holding a space, always caring for those who cared for us. For my Uncle Rene, who would also show up—though usually a full day late—we miss you. We wish you were here with us. Thank you for the love and support you showed me all through the years. To the rest of the Reyes family, and, by extension, to the Zaragozas—and, when I feel generous, the Contreras family—we are a large, loud, but most importantly caring, loving, and giving family. I am blessed to be born into this family.

Thank you for all those friends and colleagues who appear in this book. There are so many stories to tell about so many incredible people, I wish I could fit in more. But I want to take a moment to name those who called me to life. To the Christian Brothers, specifically Br. Patrick Dunne, thank you. To all those kids I grew up with: Jesse, Sammy, Luis, Sarah, Aimee, Yvette, Luis, Jorge, Patrick, Stephen, Gabe, Brandon, Angel, Carlos, and so many more. To those who I ran with in high school, both on the playground and at school: Raul, Dennis, Dante, Jose, Chris, Lamar, Steve, and your families and life partners now, thank you for walking alongside me in troubling times. A special thanks to Raul and Marisol Rico for the love and care they have always shared toward me. And for Lemec and Tara Thomas for being lifelong friends who continue to walk a Christian life that inspires me to do better. To those who are no longer with us, we love you and we miss you.

To those members of *Nueva Comunidad* who walked with me on a longer process of healing, and for all those who were healed by that space, thank you. For the one who appears as Michael in this story, I hope that you find peace and love in your life. Your brilliance is beyond anything I have experienced in the university. To the women in the packing sheds, specifically Yisenia and Edythe, thank you. You not only reminded me that there were options during our little Bible studies, but you encouraged me to try new things. To those in the fields I labored alongside and will continue to, thank you for surviving and continuing to survive for the next generation. To all those young people who I came across in gang intervention or prevention programming, thank you for your lives!

Of course, a deep thank you to my mentors, Frank, Sheryl, and Santiago. I knew that from the very outset my story, my family, and my body would be cared for in a doctoral program because of all of you. You liberated my mind and my ability to write and think from the very material circumstances that are so dear to me. To those educators who supported me in Boston, such as Bryan Stone, Pamela Lightsey, Mary Elizabeth Moore, Shelly Rambo, Cristian De La Rosa, and so many others, thank you for helping me to find my voice in what was a depressing and isolating time. For those classmates who labored through and bonded during our work together, thank you. To Annesa Williams-Meis, Tena Williams-Meis, Altagracia Perez-Bullard and Cynthia Perez-Bullard, thank you for being such incredible and inspirational people. To classmates who picked me up when I was at the bottom like Blake Huggins and Alex Froom, thank you. While of course we talked about our work, so much of why I felt connected to you all was about those things that happened outside of the classroom. Thank you. It saved me.

Thank you to those who sponsor and believe that I have a story worth telling. To Dori Baker for identifying me as an author and helping me think through what telling this story might look like, and for Callid Keefe-Perry and Brian Bantum for making connections between people who are doing incredible work and taking the time to help me with the story. To the family that is the Forum for Theological Exploration, thank you for getting behind me as an individual long before you knew who I was or what I was about. Thank you to Ulrike Guthrie, my editor, who helped me find the words and phrases I was actually trying to use. Trauma disrupts how one recovers the language for an event, and this book was a testament to a community that heals and mends the pieces of a broken body back together.

I want to thank those who do not appear in this book, yet who informed how I think about my own story. To all those students I served alongside at Northeastern University and Trinity Lutheran College: you taught me so much more than I could ever bring to a classroom and an administrator's table. To those spiritual advisors and faculty I served alongside at both institutions: I am thankful for your caring presence. For those administrators of color who held it together when things were a little too "real": thank you. Thank you to Shaya Gregory Poku for standing up for me as we advocated for each other's strengths. To Andrea Paull, Abraham Rodriguez, and Christian Paige: thank you for taking time to build trust, friendship, and collaboration to better a community that we loved so dearly, but may not have loved us back. Thank you to my supervisors and mentors who called me to life and provided me more than just a job by asking me to bring my whole self to the work: Robert Nomelli and Michael DeLashmutt, thank you. For my new work colleagues at FTE: you are an inspiration. I have never felt more at home and alive than I do now. Your lives and stories are brighter than any one of you could imagine. I am blessed to be working now with you.

To the larger community of Salinas: that we may find peace. To all of those suffering under the weight of violence, historic or current, I will continue to work and pray for your survival. To all those suffering from mental illness, especially my brothers and sisters in the university and in the streets of my home community: your bodies, souls, and hearts are loved; loved by me and by God. These may only be words, but know I write because of a pain that I can't shake, a cloud that won't leave my head, and from a world that seems to improve at a snail's pace if at all. I want us to live! Breathing slow, life-full breaths. For the one who killed that little girl all those years ago: we are not done working. God is not done working. We have a responsibility to resurrect the lost life.

Finally, I want to acknowledge that I cried to God to save me more times that I care to remember. Each time, I hoped God would reach down into my world and pluck me out of my life. There were faithful people in the world who heard a call from God. And though it may not have been immediate, God called those people to be present in a school, in a family, in a community, and to be authentically Christian. Part of this Christian call is to save lives. When we respond to that call, we then begin to catch just a small glimpse of what God hears, sees, tastes, smells, and experiences. Once you are called to life out of certain death, you cannot un-see the death around you. You cannot un-hear the cry of the marginalized, the dispossessed, and the suffering. You can taste the dry saltiness, of the pains of hunger. You can smell death on every street. You begin to experience the suffering of this world, and are now responsible to respond to those cries for God and for those who walk through a world that was not made for them. God, you called me to life through others. Thank you.

Bibliography

Abraham, Susan. *Identity, Ethics and Nonviolence in Postcolonial Theory: A Rahnerian Theological Assessment.* New York: Palgrave Press, 2007.

Alves, Rubem. *The Poet, The Warrior, The Prophet.* Norwich: SCM Press, 2002.

———. *Tomorrow's Child: Imagination, Creativity, and the Rebirth of Culture.* Eugene, Oreg.: Wipf and Stock, 2009.

———. *Transparencies of Eternity.* Translated by Jovelino Ramos & Joan Ramos. Miami: Convivium, 2010.

Anderson, Benedict. *Imagined Communities: Reflections on the Origin and Spread of Nationalism.* London: Verso, 2006.

Anzaldúa, Gloria. *Borderlands: The New Mestiza/La Frontera.* 3rd edition. San Francisco: Aunt Lute Books, 2007.

Baca, Jimmy Santiago. *A Place to Stand.* New York: Grove Press, 2001.

———. *Immigrants in Own Own Land & Selected Early Poems.* New York: New Directions Books, 1991.

Bass, Diana Butler. *Grounded: Finding God in the World—A Spiritual Revolution.* New York: Harper Collins, 2015.

Beaudoin, Tom. *Witness to Dispossession.* New York: Orbis, 2008.

Berry, Wendell. *The Long-Legged House.* Berkeley, Calif.: 2012.

Bhabha, Homi K. *The Location of Culture.* New York: Routledge, 2004.

Boal, Augusto. *Theatre of the Oppressed.* London: Pluto Press, 2000.

Brooks, David. *The Road to Character.* New York: Random House, 2015.

Butler, Octavia. *Parable of the Sower.* New York: Warner Books, 1993.

Canada, Geoffrey. *Fist Stick Knife Gun: A Personal History of Violence.* Boston: Beacon Press, 2010.

Castillo, Adela. *Mundo Mio.* Mexico: Editorial La Quimera, 2006.

———. *Sólo Amor.* New York: Orbis Press, 2009.

Cisneros, Sandra. *A House of My Own: Stories from My Life.* New York: Alfred A. Knopf, 2015.

———. "Foreword." In *The Future Is Mestizo: Life Where Cultures Meet,* by Virgilio Elizondo, ix–xi. Boulder, Colo.: University Press of Colorado, 2000.

Coates, Ta-Nehisi. *Between the World and Me.* New York: Spiegel & Grau, 2015.

———. *The Beautiful Struggle: A Memoir.* New York: Spiegel & Grau, 2009.

Coelho, Paulo. *The Alchemist.* 25th anniv. ed. New York: Harper Collins, 2014.

Day, Dorothy. *The Long Loneliness*. New York: Harper One, 1952.

Du Bois, W.E.B. "Education." *Du Bois Central*. 1915. http://www.library. umass.edu/spcoll/digital/dubois/EdEducation.pdf (accessed June 16, 2013).

Elizondo, Virgilio. *Christianity and Culture: An Introduction to Pastroal Theology and Minsitry for the Bicultural Community*. San Antonio: Mexican American Cultural Center, 1999.

———. *The Future Is Mestizo: Life Where Cultures Meet*. Bloomington, Ind.: Meyer Stone, 2000.

———. *Galilean Journey: The Mexican-American Promise*. New York: Orbis, 2010.

———. *Guadalupe: Mother of a New Creation*. New York: Orbis, 1997.

———. "Mestizaje as a Locus of Theological Reflection." In *Beyond Borders: Writings of Virgilio Elizondo and Friends*, edited by Timothy Matovina, 159–75. New York: Orbis, 2000.

Espín, Orlando. "An Exploration into a Theology of Grace and Sin." In *From the Heart of Our People*, edited by Orlando Espín & Miguel Díaz, 153–71. New York: Orbis, 1999.

———. *The Faith of the People: Theological Reflection and Popular Catholicism*. New York: Orbis, 1997.

Fanon, Frantz. *Black Skin, White Masks*. Translated by Richard Philcox. New York: Grove Press, 2008. First published, in French, in 1952.

———. *The Wretched of the Earth*. Translated by Richard Philcox. New York: Grove Press, 2005.

Foucault, Michel. *Power/Knowledge: Selected Interviews and Other Writings, 1972–1977*. Edited by Colin Gordon. Translated by Colin Gordon, Leo Marshall, John Mepham, & Kate Soper. New York: Pantheon, 1980.

———. *The Archeology of Knowledge and the Discourse on Language*. Translated by A.M. Sheridan Smith. New York: Pantheon Books, 1972.

Freire, Paulo. *Educaiton for Critical Consciousness*. 1st American Edition. New York: Seabury Press, 1973.

———. *Pedagogy of Freedom: Ethics, Democracy, and Civic Courage*. Lanham: Rowman and Littlefield Publishers, 1998.

———. *Pedagogy of the Oppressed*. Translated by Myra Ramos. New York: Continuum, 2011.

———. *The Politics of Education: Culture, Power and Liberation*. Westport: Bergin and Garvey Publications, 1985.

García Márquez, Gabriel. *One Hundred Years of Solitude*. London: Pan Books, 1978.

Glissant, Édouard. *Poetics of Relation.* Translated by Betsy Wing. Ann Arbor: University of Michigan Press, 2010.

Holland, Scott. *How Do Stories Save Us? An Essay on the Question with the Theological Hermeneutics of David Tracy in View.* Dudley, Mass.: Peeters, 2006.

hooks, bell. *Ain't I a Woman: Black Women and Feminism.* Cambridge, Mass.: South End Press, 1981.

hooks, bell. "Embracing Freedom: Spirituality and Liberation ." In *The Heart of Learning: Spirituality in Education,* by Steven Glazer, 113–29. New York: Jeremy P. Tarcher/Penguin, 1999.

———. *Teaching Community: A Pedagogy of Hope.* New York: Routledge, 2003.

———. *Teaching Critical Thinking: Practical Wisdom.* New York: Routledge, 2010.

———. *Teaching to Transgress: Education as the Practice of Freedom.* New York: Routledge, 1994.

Ilibagiza, Immaculée. *Left to Tell: Discovering God Amidst the Rwandan Holocaust.* New York: Hay House, 2007.

Isasi-Díaz, Ada María, and Eduardo Mendieta. *Decolonizing Epistemologies: Latina/o Theology and Philosophy.* New York: Fordham University Press, 2012.

Isasi-Díaz, Ada María, and Yolanda Tarango. *Hispanic Women: Prophetic Voice in the Church.* New York: Harper & Row, 1988.

Keefe-Perry, Callid. *Way to Water: A Theopoetics Primer.* Eugene, Oreg.: Cascade Books, 2014.

Lake, Alison. *Colonial Rosary: Spanish and Indian Missions of California.* Athens: Ohio University Press, 2006.

León-Portilla, Miguel. *Aztec Thought and Culture: A Study of the Ancient Nahuatl Mind.* Translated by Jack Emory Davis. Norman: University of Oklahoma Press, 1990.

Lugones, María. *Pilgrimages/Pereginajes: Theorizing Coalition Against Multiple Oppressions.* Lanham, Md.: Rowman and Littlefield Publishers, 2003.

Maldonado-Torres, Nelson. *Against War: Views from the Underside of Modernity.* Durham, N.C.: Duke University Press, 2008.

Marshall, Howard. *The Gospel of Luke : a Commentary on the Greek Text* Part of the New International Greek Testament Commentary. Grand Ripids, Mich.: Eerdmans, 1978.

May, Melanie. *A Body Knows: A Theopoetics of Death and Resurrection.* New York: Continuum, 1995.

McCarthy, Cormac. *The Road.* New York: Alfred A. Knopf, 2006.

Memmi, Albert. *The Colonizer and the Colonized*. Boston: Beacon Press, 1991.

Merton, Thomas. *No Man Is an Island*. Boston: Shambhala, 2005.

———. *Seven Story Mountain*. New York: Harcourt, 1976.

Mignolo, Walter. *Local Histories / Global Designs: Coloniality, Subaltern Knowledges, and Border Thinking*. Princeton: Princeton University Press, 2012.

———. *The Darker Side of Western Modernity: Global Futures, Decolonial Options*. Durham, N.C.: Duke University Press Books, 2011.

———. *The Idea of Latin America*. Malden, Mass.: Blackwell Pub., 2005.

Minh-ha, Trinh. *Elsewhere, Within Here: Immigration, Refugeeism and the Boundary Event*. New York: Routledge, 2011.

Mohanty, Chandra Talpade. *Feminism Without Borders*. Durham N.C.: Duke University Press, 2003.

Moraga, Cherríe L. *Loving in the War Years: Lo Que Nunca Pasó Sus Labios*. Cambridge, Mass.: South End Press, 2000.

Morrison, Toni. *Beloved*. New York: Vintage International, 2004.

Nanko-Fernandez, Carmen. *Theologizing in Espanglish*. New York: Orbis, 2010.

O'Connor, Flannery. "The Grotesque in Southern Fiction." In *Collected Works*, by Flannery O'Connor, 813–21. New York: The Library of America, 1988.

Ochs, Carol. "Miriam's Way." *Cross Currents* Winter (1995): 493-509.

Palmer, Parker. *A Hidden Wholeness: The Journey Toward an Undivided Life*. San Francisco: Jossey-Bass, 2004.

———. *Let Your Life Speak: Listening for the Voice of Vocation*. San Francisco: Jossey-Bass, 2000.

———. *The Courage to Teach: Exploring the Inner Landscape of a Teacher's Life*. 10th anniversary edition. San Francisco: Jossey-Bass, 2007.

Paz, Octavio. *The Labyrinth of Solitude*. Translated by Lysander Kemp, Yara Milos, & Rachel Phillips Belash. New York: Grove Press, 1985.

Petrella, Ivan. *Beyond Liberation Theology: A Polemic*. London: SCM Press, 2008.

Poling, James. *Rethinking Faith: A Constructive Practical Theology*. Minneapolis: Fortress Press, 2011.

Prakash, Madhu Suri, and Gustavo Esteva. *Escaping Education: Living as Learning within Grassroots Cultures*. 2nd edition. New York: Peter Lang International Academic Publishers, 2008.

Reyes, Patrick B. "Alisal: Theopoetics and Emancipatory Politics." *Theopoetics* 2, no. 2 (Forthcoming).

————. "Blood in the Soil: Liberating Space, Identity and Farm Workers in the United States." Edited by Kyle Thompson. *Claremont Journal of Religion* 1, no. 2 (2012): 68–84.

Rivera, Luis. *A Violent Evangelism: The Political and Religious Conquest of the Americas.* Louisville: Westminster/John Knox Press, 1992.

Rivera, Mayra. *Poetics of the Flesh.* Durham, N.C.: Duke University Press, 2015.

————. "Thinking Bodies: The Spirit of a Latina Incarnational Imagination." In *Decolonizing Epistemologies: Latina/o Theology and Philosophy*, edited by Ada Maria Isasi-Díaz & Eduardo Mendieta, 207–25. New York: Fordham Press, 2012.

————. *The Touch of Transcendence: A Postcolonial Theology of God.* Louisville: Westminster John Knox Press, 2007.

Roberto, Goizueta. *Christ Our Companio: Toward a Theological Aesthetics of Liberation.* New York: Orbis, 2009.

Rodriguez, Richard. *Hunger of Memory: The Education of Richard Rodriguez.* New York: Bantam Books, 1982.

Rogers, Frank. *Practicing Compassion.* Nashville: Fresh Air Books, 2015.

Said, Edward. *Orientalism.* New York: Vintage Books, 1978.

————. *Culture and Imperialism.* New York: Vintage, 1993.

Sandoval, Chela. *Methodology of the Oppressed.* Minneapolis: University of Minnesota Press, 2000.

Segundo, Juan Luis. *Liberation of Theology.* Translated by John Drury. Eugene, Oreg.: Wipf and Stock Publisher, 2002.

Smith, Andrea. "Decolonizing Theology." *Union Seminary Quarterly Review* 59, no. 1–2 (2005): 63–79.

Smith, Linda Tuhiwai. *Decolonizing Methodologies: Research and Indigenous Peoples.* 2nd edition. New York: Zed Books, 2012.

Tamez, Elsa. "Hagar and Sarah in Galatians: A Case Study in Freedom." *Word & World* 20, no. 3 (Summer 2000): 265–71.

Taylor, Barbara Brown. *The Preaching Life.* Cambridge, Mass.: The Cowley Publications, 1993.

Taylor, Mark Kline (Lewis). *Remembering Esperanza: A Cultural-Political Theology of North American Praxis.* New York: Orbis, 1990.

Thurman, Howard. *For the Inward Journey.* San Diego: Harcourt Brace Jovanovich, Publishers, 1984.

————. *Jesus and the Disinherited.* Boston: Beacon Press, 1976.

Tillich, Paul. *Systematic Theology.* Vol. 1 of 3 vols. Chicago: University of Chicago Press, 2012.

Tinker, George. *Spirit and Resistance: Political Theology and American Indian Liberation.* Minneapolis: Fortress Press, 2004.

Torre, Miguel A. De La. *The Politics of Jesús: A Hispanic Political Theology.* London: Rowman & Littlefield, 2015.

Tupac Shakur, "Life Goes On." *All Eyez on Me.* Death Row Records, 1996, compact disc.

Williams, Delores. *Sisters in the Wilderness: The Challenge of Womanist God-Talk.* 20th anniversary edition. New York: Orbis, 2013.

Wink, Walter. *The Powers that Be: Theology for a New Millennium.* New York: Double Day, 1998.